# ELMER McCURDY

To Carter,

With great admiration
for your work, from
a fellow poet.

All the best,

Mark Svenvold

5-16-05

# ELMER McCURDY

## THE MISADVENTURES IN LIFE AND AFTERLIFE OF AN AMERICAN OUTLAW

## Mark Svenvold

BASIC

BOOKS

A Member of the Perseus Books Group
New York

Published by Basic Books,
A Member of the Perseus Books Group

Designed by Trish Wilkinson

The Library of Congress has cataloged the hardcover edition as follows:
Svenvold, Mark, 1958–
    Elmer McCurdy : the misadventures in life and afterlife of an
American outlaw / Mark Svenvold.
    p.   cm.
    Includes bibliography references and index.
    ISBN 0-465-08349-8
    1. McCurdy, Elmer, 1880–1911.  2. Outlaws—United States—Biography.
3. Brigands and robbers—United States—Biography.  4. United
States—History—20th century—Biography.  I. Title.
HV6448 .S87  2002
364.15'52'092—dc21                                        2002008664

Paperback ISBN 0-465-08349-8

03 04 / 10 9 8 7 6 5 4 3 2 1

For Martha and Livia, always

*If you didn't see the six-legged dog,*
*It doesn't matter.*
*We did and he mostly lay in the corner.*
*As for the extra legs,*

*One got used to them quickly*
*And thought of other things.*
*Like, what a cold, dark night*
*To be out at the fair. . . .*
                                —CHARLES SIMIC


*The dead advance as much*
*as the living advance.*
                                —WALT WHITMAN

≈ 1 ≈

# Re-Entry

In December of 1976, Detective Daniel P. Sallmen of the Long Beach Police Department arrived at the office of the Los Angeles County Medical Examiner–Coroner holding a severed arm as if it were a baguette in a brown paper bag. It had been found, along with the rest of a mummified body, in a Long Beach amusement park fun-house ride called the "Laff-in-the-Dark" and had caused a bit of a commotion. The Fire Department had been called. Homicide had been called. Arriving at the scene, Detective Sallmen thought it best to have the arm checked out, so he put it in his cruiser, and together the arm and the man made their weird way north up the Long Beach Freeway to East Los Angeles. By the time they arrived at the Coroner's Office, it was mid-morning and all was in full swing on the security floor.

Sallmen walked down hallways lined with bodies awaiting autopsy. In the rooms on either side, the grim business was being performed at top speed upon dozens of the dead who lay on their backs while technicians, their faces hidden behind special masks that filtered the septic, stinking air, busily sawed and cracked and eviscerated, lifting out and weighing their subjects by the yard and bucketful. Here everything looked more like the work of wolves than of science, with the attendant screams of power tools and Stryker saws.

"Doc," Detective Sallmen said, approaching the desk of Joseph Choi, the senior deputy medical examiner, who was busy catching up on some paperwork, "I brought something to show you." He took the arm out of the paper bag. It had been spray-painted the color of orange highlighter. "I want to know if this is a real human arm or the arm of a mannequin. It fell off of what was supposed to be a mannequin."

Choi had been hired by the chief medical examiner, Thomas T. Noguchi, in 1969 and had developed a reputation for careful and exhaustive work in a number of celebrity deaths and high-profile murders—among them the case of the Hillside Strangler and the Skid Row Slasher. He examined the arm. The joint and the muscle tissue, which looked like pemmican, was clearly mummified. The skin, beneath many layers of paint, was dark brown. It was definitely a human arm and not the arm of a mannequin. Choi guessed that it belonged to someone of South American, Indian, or Mexican extraction. The cadaver may have been smuggled across the border and sold to a medical school. Such things were not unheard of. He ordered the rest of the body back to the Coroner's Office and notified Noguchi, who asked Choi to perform an initial examination.

The body was listed as "the Decedent," in official coroner's parlance Dead Body Case #76-14812, and then photographed from head to foot and prepared for autopsy alongside several other bodies in a small room adjacent to the main action on the security floor. Word soon got around about John Doe #255, the fun-house mummy, about whom so little was known that the autopsy, performed by Dr. Choi on the morning of December 8, took on the character of an archaeological dig. Indeed, with its smooth, darkened skin and gaunt face, drawn into a grimace, it looked Neolithic, like something pulled out of a peat bog, an ice cave high in the Andes, or the sands of Wadi Kubbaniya. As Choi began the examination, his first and most basic question—the time of death—seemed to have less to do with clocks and calendars than with ages or epochs.

The body had surfaced at a location shoot for the television show *The Six Million Dollar Man*. The show's fictive hero was Colonel Steve Austin, a former Air Force test pilot, whose body, after a spectacular plane crash, is, at great government expense, retooled and "bionically" retrofitted with enough high-powered, high-tech gadgetry to enable him to run faster, swim deeper, and see farther than anyone alive, all in the service of countermanding the many evils stalking the American dreamscape in the 1970s.

There were missiles to contend with, for starters, lots of nuclear missiles, constantly falling into the wrong hands. Sometimes the nuclear threat was combined with other anxieties of the time, and in one episode Steve Austin would be forced to choose between using his bionic powers to help an evil doctor mine a substance called *dilanthium*, which would provide the Earth with a new energy source, or standing by helplessly as the doctor detonates a nuclear bomb. In this way, week after week, the nuclear crisis might be combined with the energy crisis and the environmental crisis as the main characters met over drinks to discuss "the computer who has gained control of the nation's money and all its secrets," or "the new Soviet probe which has crash landed in Wyoming," or "the land developer who has visions of becoming the new energy czar of the world."

The episode being filmed that week at the fun house, "The Carnival of Spies," called for Steve Austin to tail an East German rocket scientist who had slipped away from a California convention in order to shoot down an experimental U.S. military bomber from a ground-to-air missile site that had been installed, diabolically, in a fun-house carnival ride. The previous month, location scouts from Universal Studios had leased the Laff-in-the-Dark, and by December, film crews had descended upon an old seaside amusement park that had seen better days.

Indeed, the Nu-Pike Amusement Park, or "the Pike," had until recently bustled with beer-swilling, tattoo-bearing sailors on shore leave in their dress whites, flocking together like foul-mouthed swans or strolling paired up with local girls carrying giant, powder blue stuffed elephants. But the fleet had moved, and with it had vanished the rolling sounds of Skee Ball, the *rat-a-tat* of the penny arcade pinball machines and shooting galleries, the high-pitched screams cascading from the roller coaster, the *thump . . . clang!* of the high striker mallet, and the ever-present, ongoing grind of the concessionaires.

Now there was nothing but candy wrappers blowing flat against a chain-link fence, and a man named Chris Haynes and his companions from Universal Studios working against a feverish shooting schedule to prepare the Laff-in-the-Dark for the few shots that would be filmed inside. The Laff-in-the-Dark was a sort of "love canal," through which couples were pulled in a small car along a track that led into a dark, howling maze filled with coffins, skeletons, creepy things that brushed against one's face and arms, and pop-up goblins and ghouls. The dramatic irony of "The Carnival of Spies" episode would be that the carnival-goers, screaming with delight inside the Laff-in-the-Dark, were having fun while Steve Austin, cool under pressure but running out of time, battled his way through the selfsame ride, fending off the goblins that now seemed to conspire with a foreign, conniving Communist power and its missile guidance system about to give the United States' B-1 bomber program a swift kick in the payload bay.

Chris Haynes had spent the early part of the morning hauling props through what looked like the insides of a very large magician's box—with all the things you're not supposed to see, all the trap doors, the false fronts, the darkened felt, the plastic masks, the fake hair, the tracks for the cars veering left then right around blind corners, all the spook-house fright machinery now suddenly exposed in the glare of work lights. The tracks snaking through the interior led, at one point, to a mannequin hanging from a wall with a noose around its neck. The work crew had begun talking about the mannequin immediately, with its strange glow-in-the-dark paint-job. For the carnival riders, it seemed, the effect would be one of misdirection: You would race headlong in the darkness toward a creepily glowing figure that seemed to hover in mid-air. At the last possible moment, floodlights would shine upon the hanged man, there would be a taped scream, and then the car, making a swift ninety-degree turn, would continue on to the next frightful thing.

A few of Chris's crewmates began poking at the hanged man. It seemed as light as balsa wood and stirred in the slight breeze of workers passing by. Someone guessed that it was made of papier-mâché. Chris stopped for a moment, then walked over to it and pulled on its arm, which snapped off. There were no hooks or wires to reattach the limb. The arm's cross section was not solid like a cut potato, as with most plastic or plaster mannequins, but dark and textured, almost shredded, like beef jerky, and in the center there was something that looked like bone. He brought the arm over to one of the guys and pointed at the bone.

"Does *that* look like papier-mâché?" he asked.

Just to make sure, the two walked back to the dummy, which was unclothed, and Chris checked between its legs. Sure enough, he was staring at a complete male package, shrunken and mummified, but all there. Not a version nor a simulacrum, but the male genitalia, woeful and sad, with a faint sprout of pubic hair. This was not "anatomically correct." This was anatomical. This was anatomy, the body itself, a completely desiccated, mummified human body.

Nobody was in a big hurry to retrieve it. Other matters seemed more pressing. Chris led an off-duty police officer working security for Universal Studios to the mummified corpse. For a moment the officer considered the body in its noose.

"Just what Long Beach needs," the officer said, "Another dead sailor," then walked out the door.

The safety officer for the Long Beach Fire Department noticed the laughing cop.

"What's he chuckling about?"

"We got a *body* in there," Chris said.

The fireman went inside for a few minutes, and then, according to Chris, came outside mulling something over.

"Hey," he said, suddenly. "I ought to give the paramedics a call."

Decades later, the *Los Angeles Times* reported that by mid-morning of December 7, 1976, paramedics for the Long Beach Fire Department had been summoned by a 911 call. Their sirens blaring, their lights flashing, they sped to the Pike in a full-out race to respond to a reported *case of severe dehydration*. The paramedics, once they realized they'd been had, took the joke fairly well, then brought doughnuts back to everyone at the station and had a good laugh about the mummy. The source for the story was Chris Haynes, who later allowed that he had not witnessed the prank himself but had heard about it from people who had. Years later, Detective Sallmen remembered nothing of the matter, nor did anyone from the Long Beach Fire Department. Whether or not the newly found mummy became the object of an elbow-to-the-ribs, interdepartmental prank—*Severe dehydration!*—one thing is certain: There is a gap in time of at least twelve hours from the morning of the 7th, when Chris reported the cadaver, to the following morning of December 8, when the boys at the Fire Department decided the case warranted a call to the Long Beach Police—time enough, perhaps, for a little malarkey. Had it been a corpse of more recent vintage, there would have been hell to pay for such a dilatory response, but, as any cop or fireman knows who crosses the line of propriety and duty for the amusement of his fellows, hell would take a check. Soon enough, the mummy would make its way to Dr. Noguchi at the Coroner's Office.

Even today, if you want to reach Dr. Noguchi, you must first listen to a mellifluous telephone receptionist gamely string together, for perhaps the hundredth time that day, the unwieldy name of a Southern California law firm that sounds vaguely like the hurried itinerary for a bus tour of the great beer kings of the Rhine. You are then put through to an amicable and equally smooth-voiced gentleman who runs interference for his old friend Noguchi, screening, one supposes, the many crackpots who want a piece of the man who is known to have examined, with a very large magnifying glass, every square millimeter of the body of Marilyn Monroe.

Noguchi is the one whom fate seems to have chosen to handle, probe, measure, weigh, and, with scalpel and saw, in the most graphic manner imaginable, dissect and physically dismantle the sculpted beauties and adored specimens of the cultural dreamscape, the gods and goddesses of an era. It was his job, over the course of several decades beginning in the early 1960s, to delve into "the five Ws" of a coroner's inquest, which, in Los Angeles County, often amounted to a "Who's Who" of the who, what, when, where, and why of death. He is the man who told us things we did not especially want to know about

Sharon Tate, Natalie Wood, Jim Morrison, Janis Joplin, William Holden, and John Belushi, among many others.

Today, sixteen years after a stormy exit from the department (he was never officially fired but "administratively reassigned," shunted off to an academic post at the University of Southern California), Noguchi still speaks of the Coroner's Office in the present tense. Indeed, the best part of him has never left the place. His legacy, the Forensic Science Center, which opened in 1972, introduced state-of-the-art technology that became standard equipment in forensic medicine. For Noguchi, the case of the fun-house mummy became an opportunity to experiment with an identification procedure known as "medial superimposition," which used the new technology of video cameras wired through a special effects blender. But the case would also offer Noguchi an opportunity to pursue a second but equally abiding interest in public relations, specifically, in raising public awareness of the role the Coroner's Office played in everyday life. However enlightened his motives may have been, there was seldom anything ordinary or "everyday" about life and death in the glare of the Los Angeles media vortex, and Noguchi soon ran into trouble. For good or ill, it was Noguchi's perceived penchant for media exposure that would make his career a cautionary tale of the hazards facing those who would presume to expose to the leveling light of science the processes of celebrity apotheosis.

Consider Marilyn Monroe, whose body, by the time of her death in 1962, had worked its way into the overheated imagination of anyone who read a certain issue of *Playboy* or watched *The Seven Year Itch*. Her image, as Andy Warhol famously reminded us, had so deeply entered the territory of the cultural unconscious that her likeness has recurred in generational shock waves. Now imagine Thomas Noguchi making his Y-incision on that same feminine form, pulling the skin of the face over itself, weighing the heart, severing the sternum, and not only will you have an idea of the invasiveness of every standard autopsy, but you will have an idea of his profession's indifference toward American iconography.

For Noguchi, the search for the truth was paramount; all bodies were treated equally in the autopsy room. But his press conferences about the dead and famous revealed a double standard, and his first high-profile case, the announcement of Marilyn Monroe's stomach contents—massive quantities of Nembutal and chloral hydrate—set a pattern he couldn't live down. His decision to hold news conferences for "celebrity" deaths such as Monroe's made practical sense, in that the most amount of information would be disseminated in the shortest amount of time with the least amount of confusion. But he chose to place himself at the center of each dark revelation about ourselves, and in so doing Noguchi paid the price of the messenger bearing bad news. Indeed, his career seems defined by a paradox: His passion for the truth seemed to have made him immune to the aura of celebrity, but he was not, ultimately, immune to the magnetic pull of tinsel town. He began to appear regularly on radio and TV news. The television show *Quincy* used Noguchi's office in its first four episodes, Noguchi providing technical assistance.

As the body count of 1970s superstars grew, Noguchi was dubbed, derisively, yet not without a trace of envy, the "Coroner to the Stars." And it was into Noguchi's celebrated jurisdiction, a

town fueled at every level by the conspicuous display of proxim-
ity to *the action*—busboys with headshots, dentists with film
scripts, vanity plates, cars, wives, dinners, drugs, all compasses
slightly and secretly atwitter to the true north of *the business*—it
was into this realm that the anonymous, Laff-in-the-Dark
mummy found itself on a cusp, of sorts, the uncomfortable,
pointed end of something.

By the hand of another, by one's own hand, by accident, kneeling, hanging, found floating in a pond or pool; by the sword, by
the slice of a blade of a motorboat, by the gun, by a rope, by a
cord; found in a cleft, a cave, a car—with a note, without
a note—with a bullet in the head: *It is the duty of the coroner to inquire* after any and all within its purview. For the Los Angeles
County Coroner's Office, this meant *death*, as per Section 27491
of the Government Code, State of California, *in whole or in part
occasioned by criminal means.* It also meant accidental death, the
many ways thereof; death without medical attendance; death
during continued absence of an attending physician; and, of
course, questionable death—strange, unusual death—the kind
that gets written up in the papers, or presented at the annual
convention of the National Association of Medical Examiners.
The titles for these papers on unusual death suggest the predicament of writers facing an audience that has seen just about
every form of mishap, murder, and mayhem under the sun.
Some opt for the straightforward approach and are thus unintentionally funny, like a klatch of oddball public-access television shows: "Homicide with a Bow and Arrow—Then and

Now," for instance, or "Gunshot Wounds of Today," or the win-
some "Dental Identification Workshop." Other titles barely contain a grim, Edward Gorey-esque glee: "Homicide and Flower
Arrangements," for example, shares a certain presentational zest
with "Shaving Cream on the Wrong Cheeks," and "Dirty Div-
ing: Sudden Death of a Scuba Diver in a Sewage Plant."

So various and odd were the ways of leaving this world—
"Autoerotic Fatalities by Electrocution," "Spelunking Deaths in
Florida"—and so common were the deaths by gunshot in this
latter part of the century, that the demise of the anonymous
mummy so long ago, however it may have happened, was bound
to seem like some quaint form of release—and yet here, and ever
so strangely, he arrived and was placed alongside all the others,
in this clearinghouse, this Grand Central Station of the dead.

How to describe the halls through which McCurdy passed—
this processing plant, this factory built in the interests of justice
and of public health, the dead arriving in great numbers, the
equivalent of a full busload each day of those who do not go gently? It was like walking in the aftermath of a very large, riotous
toga party in some crowded apartment, only all the guests were
dead—but somehow the catering staff seemed unaware of this
and was going full throttle in the kitchen, banging away with
their pots and their pans and their electric knives, the waiters,
talking amongst themselves, wearing blue scrubs and breathing
masks, moving blithely with big steel gurneys among the guests,
who lay as quiet as stones, semiclad in sheets, as limp as rag dolls
but lifted with great effort, like heavy pieces of furniture.

This was the disquieting bustle of the security floor where
McCurdy lay, looking by comparison like a burnt ember. Here

one could not, literally, stand in one place for more than ten seconds without being nudged aside by a masked, blue-clad technician bearing a body on a gurney: a tall Asian man, say, his body puffy, turning the color of an olive loaf. An obese black woman, an emergency room breathing tube still taped to her mouth. On her right temple, a dark bullet hole as wide as a pencil, and two more bullet holes on her right side. MGW—multiple gunshot wounds. A blond woman lying on a gurney, an investigator rolling her head toward him to better see her face, her head turned with ease, as if she were a drugged sleeper, then rolling back to the wall with a little clicking noise. Gone was the boundary-setting sense of "personal space" that would prevent one from gawking. Here on the security floor, the dead bodied forth, becoming wholly body, each an occasion for pronominal confusion, each no longer "she" or "he" but an object of regard, an "it," this the first sign of the process into which we are vanishing, beyond grief and history.

The mummy, too, like every other body, was now the fact and the frame, the physics and trajectory of a story to be opened and read, the body an epilogue of sorts, a cipher wherein the blunt physical details—the what of color, texture, and chemistry—were put into the service of discovery, cause, responsibility, justice—who did what to whom, and when, and how. All of this was contained for Dr. Joseph Choi, a reader of manifest patience, in blue scrubs and mask, his knife in hand, bent to his task, trained in the earliest act of modern medicine, a procedure whose root means "to see for one's self."

*The body,* Dr. Choi wrote, *is completely mummified. The nose and facial features appear to be Caucasian.*

Yet a difference began to settle in over the examination table. A crowd began to gather. Few could resist the temptation to satisfy a little professional curiosity. After all, this particular *post* had been spectacularly delayed. By mid-morning, Choi had a jocund audience observing his every move. Detectives from Homicide stopped by to watch, coroner's investigators floated in, along with Dr. Dean Wisely, the chief of forensic medicine. Bob Dambacher, chief of investigations, took a break from his busy schedule, standing alongside other police officers and medical technicians, to linger over the mummy.

Each in his own way, and to a greater or lesser degree of training and expertise, made it his daily business to be a solver of puzzles, and everyone had a pet theory about the one that lay before them now—who he was and how he had died. Each theory pitched the mummy backward and forward along the arc of time. On principle and from hard experience, few would allow that the mummy was ancient. They'd seen strange things at the Coroner's Office, but nothing *that* strange. Nevertheless, the part of modernity to which the body belonged was a question that reached back, potentially, hundreds of years. There was a lightness, a levity in the air, a sense of relief from the usual grind. For a moment, among the multiple gunshot wounds, the strangled and the abandoned, the overdosed and the variously, violently dead, it almost seemed like the circus had come to town.

Choi, meanwhile, at the business end of things, was carefully and deliberately trying to remain the calm locus of the show, notwithstanding all the backseat commentary from his assembled colleagues. He had his hands full. Everything about the case seemed to tilt the proceedings in the direction of the ribald. First of all, there were several coats of spray paint covering every inch of the body, which glowed faintly for a moment with each flash of the coroner's camera. Then there was the noose around the neck, which was clearly a prop, an obvious—and unlikely—cause of death, but which amusingly called attention to itself. One can imagine Dr. Choi, stooped over, following a standard protocol that he had practiced thousands of times, meticulously surveying the exterior of the body with a very large magnifying glass, while others, waiting for that particular visual effect to sink in, would now and again, in mock-helpful tones, casually mention the noose.

*The neck is not remarkable,* Choi wrote. *The arms are not remarkable.*

Then, of course, there were other odd details that narrowed the field of speculation considerably: the modified Y-shaped incision above the clavicle indicated that the body had been previously autopsied. Choi was, in effect, performing an autopsy upon an autopsy. What intrigued everyone, however, was that the body, although light, was as hard as a tick. It was a rare procedure that precluded the use of a knife of any kind, but this was such a case. It would require an instrument with a high-speed vibrating blade, a Stryker saw, which was normally used to open up the skull. Could a body in such condition be examined at all without shattering it to pieces? As Choi finished his initial examination, something caught his eye: a small dimple or depression in the tissue just beneath and to the right of the right nipple. Choi raised an eyebrow and said, only half in jest, "Maybe he got a gunshot wound here."

Dr. Wisely scoffed. If anything, it was probably an old hole for a chest tube. Wisely and Choi, it seemed, were both guessing the body was from some part of the previous century, but they amiably disagreed about the cause of death. It seemed far more

likely to Choi's superior that they were looking at a victim of tuberculosis—a common enough disease in the nineteenth century. He'd had a chest tube inserted to drain the fluid. He'd probably died in a TB hospital. Choi demurred but kept on working
anyway, looking for further evidence of a gunshot wound. Both
men knew that determining the cause of death would help the
doctors establish the general time period of its occurrence. As
the day progressed, more clues unfolded, but for now, Wisely
championed his tuberculosis theory and joked with his colleague
in mock concern.

"Careful, Choi. You'd better wear your mask!"

Before starting the Stryker saw, Choi called for an X ray,
which might resolve the matter then and there, revealing, on
the one hand, the signature calcification of tuberculosis in the
lungs—as white spots on film—or perhaps disclosing a bullet
lodged in tissue. But the results of the X ray startled everyone:
The film was entirely white. The body was packed with radio-
opaque material, which had fogged the X-ray film, obscuring all
traces of a bullet or evidence of TB. In a moment typical in
forensic science, the clues of the body had baffled the expectations of the examiners.

The modified Y-shaped incision, for starters, was an old-
fashioned technique used in the last century. Choi knew, moreover, that, starting around the time of the Civil War, undertakers
had begun to pack dead soldiers with arsenic, a heavy-metal compound, to preserve them for the long transit back home. Abraham
Lincoln's body was among the first to be preserved using arsenic
embalming fluid, instead of a packing compound, which kept the
presidential corpse in fairly presentable condition. The body had

been viewed by hundreds of thousands—with ever-greater appli-cations of undertaker's makeup toward the end of its long journey by train from Washington, D.C., to Springfield, Illinois. Choi concluded that the Y-shaped incision, and the two embalming su-tures in the groin, set a rough, far limit for the time of death. This was not an ancient corpse; it could in fact be no older than the Civil War. The presence of arsenic also set a useful near limit, in-dicating that the body could be no closer to the present than the 1930s, when the use of arsenic for autopsies fell into disfavor.

There was only one thing to do now, and that was to enter the body itself. Choi took his Stryker saw and began a long, ar-duous, and noisy process of opening the corpse along the old suture lines.

*The brain is mummified and like a rock.*

He found that the other internal organs were also hard as rock and almost perfectly preserved by the arsenic. The coronal and sagittal suture lines of the skull indicated that the decedent was between forty and fifty years of age at death. Later analysis of a part of the pelvis called the *symphysis pubis* put him closer to forty, with a degree of error plus or minus six years. With his Stryker saw Choi then carved out nearly the entire lung, the right periphery of which showed evidence of hemorrhage, but no sign of a penetrating wound. He noticed another telltale de-pression on the right lobe of the liver, however, which looked to him like the mark of a gunshot wound. That gave him two points along an imaginary line he could track through the body, one at the chest and one at the liver.

In the early afternoon, Choi found along this same line a copper fragment imbedded in the left hip bone. The fragment was part of an antique bullet assembly called a gas check, which was used to contain exploding gases inside a rifle. Sergeant Lee Kruman, a ballistics expert at the Los Angeles Police Department, told Choi that the gas check was for a 32-30 caliber bullet from a gun with a barrel with six right rifling. He added that this type of gas check was first used around 1905. The death, however it may have happened, could not have occurred before that year. Since gas checks were discontinued just prior to World War II, the new, adjusted time of death had now been narrowed considerably. Sometime between the years 1905 and 1940, a bullet ended the life of John Doe #255, a man in his mid thirties or forties. The bullet entered from the front of his right upper chest and traveled along the torso, lodging in his left hip. For a wound to make an entrance into the body at such a steep angle, about 30 degrees, one would have to be shooting downward, almost directly overhead. Or one would have to be shooting from ground level, the gun barrel inclined upward above the horizontal, while the decedent lay facing you on his stomach, in a location that was elevated above ground, perhaps firing back.

Late in the day came the biggest surprise of all. While removing the jaw, mandible, and teeth for a routine dental analysis, Dr. Choi pulled from the back of the mouth of the deceased a single, green, corroded copper penny dated 1924 and several ticket stubs, one giving an address on the Pike and another that read "Louis Sonney's Museum of Crime, 524 South Main Street, Los Angeles." After all the careful speculation and surmise, after the body had been completely dismantled for any possible clue to its identity, the biggest clue came straight from the mouth of the corpse itself, like a laconic joke delivered in perfect deadpan.

Detectives immediately set to work tracking down Louis Sonney. On December 9, the medical examiner issued a press release
announcing the discovery of the fun-house mummy, stating the
official cause of death by gunshot wound, and closing with a request for assistance in identifying the body. The announcement
did not sound hopeful about the prospect.


Newspaper coverage of the mummy began as a routine call to
the Coroner's Office from *Long Beach Independent* reporter Robert
Gore. The news about the body had swept through the Nu-Pike
the day before, and Gore, knowing that one o'clock was around
quitting time at the medical examiner's, called the press officer
there to confirm a few details in time for his deadline. The next
day, December 9, when the Coroner's Office issued its official
press release, the *Independent*, with a winking, elbow-swinging
headline flourish that would become, in time, the story's base-
line "madcap" motif, flopped out the following: "Mummy at Pike
No 'Laugh in the Dark.'" The news zipped along the AP/UPI
wires and was reported more soberly the following day by the
*Los Angeles Times*, the *New York Times*, and the *St. Louis Post Dispatch*,
among others. *Variety*, however, cracked wise with the headline,
"Bionic Man Meets Dummy Mummy."
    A few days later, a second and larger wave hit the news-
stands. The *New York Times*, the *Los Angeles Times*, and dozens of
papers in between announced the startling connection between
the mummy and an unknown outlaw from Oklahoma named
Elmer McCurdy. It was all speculation, of course; the Coroner's
Office quickly made that point clear enough, hoping to slow

the number of calls flooding the office. Positive identification had yet to be established, the coroner stated dourly, but few newspapers seemed willing to let that technicality get in the way of a good story. It was perfect material for tabloids like the *Star* and the *National Enquirer*, but major city newspapers picked up the story as well. It even appeared internationally in *Der Stern*, *Le Monde*, and the London *Sunday Times*. Locally, a Los Angeles talk-show host printed up several thousand T-shirts to celebrate the discovery of Elmer McCurdy and his dual career—in life as a train robber and in death as a sideshow exhibit.

It was, perhaps, the kind of news people seemed to hunger after, a spectacular version of a dead letter story, where the post office somehow misplaces a paycheck or a love letter only to deliver it decades later. It was too remarkable to be believed, but it was entirely true. It was a wonder that simultaneously engaged two great reservoirs of empathy and interest from two extremes of the American mythographic landscape. The Bionic Man, the most recent figure from the myth of technological progress, indirectly rescuing a mythic figure from the American West, the renegade, the desperado, the outlaw. At the heart of the story was the fact that this vestige of the past had been in limbo, had been erased from memory and from history, but unlike so many of the countless, unremembered dead, each with a human story that had run its course then vanished without a trace, this one had been found, brought back from limbo, and placed in time and space. From the cloud of oblivion into countable, component time, it was a miraculous re-entry.

It was a story, too, that had emerged, flashed briefly across the wires, and was then swept away and forgotten. As a boy, I'd missed the story completely. Twenty-three years later, in 1999, as the great odometer was about to turn over the zeros to usher us into a new century, a new millennium, I wanted to write about McCurdy's life and spectacular career in death. But I was a latecomer, it seemed, to the Elmer McCurdy story. There was the fact of BBC documentary called "The Oklahoma Outlaw." There was a professor of theater in Kansas who had been bitten by the McCurdy bug and spent eight years researching his subject before he died. There was a Celtic folk band, "Mustard's Retreat," that had released a CD containing a five-minute mini-epic entitled "The Ballad of Elmer McCurdy" and another piece by oddball songwriter Brian Dewan that got most of the details wrong but was clearly inspired by the McCurdy odyssey. A bed-and-breakfast entrepreneur in Guthrie, Oklahoma, offered the drama-starved citizens of the prairie something called a "Murder Mystery Weekend" that featured a séance at the grave of Elmer McCurdy—for those whose idea of fun was to dress up in western clothing and play make-believe with strangers. In the unlikely event that you were swept up in an Elmer McCurdy frenzy, you could plunge into the deep arcana of the Internet, where McCurdyana seemed to proliferate like a virus. There was even a McCurdy poet-laureate, Glenda George, whose slender volume of experimental poems contained lines I was not about to experiment with anytime soon: "Elmer is aroused by the sight of the loco," sang the poet, and, in a line that would have puzzled the man himself, "Elmer is masturbating in the dawn." There was even a rumor of a screenplay in circulation. Indeed, I had the disquieting sense that an unlikely field of McCurdy Studies now burgeoned forth like so many flowers on the prairie.

It was time to get going. It was time to cast the wide net. It was time to unleash the many-tentacled grasp of the interlibrary loan system. It was time to hit the road, to pound the pavement, to stain my sleeves in the archival dust of the past, to coax out the truth, the heart of the Elmer McCurdy story, whatever that might be.

## 2

# The West That Wasn't

It wasn't Horace Greeley who first said "Go west, young man," but John Babsone Lane Soule in the *Terre Haute (Ind.) Express* of 1851. Greeley so liked the sentiment that he used it in a *New York Tribune* editorial, and so it was fixed in the American consciousness as a Greeley-ism. For his part, Greeley made a judicious effort to call John Soule upon the national stage in order to shine the light of acknowledgment upon him, but, for all intents and purposes, Soule has vanished from history, and it is Greeley, the man at the helm of nineteenth-century pubic opinion, who mouths his words. "If you have no family or friends to aid you," Greeley's editorial continued, "and no prospect opened to you, turn your face to the great West, and there build up a home and fortune."

Greeley's phrase tapped into an occidental inclination at least as old as Seneca, a belief that civilization was marked by westward advancing periods, an inevitable cultural shift that found the center of the civilized world first in Persia, then Egypt, then Greece, then Italy. It was a belief that thrived in the heart of the Augustinian City of God, that spoke in the eleventh-century scholar Rodulfus Glaber's image of Christ at Golgotha, his face turned westward. Archetypal in its sway, it fueled the motto of Charles V, *Plus Ultra*—You can go beyond—under whom Columbus sailed, and it informed John Foxe's *Book of Martyrs*, which in 1563 proclaimed the reign of Queen Elizabeth as the inescapable final destiny of Western Civ, after which the aforementioned seat, with the help of Walter Raleigh and others, daintily jumped westward, to America. "Westward the Course of Empire takes its Way," wrote Bishop George Berkeley in 1726, prefiguring that century's great utopian experiment. It was a cardinal direction, as it were, a political, economic, and cultural directive of heroic proportions, an instinct for farthering and furthering as strong and seemingly self-evident as the pull of gravity or the flow of water.

Writing about the drift westward became a genre that would include, among its earliest contributors, Pedro de Castañeda, a diarist who accompanied the army of Francisco Coronado. Castañeda's account of the journey into the heart of North America in 1542 shows signs of a mind made unwell by the prairie. "The land is the shape of a ball," he wrote, trying to get his mind around the vast plains that would become Kansas and Nebraska. Nearly every major and minor writer of the nineteenth and early twentieth centuries wrote about the American west, from the most prominent of point men, Meriwether Lewis and William Clark (*The Journals*, 1804–1806) to Washington Irving (*A Tour of the Prairie*, 1832) and dragoons of English clerics, lords and ladies, venture capitalists, newspapermen, gadabout dandies, and deputy postmasters general on holiday, who added to the growing catalog of description and travel their own westering impressions. The sheer number of such accounts suggests a shift-ing, unpinpointable quality about the west. By the time Greeley tossed his valise into the ring in *An Overland Journey from New York to San Francisco in the Summer of 1859*, and two years later Mark Twain in *Roughing It*, the west was becoming, among other things, a destination for people who, as a little *divertissement*, sought to put the *travail* back into travel—that others might read of it in the comfort of their own homes. While Twain mined a mother lode of western Americana, others were building a road directly through *terra obscura* itself. The Hundredth Meridian Ex-cursion of 1866 brought a group of dignitaries and their families to Cozad, Nebraska, the westernmost point then yet reached by transcontinental construction crews of the Union Pacific line. The excursion participants "camped out" under the stars and were entertained by Pawnee Indians who performed evening war dances by firelight, staged an early-morning wake-up raid, and acted out an elaborate "battle" between Sioux and Pawnee warriors. The Indians were paid with gifts thrown from the train, which prompted an unscripted second skirmish. By 1900, you could pass from east to west by car like some latter-day cowboy, eat a little trail dust, gape at the last remaining buffalo, and com-pile for those who followed in your tracks a list of essentials: "First, a coat and *pleated* skirt of a material that does not show creases; an evening dress of black jet or cream lace; a taffeta duster; and a comfortable fur coat." So wrote Emily Post in *By Motor Car to the Golden Gate*.

As the west was transformed, it acquired a mythic potency keyed to a particular American palette and fueled by a growing anxiety, especially in the years following the famous thesis of

Frederick Jackson Turner on the significance of the frontier in American history, the great postmortem on the west. Turner's essay was delivered in conjunction with the Chicago Columbian Exposition in 1893, a few years after the census declared the wild American frontier officially "closed," that is, bought, sold, divided, subdivided, leased, gated, and demarcated into sections and ranges, the legal latticework of ownership and tenancy. By chance, Chicago in that year became a vortex of sorts, a congeries of cultural observers, each perhaps dimly aware of the other, each in his realm a showman who would remain synonymous with the furtherance of American nostalgia about the west: Across the street from Turner's lecture, under a covered grandstand that could hold 18,000 people, *Buffalo Bill's Wild West and Congress of Rough Riders of the World* wowed the fair-goers for a solid two hours twice a day, every day, rain or shine. A young man from Claremore, Oklahoma, attending the spectacle, was sufficiently impressed by the rope tricks of Vicente Oropeza to begin developing his own roping routine that would become the trademark of Will Rogers. Samuel Clemens was also in town that season poking around for magazine work. His long, agonizing misadventure with the Paige typesetter had brought him to the brink of bankruptcy, and the nation itself would soon plummet headlong into financial panic. Clemens stayed in bed, knocked off his feet for eleven days by a bad cold brought on by overexposure, it seemed, to what he once had celebrated as "the drive and push and rush and struggle of the raging, tearing, booming nineteenth century."

These interpreters of the west all drew attention to its demise, and each version drank deeply from the well of nostalgia, implicitly condemning the present as a fallen state inhabited by modern epigones, riding model Ts, dreaming of a fenceless prairie. Turner's writing furthered the belief in a land and its people that contained whatever had been authentically American, uncontaminated by European decadence. The ephemeral west, to borrow historian Robert G. Athearn's well-wrought phrase, remained a powerful chimera on the horizon that many, including westerners themselves, attempted to describe despite the annual declarations of its passing. The trouble was, as Greeley and others discovered about the mythic west, wherever you went to find it, there it wasn't.

In 1880, thirty years after Greeley offered his advice, eleven years after the completion of the transcontinental railroad, Elmer McCurdy was born in Washington, Maine, out-of-wedlock to seventeen-year-old Sadie McCurdy and an unknown father, possibly Sadie's cousin, a man whose name—Charles Davis—became one of Elmer's aliases in later life. According to Richard Basgall's *The Career of Elmer McCurdy, Deceased*, Sadie's brother, George, and sister-in-law, Helen, adopted and raised Elmer to protect Sadie from embarrassment. George's death of tuberculosis, in 1890, when Elmer was ten, forced the family to move to Bangor, Maine, where George's brother, Charles, helped the two sisters find jobs in town. Here in Bangor, Sadie began to take responsibility for raising her own son. This required that they reveal to Elmer that his "mother," Helen, was really his aunt, and that his "Aunt" Sadie was really his mother.

Basgall, a Kansas drama professor who spent eight years caught up in McCurdyana, and who remains a sort of founding father of Elmer McCurdy studies, traces the beginning of Elmer

McCurdy's problems to this initial disclosure, after which, according to one observer who knew the family, the young McCurdy "became unruly and rebellious." He seemed resentful and found temporary solace in the bottle, setting a pattern of drinking and troublemaking that dogged him the rest of his life. At fifteen, he started a fight in a bar, the story reported in the local *Belfast Age*. Later, he moved in with his grandfather, Harden, who helped him find an apprenticeship to a local plumber. In time, Elmer became known as an expert plumber who made a comfortable living, but by 1898 the economy of Bangor began to feel the effects of a major worldwide recession. This downturn left millions jobless and set thousands of young men on the road looking for work. Businesses closed. People went hungry. Helen and Sadie lost their jobs. It was a worrisome time, and a sad measure of the grinding burden she bore that in August of 1900 Sadie died of a ruptured ulcer. A month later Harden died of Bright's disease. With little left to hold him in Bangor, Elmer set out for the open road, following an itinerary that Horace Greeley seems to have uncannily predicted so many years earlier. "The active, aspiring mechanic," Greeley wrote, "born in Maine or New Hampshire, migrates to New York or some other Middle State soon after reaching his majority; reaches Illinois or Missouri two or three years later; and will often be found traversing Montana or Illinois before he is thirty." It was this route—or something very much like it—that McCurdy followed, spending some time along the eastern seaboard, then making a big right-hand turn and heading west.

He was not alone, for in the period between 1870 and 1910, more than 7 million people migrated to states west of the

Mississippi, at a rate that reached, as one observer described it in 1904, almost 400,000 migrants a year. During this period, more young men went west than ever before, as did more young women, more families, more of just about anybody of any age, sex, and race willing to risk the trip. When they arrived they began fencing, planting, and attending more civic meetings than had been held in all the prior history of the continent. Iowa and Missouri were emptying of people who were heading farther west, while in the two decades prior to 1900 the population of Oklahoma increased over 1,000 percent. McCurdy joined the ranks of hundreds of thousands, all seeking the westward geographical remedy, a growing population of "floaters," cast adrift by the chronic economic conditions of a nation undergoing severe growing pains.

Never have things been so bad for so many, nor so good for so few. The period coincided with the most spectacular accumulation of capital in the fewest hands that the world is ever likely to see. By 1900, with a population of 76 million, a scant fraction of 1 percent—between 25,000 and 40,000 people in the United States—owned half of the country's wealth. It was the era of the booming industrialists of steel, of railroads, and of coal—whose names we know from the marble columns, the grand estates, and the endowments they have left behind: Rockefeller, Carnegie, Frick, Morgan. The industrial capitalist, according to an observer of the time, would just as soon "sell his service to whom he pleases at what price may suit, and if by doing so he ruins men and cities, it is nothing to him." It was an era plagued by financial panics often caused by the overreaching expansion of capital. The Panic of 1837, the result in part of a crash in land speculation, drew the nation into a depression that lasted for years. The Panic of 1857 was in part the result of overcapitalized railroads. The Panic of 1873, again the result of railroad building, pitched the economy into a twenty-year period of socioeconomic instability at a time before safety nets, before unions, before unemployment insurance, social security, retirement pensions, and other protections for working people.

Greeley's westward advice, meant for those of a particular time, was felt in the gut by millions throughout the century, millions facing the stark options of suffering and death. Although some historians dispute the significance of these economic downturns, pointing to figures suggesting that over 85 percent of the entire labor force has remained at work in every decade from 1789 onward, few dispute the depths of the catastrophe that occurred in 1893, when the Philadelphia and Reading Railroad declared bankruptcy. The news brought on a financial collapse in which 500 banks and 16,000 businesses failed, and 3 million people lost their jobs. Among those affected was the McCurdy household in Bangor. Sadie McCurdy, dying on her feet, became a door-to-door seamstress. The ensuing depression lasted the rest of the decade, creating a desperate atmosphere in which people with little left to lose seemed willing to rush all over North America chasing even the faintest hope of opportunity. It was a westward trend that at times took the form of a stampede, for gold, for silver, or for the very ground itself.

As farmers throughout the world had long known, it required precious little land—perhaps a fertile acre or two—to raise enough crops to support an entire family for a year. The American homesteader, if he proved up on his allotment of 160 acres, stood to make an 8,000 percent gain above and beyond the two acres required for his own subsistence, to say nothing of surplus crop yields and increases in the value of his land above the standard $1.25 per acre. Land, then, was the original poor man's gambit, and the homesteader, that redoubtable American icon, was thus by default and definition a speculator, a mule-driving, stump-busting, hoe-tilling value-added player of the prairie, one liable to drop everything at the news of more free land farther west.

In September 1893, newly appointed U.S. Marshal Evett Dumas Nix described one such occasion, the opening of the Cherokee strip in the Territory of Oklahoma, where an estimated half-million people had amassed in the hope of settling one of the 35,000 available claims: "There were poor souls, their dilapidated wagons crammed with dirty children and drawn by starved beasts that were poorly fitted to contest against the strong men and animals who would take the lead; there were penniless drifters, afoot, and there were carts, buggies and wagons so dilapidated that one expected them to fall apart at any moment. There were old men and women . . . many of them penniless, with wasted years behind them, and they were here to make a last attempt to accomplish and accumulate something for themselves."

The rush for free land began at noon on September 16 at the sound of a gunshot. In the smoke of prairie fires that had been set the night before, one witness described how a solid mass of wagons, buggies, carts, and horsemen standing knee to knee as far as the eye could see began to spread out like a vast fan. A young woman ran out from between the galloping men on horseback, crossed the line, and sat down as hordes streamed past her. She was only a few yards into new territory, but she held her claim. A half mile ahead, through the dust and smoke, the horsemen were speeding out of sight, the landscape littered with overturned buggies and wagons, stray horses running every which way, belongings scattered over the prairie. It was a breathtaking event from which Oklahoma got its nickname, "the Sooner state," derived from those who tried to sneak across the heavily patrolled boarder prior to the shot of the gun.

By the turn of the century there were many "wests" to choose from, and few of them were wild. Most, in fact, were rather mild. Everywhere there arose a great passion for the heft and line of order: the laying out of streets, the construction of schoolhouses, firehouses, jails, and other public works, which became objects of a new kind of western civic pride. A booming era was upon the land. The mild west was born. The older, well-plowed west of the mid-prairie states was swelling with a new wave of recent settlers, who profited from the hard-won experience of the rough-hewn generation who had come before. The young man who went west, as Charles Moreau Harger observed, "goes into very different circumstances. He rides in a comfortable railway coach to the very locality where he is to reside. He drives out to his new home in a buggy, instead of toiling over the way in a 'prairie schooner.' He is close to market and to well-appointed stores. Perhaps he has free rural delivery of mail as soon as he has built his house."

Harger, no doubt, had someone other than McCurdy in mind when he wrote this in 1904. Riding up to a "new house," of course, was out of the question for McCurdy. The trip alone by passenger train would have cost him a month's wages. More likely, McCurdy hopped a freight car and spent a dirt-choked, dangerous, but exhilarating week or so on the Pennsylvania railroad, then headed southwest on the Santa Fe line. Whatever route he took, during that summer, an estimated 60,000 men rode the rails, some, like McCurdy, looking for work, others following the whim of hap and circumstance.

He merged into a floating population of tramps and hoboes, most of whom, as historian Kenneth L. Kusmer has noted, were nothing like the stereotype described in the *New York Tribune*: "indigent foreigners . . . drift[ing] naturally into the lowest employment of the depraved indolent." Rather, they were very much like McCurdy himself: young, white, single, native-born American men, nearly half of whom, like McCurdy, were skilled or semi-skilled tradesmen. Nine in ten could read and write. An increasing number had gone to college or business school or were members of the professional class. In 1904, Robert Hunter described one such down-at-heels tramp who had been an editor "with a large and first-class publishing house. The books of some of the best American writers received his approval before they were published." They were, in Hunter's words, "accidental vagrants," part of a huge reserve of labor on the move. In 1900, one-fifth of all workers in the United States were out of work from one to twelve months. Like McCurdy, they were "reacting to the social conditions of their lives, much of it either directly or indirectly a product of industrialism," but, as Kusmer adds, they were not necessarily victims of capitalism. One study in 1904 suggested that most, like McCurdy, had voluntarily left their jobs at least once

during the previous six months. The degree to which their departure had been voluntary depended, of course, upon one's
point of view. By the 1890s the railroads—the main component of the American industrial machine—fed raw materials to
factories and shipped finished goods. Automation, overproduc-
tion, and child labor brought unemployment. The factory system displaced thousands of workers and made them account-
able to the time clock and to an assembly line that dictated
their movements down to the very second. And while it was
true that wages for such work rose, untold thousands of men
and women opted to look elsewhere for employment. Was this
voluntary, or had the choice for meaningful work been taken
away? Thousands answered the question with their feet, working when they wanted, when the wages or conditions were
right, then moving on. "To save a few dollars," the *New York
Times* reported, they hopped freight trains and "beat their way
from town to town in search of work."

Such travel was dangerous and unpredictable. McCurdy
would have spent long, gaping hours waiting track side for
something to happen, punctuated by minutes of blind excite-
ment. He moved through a system ill designed for passenger
comfort. A misstep could prove deadly, yet one might need to
move quickly at any time to avoid being shunted off to some
godforsaken spot for hours or days. Company detectives or
yard bulls were always ready to throw tramps in jail. Nevertheless, McCurdy would have found in the hoboes he met a
kind of temperament, a mixture of mood and motive, that
matched his own life experience thus far. In a world of aliases,
hobo monikers, codes that preserved anonymity, and the gen-

eral reticence of the time that shielded each from the other, it's unlikely that McCurdy would have learned much, if anything, about his traveling companions. But a number of different surveys taken at the time reveal that many of McCurdy's hobo contemporaries knew firsthand about the death or desertion of a parent, about abuse and neglect, about broken homes and other dislocations of identity that so often serve to stamp some with an abiding ironic distance from the purported order that governs most men's lives. And now he was in the company of men who made it their business to flout that order. Stealing a ride on a freight train became a point of honor, and if they rode on the very back of the beast that had displaced them, at least they rode for free.

The west that McCurdy found when he arrived in Iola, Kansas, in 1903, was making a desperate bid to erase every last trace of wildness from itself. The city fathers of Iola aspired, in fact, to erect a great center of industry fueled by the fifteen-square-mile reserve of natural gas that lay a thousand feet beneath the town. The size, quality, and probable permanence of the Iola gas fields, according to experts of the time, were unequaled by any other gas field in the world, promising that "no one now living will ever see the time when this gas field outlives its usefulness." Within a decade of the first deep well strike in 1893, the town that once used a team of draft horses to drag its main street with a railroad iron had seventeen miles of paved streets, thirty miles of sidewalks, indoor plumbing, sewer, gas, electricity, a water and light plant, a telephone system, an electric trolley system, five public schools, a federal building, and a modern hospital. If Jesse James had still been alive he could have read about his exploits in the public library and stayed at the YMCA. Iola had an opera house. It had an amusement park. Though Allen County was dry, Iola itself was flush with speakeasies with names like The Eagle, Red Light, and The Blue Front that ran on the sly.

Iola boosters, churning out brochures and promoting the town in national magazines, offered twenty years of free gas to any industry that would set up shop there. The offer caught the attention of the big zinc-mining companies eighty miles to the south, a complex of mines and smelters that made up a $155 million a year industry, in today's money. By 1902, new smelters built just outside Iola were all burning free gas night and day, producing 40 percent of the world's supply of zinc. When McCurdy arrived, there were eight smelters, one rolling mill, five brickyards, an iron foundry, and a sulfuric acid factory. Clearly, this wasn't the west of yore. This wasn't even Kansas, anymore—but something more akin to Elizabeth, New Jersey. In this new, highly revised version of itself, the old west had been nearly obliterated, easternized: Iola had a suburb southeast of town named Brooklyn Park.

Soon there was a glass factory, an ice plant, and several cement factories, all run on natural gas, and the town, seemingly drunk on its rich supply, reached new heights of profligacy. The local chamber of commerce organized a gas carnival and county fair where new uses for natural gas were displayed to thousands of fair-goers. The town of La Harpe, six miles east of Iola, greeted incoming visitors with screaming, gas-blown whistles from the gas-fueled smelters, gaslights aflame in every door and yard, and, across the town's main street, a huge fiery sign of flaming gas letters that read, *There Are Others*, like some veiled message across the darkened prairie to neighboring Oklahoma. In Iola, the conventioneers had other opportunities to witness flame and fiery eruptions from its gas-happy citizens, whose flame-spewing cannon shot fire-salvos fifty feet into the air from the courthouse square, the entire eight city blocks of which was lit by gaslight until dawn.

More than 500 houses were built the year "Frank Curtis" arrived (some guess the alias helped McCurdy avoid anti-Irish sentiment), and these new homes all required gas lines and plumbing. Working for William Root, a church-going Iola booster and owner of the Eagle Cornice Works and Plumbing Shop, McCurdy made good money, putting in ten, sometimes twelve hours a day. As "Curtis," he seemed caught up in the spirit of community building, joining the volunteer fire department, where he earned fifty cents for each call, a dollar if he was required to actually fight a fire. He became a member of the local trade union and participated in several town meetings. He was even seen walking with the daughter of a prominent merchant.

The town boomed. Newspapers advertised Handsome Oak Davenports (fancy five-color, velour-covered, tufted models with steel springs, $2.00 cash, $1.00 per week), gas ranges, and rebates for railroad fares. An ad for a furniture store shows a group of working men in corduroy pants and bowler hats, their shirtsleeves rolled up to the elbows. It's Friday, when the eagle flies. One man smokes a celebratory pipe and contemplates a full-page newspaper ad for a furniture store while two men behind him study the merchandise over his shoulder—the stoves and the clocks and the beds and the sewing machines, all the gizmos of domestic bliss hovering at the dawn of the consumer era. And there in the paymaster's line, the men gaze at the fancy ad with all the intensity of money already spent. One man leaving the paymaster's window, his hat tipped jauntily on the back of his head, counts his wages. "You Get Married," the ad enjoins, "We'll Feather the Nest."

If there was a time in McCurdy's life when he might have taken up that advice, might have been drawn into a community by its infectious optimism and the blandishments of manufactured desire and the everyday wonders of revolving credit, by the shy laughter of a young girl and the promises thereof, this was the time, and Iola was the place. An Iola paper described Elmer as "an industrious young man who had gained access to the better society circles of Iola, who classed among his friends many of the well known people of the town." This would have felt good to him, making his own way, would have reminded him of Bangor, with Sadie singing in the kitchen and Elmer putting his days in, collecting a decent living wage. But he was a young man, alone in the world, and Iola, despite its promise, offered darker temptations for those who needed them—and he was, after all, rudderless and orphaned. A disquieting pattern began to emerge. His employer at the plumbing shop later acknowledged what he called McCurdy's "addiction to drink," and it was during a drunken conversation with a fellow plumber that McCurdy admitted that he was living under an alias, saying that he'd killed a man in a barroom brawl in another state. Whether this was true or just the blustering of a young man counting coup in a local speakeasy, nobody knows for sure. What is known is that William Root got wind of the rumor and later confronted McCurdy about his real identity and about the alleged murder. McCurdy acknowledged his true identity but denied the murder story. It was all too much for William Root, though, who in February 1905 fired McCurdy.

Root's action underscores the profound change that had taken place in the world that McCurdy inhabited. Fifty years earlier, for a man to have an alias and a shadowy past were features that provoked little comment. Life was hard. A good man could get into a bad scrape. What mattered back then, it seems, was what one could do in the here and now, and by these standards, the always ongoing, eternal present-tense standards of the old frontier, Elmer McCurdy would have been a model citizen. But more had changed about Iola than can be measured in the manufacturing statistics of the Kansas State census. Iola had become genteel, was embarrassed about its violent past, and had yet to become nostalgic about rising from the muck of the plains, and McCurdy's story of a barroom murder, whether true or not, was now like an unpleasant odor. The genteel mind is made vulnerable to such revelations, and McCurdy, a plumber of dubious parentage, caught up in Iola's pretensions, must have been stung by this forced disclosure. He had been at a crossroads in his life. Iola had offered him something akin to happiness, and now the offer was withdrawn. William Root, with his two-story brick house on Washington Avenue, could not risk a scandal, and McCurdy was unceremoniously exiled from the good life that Iola had promised.

By 1905 the nation was shooting skyward in the spirit of high, steel-framed American verticality. Everything the country did to get big and tall required raw material, and someone at the business end to dig, drift, blast, heft, and haul it from the ground. Out of the strip mines of Butte, Montana, came the copper of the Carnegies, hauled out by Irish immigrants to electrify a nation, and from the mines underneath the timbered hillsides where the states of Missouri, Oklahoma, and Kansas meet came an unheralded ore that was loaded onto trains in smelted pigs, shipped east, and used as an anticorrosive alloy in just about every conceivable form of manufacture, from brass fittings to roofing tiles, medicines, and armory shells. That ore was zinc, and it was at the bottom of a mine shaft in Carterville, Missouri, with a double-pointed pick and a square scoop shovel, that Elmer McCurdy, on the cusp, as it were, the sharp, pointed end of the American technological sublime, found himself working nine-hour shifts, six days a week, loading tons of zinc ore into thousand-pound tubs.

The region had been prospected by the French as early as 1720 under the command of Bernard de La Harpe, who wrote of the Osages, "There are lead mines 12 leagues from their home, of which they do not know the usage." Settlement of what became the Tri-State District, a 1,000-square-mile region of howling wilderness, came in the 1830s as farmers arrived, attracted by the miles of rolling prairie, blackjack oak, abundant wildlife, river valleys, and superb grassland for livestock. The land could not have been more promising—an abundance of wildlife and the very ground itself offering up the metal with which game could be taken—lead melted for shot. Here legends were born of farmers tripping over dark seams of heavy, cubed lead ore of such purity—over 80 percent galena—that it could be melted on the spot or formed into 80-pound pigs and sent down the Mississippi by flatboat for trading in New Orleans. Word spread, and early, pre–Civil War mining camps flourished. In 1854, not a single cabin stood along the Shoal River near the site of Ganby, Missouri. By 1860, there were 300 shafts dug and 7,000 people.

One camp, Minersville, later called Oronogo, produced the largest chunk of pure lead ever found in the region. It lay just six feet deep and weighed 30,000 pounds. In the 1870s, some miners in Carthage were making up to $50 per day. One man, digging a well for water in his backyard, found a vein of ore that yielded $2 million by today's valuation. It was this kind of discovery—so rich and so near the surface—that stayed in the public mind, vibrating like a struck tuning fork as the country's economy seesawed up and down across the middle decades of the 1800s, and gave the region a reputation as a "poor man's camp," meaning that even a poor man with nothing more than a pick and a shovel had a chance to make a fortune. Many who arrived early did just that. Fortunes were made in the "Lucky Bill," the "Lucky Joe," the "Once More," the "Never Sweat," the "Fighting Wolf," the "Bonehead," and the "Navy Bean," names that suggest the fleeting, giddy impulsiveness of a particularized moment of apprehension—of partners hopping up and down in the mud knowing they'd never have to work again. Mining camps, then mining towns, sprang up—Galena, Blende City, Leadville, Carthage, Webb City, Oronogo, Granby, and dozens of others, with Joplin the unofficial regional center and supply depot.

And there was more. Beneath the deposits of lead lay one of the world's richest fields of zinc, which until the turn of the century had ended up in the tailing piles. As more uses were found, the price of zinc soared from $8 a ton in 1873 to $27 a ton in 1888. The zinc deposits were deeper in the ground, however, and required more capital to extract. Small partnerships merged to form large consortiums. The Davey Mine, once operated by Thomas and Paul Davey, had merged with American Zinc and by 1910 had mills and underground works in half a dozen towns in the Tri-State District, making it the largest operation in the area, and the one most likely to have employed the drifter Elmer McCurdy, who arrived too late in the game to make it big, though not late enough to make a decent wage down in the mines, where work was hard but profitable.

He would have been one among many in a crew sinking a vertical shaft fifty feet down, then cribbing the shaft with oak planks until they hit a seam of ore, then "drifting" horizontally, flaring and blasting away, following the ore, sometimes creating huge subterranean galleries fifty feet high. After a charge had been set off by the "powder monkey," roof trimmers would enter the gallery to dislodge unstable pieces of rock from the ceiling with pry bars to prevent roof cave-ins, the cause of at least half of the mine fatalities. Working as a mucker, McCurdy would have had to move 1,200 pounds of ore into a tub, or "can." It was a kind of labor that few of us today could fathom, a staggering kind of work that, by agreement, required McCurdy to fill a minimum of between 80 and 100 such cans each shift—about 60 tons of ore, all of it shoveled by hand—to remain a mucker in good standing. For this McCurdy was paid 2 cents per can, or about $2 a day—and his was often the highest-paying job in the mine, more so than hoisterman, who lowered and raised the buckets, or the pig tail, who shuttled buckets back and forth underground, or the screen ape, who broke rock with a sledge into small pieces above ground. The work was dangerous—men were crushed by rock fall or blown to bits by overzealous applications of dynamite. Hard hats were unknown. Instead, miners stuffed wadded-up newspapers into their felt hats and hoped for the best. Lead and zinc dust hung perpetually in the air as the men drilled and blasted and shoveled and trimmed and trammed their way through the earth. In time, McCurdy would become chronically short of breath, coughing, losing weight, his lungs irritated, inflamed by zinc dust, the tissue scarring. This was the onset of silicosis, or miner's consumption, which, though not contagious, was progressively debilitating and made McCurdy and everyone who worked in the mines vulnerable to tuberculosis, a disease that could be passed on from one man to an entire crew with each sip of a shared water cup.

Tuberculosis was rampant throughout the camps. An Anti-Tuberculosis League was formed, and a twenty-acre tent city was built for the victims of the disease. In a study of 720 Webb City miners, Dr. Anthony J. Lanza of the U.S. Public Health Service noted, moreover, that "after silicosis has developed, the use of alcoholic drink and patent medicines increase[d] decidedly." Alcohol consumption rose up to 25 percent. No doubt a portion of McCurdy's hard-earned pay went to the local saloons of Carterville, which could not have been any better than those of Joplin, where, according to a local versifier, "women drank and cursed like fury" and "the barkeepers sold the meanest liquor which made a white man sick and sicker." After nine dank, dark hours working ankle deep in water at the chilly bottom of a mine shaft, almost anyone might want a drink. It was, perhaps, a measure of his desperation that McCurdy tossed his shovel aside, fled the Tri-State mining district in November 1907, and joined the U.S. Army.


McCurdy was mustered into Company E, 3rd Infantry, and stationed at Fort Leavenworth, Kansas, which had been, since its founding in 1827, the first permanent fort established west of the Missouri River, the first continuously occupied settlement in Kansas, and the primary tactical base of operations for clobbering and removing the Native American tribes west of the Mississippi. By 1883, according to General William T. Sherman's final report to the secretary of war, the west was "completely open to the immigrant in regions where a few years ago no single man could go with safety." Yet the juggernaut of Manifest Destiny marched ever westward, as cavalry and infantry advanced overland to annex California from Mexico. In 1900, the imperial directive came full circle as infantry from Fort Leavenworth were dispatched into the Eastern Hemisphere, and west met east at bayonet point in the islands of the Philippines. McCurdy arrived at the post just as the expeditionary force returned from overseas.

Shortly after that, a young first lieutenant also arrived at Fort Leavenworth. A recent West Point graduate, he had passed the last few years in Washington, D.C., by day enduring postgraduate engineering school with an air of casual indifference, by night moving among the highest-ranking officials in the land. Family connections had secured for him an astonishing extracurricular appointment as aide-de-camp to Theodore Roosevelt, and thus he had seen the Philippine Insurrection from the rarefied summit of global stratagem. Roosevelt's White House deliberations over the turmoil in the Far East apparently included a request, at one point, for the junior officer's opinion on the whole matter. Thirty years later, he would come to know the Philippines all too well, first in defeat and then in triumph. He would leave much of the record of his life in flames in that far-off archipelago, only to reappear with such a vengeance that his name would become for a generation who lived through World War II synonymous with a crushing, annihilating, vindicating form of return. He was Douglas MacArthur, in age Elmer McCurdy's exact contemporary.

The two men couldn't have been more different had they come from opposite ends of the galaxy. On his army enlistment papers McCurdy recorded his occupation as "miner," although this was less than candid. He was, in fact, a skilled plumber but a tradesman nonetheless, a drifting, hard-drinking member of the working class. MacArthur, by contrast, was a creature of privilege, the son of a decorated general and a doting, determined mother, as fierce a general of her son's career as could be found anywhere. Her friends called her Pinkie. It was the sort of Social Register nickname, like Binky or Bunny, that signaled an ever-so-brief excursion into the ridiculous—a ruling-class indulgence. The apple did not fall far from the tree. A photograph taken in 1906 shows MacArthur holding a pipe, seated outside in a folding chair encamped somewhere, his legs crossed, pants tucked neatly into shin-high boots. There are weeds underfoot upon which planks have been thrown, and there's the vague suggestion of a tent in the background. He looks into the camera as if he were a huntsman on tour in the Congo, with an air of supreme entitlement, as one to whom great things were about to happen, *in Milwaukee*. Indeed, both he and his father found themselves shunted off to undistinguished assignments in that city, where the family lived together in a large house and tried not to imagine themselves in exile. Under the command of Major William V. Judson, Douglas MacArthur was primarily focused on passing his postgraduate engineering exams and could barely contain his contempt for the work that Judson asked of him. He shirked his responsibilities, disappeared from the drafting table.

Judson, with an aim to readjusting MacArthur's hauteur, ordered him upstate to Manitowoc and gave him a task large
enough to absorb his burgeoning ego: the reconstruction of
Manitowoc Harbor. Instead, MacArthur bridled at the assignment. The two men were at loggerheads until April 1908, when
MacArthur was hastily reassigned, again with the help of a family
friend, to Fort Leavenworth, where he was placed in command of
Company K, the worst, most dispirited group of soldiers of the
twenty-one companies on the post. MacArthur flourished in his
first taste of command. In July of that year, Major Judson had
his revenge, however, submitting an official report so damaging it
threatened to ruin MacArthur's career as an officer. Judson wrote
that MacArthur "exhibited less interest in and put in less time
upon the drafting room, the plans and specifications for work
and the works themselves than seemed consistent with my in-
structions." Of the assignment to Manitowoc Harbor, Judson
stated that MacArthur had "remonstrated and argued verbally
and at length against assignment to this duty, which would take
him away from Milwaukee for a considerable portion of time."
This was about as far as one could go without actually charging
MacArthur with insubordination, but Judson wasn't through yet,
adding a damning final assessment: "Lieutenant MacArthur," he
wrote, "while on duty under my immediate orders, did not conduct himself in a way to meet commendation, and . . . his duties
were not performed in a satisfactory manner."

MacArthur tried to convince the chief of engineers to ex-
punge Major Judson's comments from his record, but in so doing he seemed only to confirm in the minds of his superiors Judson's implied opinion, that MacArthur was an overindulged

pain-in-the-ass to have under one's command. Things looked so bad, it seemed, that Pinkie, without MacArthur's knowledge, solicited the head of the Union Pacific Railroad, Edward H. Harriman, for a position on her son's behalf. For his part, MacArthur threw his considerable energies into the command of the hapless Company K, marching them, riding horseback with them, setting speed records for the construction of pontoon bridges (one soldier died in the effort), and winning commendations. But still, it was clear that his thoughts lay far beyond his purgatorial moment there in Kansas. A fellow officer recalled him in front of a Fort Leavenworth drugstore, "standing a bit aloof from the rest of us and looking off in the distance with what I have always considered in other people to be a Napoleonic stance." Working with the Engineering Corps, MacArthur soon gained a considerable reputation as an explosives expert. He wrote a demolitions field manual and designed a two-week curriculum of instruction for military demolitions.

And in the fall of each year, with the leaves changing in the cottonwoods, and geese on the fly, MacArthur gave his two-week course, followed by demonstrations in "demolishing things with dynamite, rack-a-rock, [nitro]glycerine and the various other concoctions known only to the blasting world." He'd leave the post for Fort Riley, Kansas, with a handful of men whom he'd personally trained. The nine men accompanying MacArthur in September 1910 included two sergeants, a corporal, and six privates from Company K. It's not known if MacArthur ever used enlisted men from other companies, such as McCurdy's own Company E, to help with the demolition training, but it is possible that McCurdy was chosen for such service. If so, he would have learned quite well indeed about charge placement. Had he been merely a casual observer of such a course, he may have learned the rudiments of handling and setting off explosives in the field. MacArthur's course coincided every year with the end of the annual August march to Fort Riley, in which McCurdy did participate. In any case, McCurdy entered the army a plumber and a shoveler of zinc ore; within months of his discharge he was blowing up things with nitroglycerin. However it may have come about, it seems likely that MacArthur, the future five-star general, "having written the standard Army text book on demolitions," had a hand, directly or indirectly, in the education of Elmer McCurdy.

Late September 1910 saw the invasion of the old army town by a different sort of army. First came the advance cars filled with teams of litho-men, paste-makers, press agents, and bill-posters, who hit, daubed, and tacked their way through the gut, the center of town, then worked outward until every likely surface bore the yellow and green colors of the so-called flying squadron, the first section of trains, carrying the cookhouse, the baggage cars, the blacksmith shop, the menagerie, and the lay-out crew for the Adam Forepaugh and Sells Brothers Big United Shows. Next came the heavy section, with all the seats and canvas, center poles, quarter poles, spikes, spike drivers, gear and tackle, and anything else that was part of the big top. Other trains followed, carrying every conceivable and every inconceivable apparatus—each move carefully choreographed.

The circus had already been through Ohio twice, all of New England, including McCurdy's hometown of Bangor, Maine, eastern and western Pennsylvania, upstate New York, and was making its way back through the Midwest bearing down on Leavenworth. With the exception of three stops—Cambridge, New York City, and Philadelphia—the Forepaugh and Sells Shows played in a different town each night, often hundreds of miles from where it had been the night before. The train for the circus was a mile long, every night loading and every morning unloading, among other things, about 1,000 people, including 50 clowns and 350 other performers, 600 horses, a menagerie of 150 other animals, and 10 acres of canvas tent—enough people and equipment to make a splash in most American towns, which was the point, after all. The scale of the undertaking was such that will never be repeated again, and the Forepaugh and Sells circus was just one of three great companies traveling the country that season under the aegis of Ringling Brothers.

I like to imagine Elmer McCurdy with his army buddies, on leave from the post, perhaps sharing a pint of whiskey between themselves, lushed up and weaving through the circus grounds of trampled grass and sawdust, the crowd milling past the constant, ongoing grind of lemonade stands, grease joints, and candy butchers. Perhaps they'd stop to watch the lightning-swift hands of the gaffs and broad tossers working the grift. Perhaps they were drawn, as everyone else was, by the billowing, "big white city" of the big top, once inside climbing high to the cheaper blue seats to watch the Three Alvos, or the rumble of Dan Curtis and his sixty-one horses galloping headlong yet staying in perfect synchrony, or the iron-jawed Soaring Richards Sisters, spinning in unison, dangling overhead by ropes clenched in their mouths. J. J. Richards and his band would be playing and the madcap clown car backfiring, elephants would be running around the hippodrome, and trained seals would be balancing globes on their noses. I like to imagine them back outside working their way through the men in derbies and porkpie hats, the women holding their long, Gibson Girl dresses out of the mud, McCurdy and his friends, feeling full for it, approaching the gaudy banners of E. J. Kelly's sideshow exhibits. They would watch a free demonstration of something unusual on the stage—a man shoving a ten-penny nail up his nose, perhaps. And then the carnival talker would tempt them with a shrewdly timed and precipitous drop in the price of admission, and McCurdy and his friends would buy a ticket and go inside. There they would see the lady sword swallower, the tattooed man, the strong-jawed nail breaker, the snake charmer, Levis's Live Rooster Orchestra, and if it were a true 10-in-1 sideshow, a mummy whom the lecturer would claim was the body of Billy the Kid, perhaps, or John Wilkes Booth, or some other long-dead outlaw. I like to hold Mc-Curdy here in my mind, in this imagined but not entirely improbable encounter, and wonder what thoughts, if any, occurred to the young private, a few weeks away from his discharge from the army, standing there before a mummified corpse.

## ∼ 3 ∼

# Help Wanted

RAILWAY mail clerks wanted. Average salary: $1,100. Common School education sufficient. Send name immediately. WANTED car carpenters experienced rebuilding freight cars; steady work; fine wages; no trouble. Ottawa Car Works. WANTED twenty laborers on Whitehead and Blacksnake sewers; good wages. Dishwashers WANTED at The Stag. WANTED reliable and sober man to take orders. References required. Active man WANTED who can do carpenter work and is handy with horses. WANTED good second butcher. Ambitious young men to become traveling salesmen; experience unnecessary. Write for particulars. WANTED good sausage and casing man. WANTED A baker, at once. WANTED Blacksmith. WANTED Sawyer. WANTED Chicken picker. WANTED Boy with wheel. WANTED Everyone to know you can see a one-hour performance of moving pictures at Princess Theater. Admission, five cents.

An afternoon at a nickelodeon might have been a good way to pass the listless days following McCurdy's discharge from the

army. During the previous three years, he seems to have
blended into the background of the regimental fabric to the
point of invisibility, distinguishing himself nowhere and at
nothing. He served in a machine-gun detachment under the
command of Captain Charles H. Murphy but for the most part
remained almost entirely below the radar of the *Fort Leavenworth
News*, the paper that regularly reported even the smallest pertur-
bation of camp life—things like hangovers and sprained ankles.
Soldiers deserted frequently or were absent without leave. The
affair of Private Dunlap, who "went to Kansas City a few days
ago and forgot to come back," was a typical rendering of such
truancy. McCurdy, for the most part, seems to have kept his
nose clean, although he was the subject of disciplinary action at
least once in his tenure. "Private McCurdy has been relieved
from extra duty as laborer in the Quartermaster Department,"
the *News* reported in the spring of 1910. On November 7, he received an honorable discharge from the army. Four days later,
the paper reported on his exit from service in the dry, coded
language of military understatement: "No re-up for him."

A change of season was upon him. November had arrived,
blustery, indecisive, sending rains one day and unseasonably
warm weather the next. The help wanted ads in the St. Joseph
papers were filled with the kind of jobs that made one sink
deeper into one's seat at the bar. Four and a half million people
were unemployed across the country, and to that figure was
added McCurdy, whose most recent job qualification as a
machine-gun operator and novice blower-up of bridges may
have lent a sardonic note to the time he spent drinking away his
discharge pay, in St. Joseph, the thriving river city that had been

the likely destination of his army furloughs. His exit papers noted his "excellent, honorable, and faithful" military service, but a constellation of resentments over life's bitter circumstances, catalyzed by a penchant for associating with a rough-and-tumble crowd of servicemen, began to shape McCurdy's imaginative energies.

Events in the next few days would suggest the direction of his thoughts. He contacted his old army buddy Walter Schoppelrie back in Fort Leavenworth, who secured a seven-day pass, ostensibly to visit relatives in St. Joseph. But on the evening of November 19, Schoppelrie and McCurdy were stopped on a side street in St. Joseph by three special officers for the Burlington line. What exactly aroused their suspicion is lost to history, but something about them looked awry.

To officers familiar with the neighborhood, the two men stood out as strangers, that is to say, drifters, of a class so often associated with petty crime that it had become a matter of course for police to stop and interrogate such men. If for no other reason, they did so in the hope that all drifters, floaters, lay-abouts, and hoboes would spread the word down the line that St. Joe was a prickly, inhospitable stopover for vagabonds. It may have been the way they were dressed—both in new, identical mud-bespattered overalls—which, the officers noticed upon closer inspection, the men wore over military uniforms. Asked to explain themselves, the two offered the kind of dodgy generalizations that only drew the officers closer, like sharks to blood.

Perhaps it was the bag the men carried and the metallic *clank* it made when they set it down. Perhaps it was what the bag contained—a force screw, a door jimmy, assorted drills and hacksaws, cold chisels, a nitroglycerin funnel, gunpowder, and a gunpowder funnel—all of which they had been lugging around with some difficulty, but to what end and purpose the men suddenly could not explain to their interrogators. The affidavit and complaint filed two days later came straight to the point, describing the evidence as "mechanical devices adapted, designed and commonly used for breaking into vaults and safes."

He had been on his own for barely two weeks, and now McCurdy faced felony charges and a two- to ten-year sentence. With little more than a dollar to his name, he could not raise bail. Walter Schoppelrie, perhaps hoping this would all blow over in a few days, wrote his commander, Captain Charles Murphy, for a furlough extension. But the letter of his arrest arrived sooner than his request to the commander's desk, and Schoppelrie, who already had a juvenile record for burglary, now faced time in the Fort Leavenworth stockade. By comparison to things going on in the world at large—rioting suffragettes slapping the British premier, the Philippine-American war dragging on, and Tolstoy recently dead—Elmer and Walter's predicament was pretty small beer, even for the local editors of the *St. Joseph Gazette*, who positioned the story among other, more alarming items—two girls killed in a runaway buggy, a lurid, quadruple murder of an entire family in Missouri. The *Gazette*'s headline was "Police Think They Nabbed Two Yeggs."

An advertisement for the Plymouth Clothing Company, a men's store in the same issue of the *St. Joseph Gazette*, features a line drawing of a pair of strong-chinned men looking directly at us—dapper, confident, comfortable in the urban scene. Their trousers are cuffed, their double-breasted winter coats buttoned to the chin. One wears a derby, the other a jaunty tam-o'-shanter. Both know how to stand in the street. They know how to hold an umbrella. This could be Wall Street, not Felix Street, St. Joseph, Missouri. Behind them, in a final, up-to-the-moment grace note, a Wright Brothers plane is visible, sailing high above their heads. In November 1910, the spirit of invention was literally in the air, and something of that spirit seems to have darted its way into the Buchanan County Jail, like a beam of mirror-bent sunlight twisting its way to the heart of an Egyptian tomb.

McCurdy and Schoppelrie had two days before their arraignment to figure out a plan. During this time, the two men underwent a jailhouse conversion of sorts, for on November 23, they stood up in court, wearing the uniform of the U.S. Army, as McCurdy declared to Judge Daniel Nies that the tools in his sack were not, in fact, the tools of a common burglar. He explained instead that they were parts to an invention that he and Walter were trying to patent, a machine-gun tripod that allowed the user to fire the gun with his foot.

By its judicious use of quotation marks around certain key words, such as "tripod" and "invention," the *St. Joseph Gazette*, which covered the arraignment, displayed an uncommon level of forbearance toward McCurdy's claim. Never mind that McCurdy and Schoppelrie had been tight-lipped on the night of their arrest: "The men are unable to explain where they got the tools, or, rather, refuse to tell," the *Gazette* had reported the next day. Now, standing before Judge Nies, McCurdy's abiding interest in a machine-gun tripod blossomed forth. According to the *Leavenworth Times*, McCurdy also claimed that he had, in fact, mentioned the machine-gun invention at his arrest, and claimed the tools as his own, to be used for that purpose. Prosecutors pounced upon the powder funnels and the money sacks, the arresting officers asking McCurdy to explain what purpose, if any, these items had to do with machine guns, tripods, or anything else. McCurdy held his ground, claiming he was using the funnel to load powder into shotgun shells for his friend Walter. And the money bags? They were simply empty coffee sacks, McCurdy said, that just happened to be lying around.

McCurdy seemed to have had the presence of mind, despite his story's transparency, to turn the procedural protections of the accused to his advantage. He asked for and received a continuance so that he could subpoena, among others, Captain Charles Murphy, his company commander in Fort Leavenworth, and other experts on his behalf. But his courtroom chutzpa turned against him the following Monday, when only Captain Murphy appeared, and to disastrous effect. "Those bits of metal," Murphy is said to have stated about the tools in question, "would have absolutely no use about any machine gun of mine." McCurdy reportedly jumped up, swearing and lunging at the captain, and had to be restrained by officers of the court. This episode was not going to blow over in a day or even a week. Judge Nies determined that there was sufficient evidence to indict McCurdy and Schoppelrie for possession of burglary tools and set a trial date for the January term.

What to make of this attempt to snooker the sober court of Buchanan County? McCurdy's performance—cobbling together a "machine-gun defense" out of a few chisels and a crowbar— attests to a bald-faced resourcefulness, a knack for pettifoggery and cunning that one associates with expensive trial lawyers. Or perhaps he was not clever at all, but made of equal measures of stupidity and grandiosity, presenting the common feature of the nascent outlaw—a thickheaded contempt or disregard for consequences—which enabled him to stand before the court and calmly present what must have seemed a preposterous defense.

It all seems a change from the model citizen McCurdy had been during his days back in Iola, Kansas. But the difference may be only one of appearance, the way light appears to bend a stick in water. There would be time, in any event, for McCurdy to pick up a few additional tips in jailhouse jurisprudence in the months to come, time to work out the finer points of the machine-gun defense. There would be time, also, to compare his resume, as it were, his life experience so far, with that of his fellow inmates, and time for thoughts of the sort that may have made the Buchanan County Jail seem less like a dead end than a threshold to bigger and better dreams.

"We went along a narrow place and got into a kind of room, all damp and sweaty and cold, and there we stopped," says Huck Finn, describing the cave, that archetypal male bonding place so reminiscent of a jail cell, where Tom Sawyer is about to initiate Huck and his group of friends into Tom Sawyer's Gang. The scene is Twain's send-up of the dime novel in *Huckleberry Finn*, with Tom Sawyer as the well-versed devotee of "pirate books and robber books, and every gang that was high-toned."

That a gang could be high-toned in the first place was an interesting take on the American outlaw, and Twain had ample opportunity to observe the phenomenon in his life, from its murderous rise in the post–Civil War west to its high-toned apotheosis in Giacomo Puccini's opera *The Girl of the Golden West*, which premiered at the New York Metropolitan Opera House in December 1910 and featured Enrico Caruso as a bandit-tenor and the soprano Emmy Destinn as Minnie, the owner of a saloon in a mining camp, "who cares for the miners and leads them in Bible studies." The opera's Italian title (*La Fanciulla del West*) suggested a mythopoetic American west that had no equivalent in Puccini's mother tongue—and little basis in reality. It was this same west that Twain exploited to great comic effect in *Roughing It* and *Huckleberry Finn*. The latter, published in 1885 when Elmer McCurdy was five years old, coincided with a period in American history when banditry in the west, in particular that variant American species, the western train robber, had emerged as a popular, almost mythic figure. For train robbery was the great leveler: the newest, fastest, and easiest way in the Gilded Age for the little guy with little inclination for honest work to stick it to the lords of capitalism.

Twain's caricature was but an exaggeration of a romance surrounding the so-called social bandits of the period. The James-Younger or the Dalton-Doolin gangs, for instance, composed of extended family members, shared the support of local farmers and ranchers and enjoyed a broad, regional following—a nineteenth-century version of a fan base. As local heroes, the outlaws were often invited to country dances and other events, and the Dalton name was enlisted on at least one occasion to boost local business: "Bill Dalton's Gang Are After You," read the banner ad of an eponymously named Stillwater grocer. "And If You Can Give Them A Trial You Will Be Convinced That They

Keep The Freshest & Best Goods In The City At The Lowest Prices." Those who nodded in approval at the news of another train robbery, who misdirected the armed posses in pursuit of the Dalton boys, who fed and offered Chris Evans and John Sontag shelter, expressed their allegiance to the idea of the social bandit, of the strong individual standing his ground against the big companies that were so often the perceived source and cause of the widespread economic hardship of the time.

Many outlaws like Jesse James and Henry Starr were acutely aware of their notoriety and actively engaged in managing and nurturing their status as social bandits in ways that a modern-day celebrity publicist would admire. Bill Dalton told a reporter for the *Oklahoma State Capital* that he was considering teaming up with Frank James to open a saloon in Chicago to take advantage of their fame. The plan never came to fruition, but it's fun to imagine the two bandits hoisting a few with Frederick Turner and Buffalo Bill Cody. Jesse James had his own newspaper apologist in John Edwards, a Missouri newspaper editor who sought to explain the James gang's predations to the public in terms of personal vengeance, of strong, decent men righting wrongs, and Bill Doolin could provoke newspapermen into rhapsody. "Doolin," the editor of the *Ardmore (Okla.) State Herald* wrote, "at present the reigning highwayman, is friendly to the people in one neighborhood, bestowing all sorts of presents upon the children . . . [and is] as fully a romantic figure as Robin Hood ever cut."

The men in the James gang, in fact, were known to write their own publicity. Just before fleeing their second job, the holdup of the Iron Mountain Railroad at Gads Hill, Missouri, in

1874, they handed the conductor an envelope that contained a vetted account of the selfsame robbery that had just transpired.

> The most daring on record—the southbound train on the Iron Mountain Railroad was robbed here this evening by seven heavily armed men, and robbed of _____ dollars. The robbers arrived at the station some time before the arrival of the train, and arrested the station agent and put him under guard, then threw the train on the switch. The robbers were all large men, none of them under six feet tall. They were all masked and started in a southerly direction after they had robbed the train. They were all mounted on fine-blooded horses. There is a hell of an excitement in this part of the country.

The legends of these outlaws, nurtured by the early image-making apparatus of the nineteenth-century graphic revolution, skewed the truth in a direction that enabled their continued popular consumption. There was also a small, specialized audience for famous western outlaws, a reader, or—more likely—a listener, for whom the outlaw myths and legends were more than forms of popular entertainment or hero worship. He could be found in the local saloon, though your eye, passing over the crowded, smoke-filled bar, would most likely pass over him, too. He was invisible, part of the backdrop of any scene, and when, after too much liquor, he made a scene and busted a few chairs or teeth, he was viewed, again, as a type, and so remained invisible. The classic photographs of him, face forward and profile—the mug shot—do not disabuse us of his invisibility. As a type, he persists through time. He is the invisible classmate who passed through your school one year, then vanished amid a swirl of rumor. He is your dead second cousin back from prison. He is the neighbor whose name you never learn.

Three years after the financial Panic of 1907, he was a shadow presence in all the papers, a fear riding just beneath the surface of life, a reminder that in an instant anyone could be cast adrift, jobless, without a safety net. A typical "advertorial" in the *St. Joseph Gazette* for Stuart's Dyspepsia Tablets, entitled "Why I Lost My Job," plays upon this fear. "In this quick age," the article begins, "our minds must be clear, rapid, active and free from outside influence or worry, or else we go down to failure with the throng of floaters who go from one place of employment to another, giving no satisfaction to others or to themselves, constantly growing older and less useful, with no ambition, no will power, and no hope."

In 1910, two such men were serving time in the Buchanan County Jail. One was Elmer McCurdy. The other was a man who, despite his circumstances, had big plans, a man for whom the legends of bygone bandits had become a sort of blueprint, a vocational guide, a talisman.

His name was Walter Jarrett, a petty burglar and a paroled, minor league bank robber finishing off a fifty-day sentence for being drunk and disorderly. Jarrett and McCurdy were in some ways a perfect match. Both liked to drink. Both were roughly the same age and size. But Jarrett, being the oldest of fourteen children, was a man who'd already robbed banks and done hard time in the Missouri State Penitentiary. In all likelihood, he projected the confidence of someone who'd been around the block, never mind that it was most recently a cell block that he was circling. Both men seemed to be on the same downward, dyspeptic slide—"giving no satisfaction to others or to themselves, constantly growing older and less useful"—that had landed them here, to spend Christmas together in jail.

Walter Jarrett had ambitions of a very specific variety. He was going to be an outlaw of the first order. He was determined to enter the realm of train robbers that began with the dastardly Frank Sparks and John Reno, who'd been credited with the world's first train robbery in 1866, continued to its early high period in the 1870s and 1880s, which included Jesse James and Henry Starr, and peaked in the late 1890s with Al Jennings, John Sontag, and also Harry Longabaugh and George Leroy Parker—a.k.a. Butch Cassidy and the Sundance Kid.

As a young boy in Missouri, Jarrett had grown up under the spell of Jesse James, who had been killed when Walter was three. According to Jarrett family legend, Walter had a bit of Tom Sawyer in him, approaching outlawry with the spirit of a romantic adventure, bordering on foolishness, that may have caused resentment in his brothers, Lee and Glenn. They also had criminal aspirations, but they were more practical-minded. At the end of his fifty-day sentence, Walter returned to his brother's cabin. Before leaving, he gave McCurdy a tip for his trial, an old trick that Jesse James often used—to subpoena friends as character witnesses. Within a few days, McCurdy had arranged for a band of former army drinking buddies from Company E to testify at his trial.

On Monday, January 30, 1911, things got off to a rocky start for prosecuting attorney Oscar McDaniel, who was able to secure only one material witness to testify against McCurdy's machine-gun defense, a local gunsmith named J. W. Batcheller, Sr. He proved testy and recalcitrant. McDaniel held up the force screw and asked his witness to state what such a tool was commonly used for. "I never saw one before," Batcheller said dryly. McDaniel then held up the long piece of metal, the jimmy, and, reminding the jury of Batcheller's experience as "a gunsmith, an expert on guns of all kinds," asked if such an object could be used on a machine gun. "I don't know much about machine guns," Batcheller said, "I only work on guns you can hunt with. You can't hunt with machine guns." For McDaniel, it was turning into a long morning.

Other witnesses for the state—a man identified as Lieutenant Powell, commander of McCurdy's machine-gun platoon, and Captain Murphy, whose testimony about machine guns had been so damaging at the initial arraignment—were detained on military business at Fort Leavenworth. For McCurdy, this was incredibly good luck. His defense attorney, public defender M. G. Moran, immediately called up the passel of character witnesses from Company E, one of whom declared to the court that McCurdy "was the best damned soldier in the whole damned army." Following this exuberant testimony, Moran leaned heavily on McCurdy's status as an army veteran with an excellent service record.

Finally, Moran called his client to the witness stand. At some point during his testimony, McCurdy went to the table, picked up the long, metal crowbar, and said to the jury, "Now, this is one leg of a three-legged mount. I'm planning to make two more just like it." The curved, business end of the bar would "act as a foot for the leg." The other end would "fasten to a metal plate with a hinge." The bolt on what the prosecutor said was a force screw would "pass through a hole in the plate, and the dogs on the nut of the bolt will clamp to a toggle on the bottom of the gun barrel." This, McCurdy explained, would "let the gun barrel rotate in any direction, as well as play up and down." The idea, he said, was "to fix up a mount that you can take down fast, carry off separate, and set up again almost anywheres."

It was a masterful appeal to the jury's imagination. By asking them, in effect, to conjure a Model T from a hand crank, it flattered their capacity to see the invisible, to complete a complex order from a few simple parts in a canvas bag. It was only a tripod, after all, that they were asked to envision. Greater miracles were being performed every day in America and not by men of science—as a pair of bicycle mechanics had proven at Kitty Hawk. McCurdy's defense thus engaged a populist, inventive spirit that put a Wright brothers plane in the background of newspaper ads, that sang, with no-nonsense technical acumen, of "dogs" and "plates" and "toggles," and that McCurdy delivered in a down-east dialect that cast him in the powerfully compelling role of a humble Yankee inventor.

The jury could not find McCurdy guilty as charged and released him. Beyond the walls of the jail in St. Joe, a novice inventor, down on his luck, might have gone any number of places to continue his quest for a better machine-gun tripod, but McCurdy's movements gave the lie to his courtroom hokum, his compass pointing him, infallibly, toward trouble. He made his way south into Oklahoma and followed Cedar Creek to a cabin owned by the brother of his jailhouse friend, Walter Jarrett.

It's hard to imagine a family more disastrously enamored with the mythic aura of legendary criminality than Walter Jarrett, his two brothers, Glenn and Lee, and their younger brothers, Buster, Floyd, and Earl. All of them seemed to share the same, doomed sociopathic crimp in the chromosomes, dangerous to themselves and to anyone who crossed them. Yet they apparently knew enough about the hazards of their nefarious trade, and the likelihood of an early death, to select the graveyard where their outlaw bones were all to be buried. It was a proactive gesture recalling the cave-borne, romantic spasms of Tom Sawyer's gang. As a group they seemed to cry out in vain for intervention from a vocational guidance counselor, flinging themselves repeatedly at outlaw fame and notoriety, only to fail or get themselves killed or locked up for life.

To seek the company of the Jarrett brothers, then, was ill advised in the extreme. It meant something that McCurdy traveled 250 miles across the entire width of the state of Kansas, then west into Oklahoma to the Jarretts' cabin, and what it meant was that he would ride with these would-be outlaws. Walter Jarrett probably played up McCurdy's experience in the army working with explosives, dubbing Elmer an expert safe blower and enlisting him in a scheme that would launch them from petty burglary into legend. In the spring of 1911, the men would break into the general store in Centralia, Oklahoma, stealing ammunition and tools that would come in handy in the next few weeks.

Northbound from Arkansas on the St. Louis Iron Mountain line, the darkened prairie must have seemed most lonesome, each slow, gliding station stop a dimly lit outpost, with place-names sounding like an alphabet blown from a hookah—*Inola, Nowata, Oologah, Talala, Watova.*

The passenger cars were filled with 250 people in varying states of slumber. One of the travelers, taking his bedtime cigar, felt the steady rolling rhythms of the train and the land moving beneath him and the breeze through the opened window parting the hair on his head. At 11 P.M., the train eased into Lenapah station, where mail was quickly loaded into the express car. The train slowly crept from the platform with great lumbering puffs, getting up to speed, while inside, H. P. Pinkney, the night mail clerk, one of legions moving like clockwork across the country that night, shook the envelopes from canvas bundles and sorted and routed the mail into pigeonholes. In America at the time, 61 million pieces of mail were distributed each day along a quarter million miles of track; each day mountains of freight and more than 2 million passengers were moved, all of it adding up to big money—a net return by today's valuation of $38 million a day for the railroad companies. And now, just up the track, plans were set for the smallest, tiniest portion of the franchise to be rerouted at gunpoint through the Osage Hills.

A few miles north of Lenapah, the train slowed, and in the middle of nowhere it came to a complete, unscheduled stop. Then came a shower of gunfire. Pinkney and his assistant hit the deck as a fusillade of bullets crashed into the side of the express car, ricocheting off the iron castings. In the passenger section, bullets whistled past the man smoking his cigar. He ran through the train shouting, "Wake up, the train is being robbed!" The shots outside left no doubt of it. Women came out of their berths in dressing gowns. Men scrambled for their trousers. There followed hurried conferences as to what to do. Money and jewelry were stuffed into cracks and crannies, hidden under seats. After a few minutes, the two mail clerks lying on the floor of the express car heard the muffled voice of the engineer telling Pinkney through the locked door, probably at gunpoint, that the "men in charge" wanted him to open up. He did. In rushed two masked men, probably Walter and Lee Jarrett, seasoned criminals who took it upon themselves to handle this critical and dangerous juncture of the holdup, when mail clerks were sometimes known to get heroic and offer resistance.

Then, according to Pinkney's later testimony, a third man, most likely Elmer McCurdy, entered the car to blow the safe. Outside, a fourth man, probably a friend of the Jarretts' named Albert Connor, compelled the engineer, together with the fireman, the baggage man, Pinkney, and his assistant, to lie on the ground. Connor then shot his rifle along the length of the train. The weapon, a Winchester, with its uncommonly loud report, like a cannon shot, froze everyone in the passenger cars. Connor worked both sides of the train assiduously, keeping such a steady covering fire that many witnesses later overstated the number of robbers that night to the press. Then the quick sound of the bandits scurrying over gravel, and a pause—*one-one-thousand, two-one-thousand*—lasting as long as it took for a fuse to reach its source, then a deafening explosion that shook the ground. The open door of the express car amplified the detonation like a gigantic sounding board.

The bandits returned to see if they'd blown the safe. Connor marched all five of his captives to the car and peered inside. No luck. Pinkney observed through smoke and shattered wood the three robbers setting a second charge to the safe, the tools of their trade—fuses, soap, dynamite—scattered on the floor around them. Connor marched the men away from the train and again ordered them to lie on the ground. Another silence, then another colossal explosion. Connor marched the train crew over gravel and splintered wood back to the car, now a little more worse for wear. Again, no luck. Connor marched the men back and ordered them to the ground.

Nothing the bandits did that night was original. The men robbing the Iron Mountain train worked from a template, perhaps it might be said a strategic, if not an officially recognized, performative tradition, which in essence consisted of a swift swoop upon a train followed by a quick gallop into the hills. But delay took the dash out of the program, and as the gap of minutes stretched into deepening night, the locomotive engine ticking away, 250 passengers in their nightshirts and dressing gowns, a captive audience, quietly deciphering from the sound of rifle fire and the thunder of the explosions the progress of events, and the crewmen being marched back and forth—when, one wonders, did the awkwardness begin to sink in? After the first hour? Did the explosion of the *third* charge of dynamite, which again failed to open the safe, provoke a few raised eyebrows, a glance at a pocket watch? Surely, into the second hour, with the safe doors still clammed shut, the pace of the robbery must have seemed, shall we say, a little tiresome?

For the robbers themselves, blasting away and getting nowhere, their elan must have been sinking like the sagging moon over the hills. What mixture of frustration, fear, and embarrassment kept Albert Connor firing his Winchester so conspicuously in the middle of the prairie night down the track and occasionally into the ground, just above the heads of the five men growing strangely familiar with the smells of gravel and explosives? In the darkness, Connor may have been unaware that he was shooting his gun so close to the men, or he may have been taking his frustration out on his captives, who could hear the rifle bullets cutting through the grass. At one point, the train's engineer vented some of his own frustration, yelling out to the man who could have shot him then and there that Connor was firing too close for comfort. Other than this moment, there would be no heroics that night.

An expert safe blower had *touch*, had finesse, used only enough dynamite to make a neat, table-sized hole in an express car. He could alter the size of the charge to open any safe, anywhere, without blasting its contents to kingdom come. McCurdy's work that night, however, suggested a greater facility for blowing up large things, like bridges or mountains. One whole side of the express car yawned open, blown to smithereens, a testament to the difficulties a novice artist faced when handling a new medium—dynamite instead of nitroglycerin, in this case—if not to say the hazards of on-the-job training. It may be that McCurdy brought both dynamite and nitroglycerin to do the job, and when the former failed, he set to work with the latter.

The fourth explosion, in any case, unhinged the door of the safe and sent it flying through the ravaged car. When the smoke had cleared, the bandits peered inside and beheld the booty, $4,000 in silver coin, almost all of it fused by the heat of four successive blasts into a glittering mass that stuck to the inside walls of the safe. The bandits were staring at what would amount today to $70,000. Yet no shovel or pick, no amount of banging or grunting or cursing, could pry it loose, try as they might, and try they did.

The night stretched on, and in exasperation, they marched Pinkney to the baggage car and ordered him to retrieve the registered mail pouch. In the distance, along the road to Oklahoma City, two lights from an automobile approached, then dimmed a hundred yards from the train. In their last few minutes, the bandits were reduced to pawing through the pouch, stooping here and there to pick up scattered coins from the floor, and resorting to petty larceny—McCurdy relieving Pinkney of his gold pocket watch. Then they walked away from the train toward the car and sped away.

It had been a busy night. The Iron Mountain train robbery made front-page headlines in the *Coffeyville Daily Journal* and other papers, but the newspapers also reported that two banks and a second train had been knocked off that same evening. In Hudson, Kansas, bandits held angry citizens at bay while the Hudson State Bank safe was blown. A watchman clobbered one robber over the head with a lantern and was shot in the street as he ran away. When a Mrs. Gus Witt, the wife of a local merchant, ran out to help, one of the bandits reportedly snarled, "Get back in your house or I'll blow your head off," to which Mrs. Witt responded, "Mind your own business. I'm going for a doctor to tend this man." As with the Iron Mountain job, the robbers used covering fire to intimidate people and a getaway vehicle to make their escape. In Curryville, Missouri, bank robbers seemed to have trouble with the safe, which took five dynamite blasts to open. In Dennison, Iowa, a masked man climbed aboard the rear of a train and mugged several of the passengers in the sleeping car, after which he jumped into the night.

Banditry, it seems, had by no means been eradicated. But there was something special about the robbery of the Iron Mountain train, which created a sensation. The criminals had used both horses and an automobile as a getaway vehicle, making them transitional criminals prefiguring the age of the gangster. The newspapers, however, seemed to pounce on the fact that the robbery *harkened back* to an earlier time: "Old Days of the Wild West Resurrected," proclaimed the *Vinita (Okla.) Daily Chieftain*. The story was news because train robbery by that time had become rare, an anachronism, a reminder of an era whose time had long passed. It was a crime that touched a public chord of nostalgia.

This was, after all, a modern world—*the* modern world— coming into being. The ancient regime was on its heels, yet all was so new and strange that even the champions and harbingers of change still put a hyphen in the word *to-day*. Everything was shrinking, getting faster, less stable. A Wright brothers airplane had flown from St. Louis, Missouri, to New York City in eleven days. The Model T Ford was rolling off the production line. Frederick Winslow Taylor's *Principles of Scientific Management* threatened to dictate down to the very second the way laborers worked in factories. Technological innovations ruptured old frames of reference, triggering new anxieties. In the same year

of the Iron Mountain robbery, the young T. S. Eliot was com-
posing the anxiety-ridden "Love Song of J. Alfred Prufrock." In
painting, the Cubist agenda of Georges Braque and Pablo Pi-
casso had dismantled solid objects. The average person no
longer understood how the simplest things of daily life
worked—the telephone, the radio, the motion picture were all
disquieting marvels. Sigmund Freud was working on other disquieting theories, and Albert Einstein, thinking about trains and
apparent motion, had shattered Isaac Newton's static universe
with the publication of the Special Theory of Relativity.

Meanwhile, McCurdy, Albert Connor, and the Jarrett brothers had been thinking about trains, too, albeit more prosaically.
They split the paltry take from the Iron Mountain job, $450,
between the four of them, money they spent in a few days of
debauchery in South Coffeyville. Their resentments would
erupt into a knife fight, reported in the Coffeyville press on
March 27, that would leave McCurdy severely slashed in the
wrist and Walter Jarrett with a hideous gash on his face. Having
had enough of Walter and Elmer, Lee and Albert left them to
fend for themselves and returned to Lee's cabin on Cedar Creek.

Perhaps it was something about the landscape around the
Jarrett cabin that made it seem such a distant, remote place that
no one could imagine the law poking around to find them. The
land, in that case, trumped the imagination. Were Lee and Albert convinced by means of the hills and hollers, the secret
dales and draws known only to them, and the vastness of the
land, the sheer distances and the separation between places,
that they were so tiny against its backdrop, so insignificant in
the larger scheme of things, that nobody would bother to come
looking for them? Perhaps it was something about the robbers

themselves, some generic quality, some gap in the criminal mind, call it denial, or foolishness, or stupidity, that led them to believe that all would be well.

The gang may have disbanded, but the Iron Mountain robbery had mobilized a corps of special agents for the railroad company, government postal office inspectors, and express company detectives, all of whom were closing in on those responsible for the holdup. It didn't take them long, nor did it take the miracles of the modern world to find the culprits.

On April 9, after learning of Walter Jarrett's return to the area, pursuing officers made a routine call on the Jarrett cabin, where they found enough evidence lying around the place to implicate the boys in the Centralia general store robbery. Glenn and Albert were immediately arrested and taken to Vinita. Two days later, postal inspector L. C. Chance visited the cabin and discovered items that nobody could claim were parts of a machine-gun invention: nitroglycerin, mixed laundry soap, dynamite, ammunition that matched the caliber of the guns used in the robbery, and bed ticking that was an exact match of a sample found at the site of the robbery. The ticking at the scene of the crime contained mixed laundry soap, used to seal up the crack of a safe after nitroglycerin is poured in. Beneath the floor of the cabin, moreover, detectives found Elmer McCurdy's army discharge papers. Albert Connor and Glenn Jarrett were brought to Muskogee, Oklahoma, and held in the federal prison there for train robbery. Glenn was later released, but the authorities were closing in on the others.

For the moment, Walter Jarrett and Elmer McCurdy remained at large. They decided to split up, and Walter headed east into Missouri where special agents picked up his trail and pursued him mercilessly. In the west of the past, a bandit could use the terrain as his principal ally, spending hours in the saddle putting distance between himself and his pursuers. But the days of the long rider were over. The telegraph and telephone had outpaced Walter Jarrett, who was found completely worn out, asleep beside his horse and his gun, and hauled back to Muskogee in chains to await trial with his brother Lee. Walter tried to escape once in the months before his trial, patiently filing away at the bars of his cell, a few minutes each day, and covering up the evidence of his work using soap and iron filings. On New Year's Eve, word somehow leaked to the jailers and his escape plans were dashed. Walter stood trial with his brother Lee and Albert Connor in January 1912. Only Walter was convicted, and he was sentenced to twenty-five years of hard labor.

The following May, Walter and four other men escaped from the government jail in Muskogee, apparently with help from someone on the outside. He remained free until that fall, when he was killed after robbing a bank in Prue, Oklahoma. He simply waited for Harvey Comer, the bank's only teller, to open up one Saturday morning, walked into the lobby, informed Comer he was being robbed, and relieved the bank of its money. Walter then forced Comer to close the bank and walk with him to the outskirts of town. The pair took a stroll outside, Comer wishing everyone they saw a good day. "That's right, son," Walter is reported to have said to Comer, "You're doing all right. I won't hurt you at all." He seemed to have finally come into his own as a social bandit. "I wouldn't take this money if it was yours," Walter told Comer. "But whatever I got will be paid back to you by the insurance companies, so it doesn't hurt you any, does it, son?" At the edge of town, Walter mounted a stolen horse and rode to his destiny. Later that day, on the same road, he was shot and killed by the owner of the horse.

Elmer McCurdy rode his horse west through April rains and gusting winds along the Oklahoma-Kansas state line. The hills of tall grass and draws choked with black jack oak looked the same on either side, but one thing had changed forever—McCurdy had crossed a different kind of border, a life threshold, and entered into a new taxonomic order. He was now a man wanted by the law, an outlaw, a designation that may have carried with it a certain biting irony, for he'd botched the job, had placed himself at great risk hoping to escape a life of hard labor, and now had nothing to show for it other than a pocket watch and his knife wounds.

And so McCurdy made his way into the Osage Nation, leaving behind a series of assumed names. He passed himself off as Charles Davis, the name of his vanished natural father. He was Frank Davis. He was Frank Davidson. In September 1911, he borrowed Frank Curtis, the name of a lieutenant from the 13th Infantry, and dropped south into the Osage Hills. But a failed outlaw had the worst of all possible worlds. He had to grub for work like everybody else *and* he needed eyes in the back of his head. For the law did not distinguish between successful and unsuccessful varieties of bad man.

## 4

# This Fair but Fated Region

I flew to Oklahoma City, rented a van, and after traveling for a time in Kansas, doubled back into Oklahoma. Highway 99 was a two-lane blacktop road built over an old stagecoach route, which itself followed an ancient complex of paths and river fords once known as the Osage Trace. It was probably along this route that McCurdy rode on horseback after the knife fight in Coffeyville, Kansas, following the Iron Mountain train debacle in April. Six months later, on October 4, 1911, McCurdy was allegedly among a group of bandits who held up another train on the Missouri, Kansas, and Texas (or M, K, & T) line near Okesa, in the heart of the Osage Hills, and fled northward. Only days after that, McCurdy was shot to death at a ranch near the Kansas state line, a short year after his discharge from the army.

As news of the shoot-out spread, most assumed that an old-fashioned sort of western justice had been served. But there were other suspects still at large who were rounded up and questioned. Two local men, in particular, one a loose cannon named Amos Hays, the other a respected farmer named Dave Sears, were grilled by Osage County Sheriff Harve Freas, yet they could not acquit themselves to his satisfaction. They were arrested and held for trial. (A fourth man, Elijah "Lige" Higgins, was questioned and released, but later used as a witness in the prosecution of Hays, his cousin.) Both Hays and Sears found Elmer McCurdy a convenient corpse, useful in their own defense, but Hays was convicted and sentenced to twenty-five years, while Sears managed to mount a more robust defense. He was also luckier. An eyewitness who claimed that Sears was one of the rifle-shooting bandits could not later pick Sears out of a police lineup. The list of witnesses testifying in Sears's behalf was drawn deeply and widely from the surrounding citizenry. Joseph Johnson, owner of the funeral parlor in Pawhuska, came to Sears's defense, as did other friends in the oil-drilling and ranching businesses. Sears was acquitted, yet to this day, his descendants are chary of discussing the matter, reporting only that his son, Charles Preston Sears, who visited his father in jail, and who may have passed messages from Sears to Sheriff Freas that led to the shoot-out with McCurdy, dropped out of school shortly after the incident and refused all his life to speak of this episode from the past.

Decades later, with McCurdy rediscovered and the light of forensic science brought to bear upon his body, autopsy results raised questions about McCurdy's role in the M, K, & T robbery. Tissue samples taken from McCurdy's perfectly preserved body showed that the outlaw was nearly dead from a combination of pneumonia, tuberculosis, and trichinosis. Suffering so badly, could McCurdy have robbed a train in Okesa, then ridden twenty miles at night on horseback to his hideout near the Kansas border? These were questions, of course, of almost no seeming historical significance, as this was just another minor dustup in the Osage. But it had once mattered very much to a group of men, whoever they may have been, flying through the hills at night on horseback. Moreover, the suspects—the guilty, the acquitted, and the dead drifter—had all been white men. That the intended target of the robbers had been a train bearing hundreds of thousands of dollars in Osage royalty payments suggested the convergence of larger lines of force and motivation, lines that I hoped to follow and develop. And so, ninety years after McCurdy's violent end, I entered the Osage.

At the Oklahoma state line, where the land began to buckle and fold, the hills are covered thickly with oak, now and again opening out onto grassland ringed by forest—what French traders originally meant by the word *prairie*. I watched cattle dozing the afternoon away as if drunk on bluestem, fescue, and Bermuda, the tall grass that makes this region so famous for grazing. Their hides were burnished browns and tans. Some of them were lying down near ponds that flashed in the sun. Sometimes I stopped to listen to the wind and the insects whizzing by, the breeze frisking my shirt, the only other sound the faraway cough and sputter of an engine driving a pump jack, its great, head-shaped counterweight nodding up and down, sucking oil from a well.

In Oklahoma, pump jacks populate the landscape in clusters or in pairs, or in lone isolation, like some unofficial flower of the industrial age. A working pump jack moves in cyclic self-absorption near the capital steps in Oklahoma City, a symbol of state pride. Here in the Osage, they appeared behind the trees, on the ridge tops, and down in the swales. They had become part of the landscape, although legally and metaphorically, they were as separate from the land and its fattening cattle as night from day. Only in a chamber of commerce sense were the pump jacks part of this landscape, for they were entirely devoted to what lay in the strata far below. Their function, if not destiny and desire, was to draw oil up to the surface, worked by means of a simple, perhaps even soothing, telekinesis that promised perpetual motion, infinite profit, world without end.

As I drove in my rental van I noticed that many of the pump jacks had, in fact, slowed down or seized up entirely, in rusting dereliction. If they suggested anything, it was a colossal, perhaps supreme indifference to a world that Washington Irving once described, in 1832, as a "fair but fated region." Theirs was a separation from any landscape, fair or otherwise, that was fated to offer itself up to their plunge and draw. Oklahoma contains much that is unintentionally symbolic in this way, and, to counter this, Oklahomans have always seemed determined to manufacture more overtly symbolic objects to shield themselves from the quandary of their past.

In Guthrie, Oklahoma, for instance, a statue at the entrance to the Oklahoma Territorial Museum stopped me in my tracks. It was a bronze sculpture by Fred Olds, whom we will meet later in this story, depicting the wedding of "Miss Indian Territory and Mr. Oklahoma Territory." Miss Indian Territory, barefooted, in a long dress blown against her left leg by the wind, her sleeves rough-hewn, her hair in twin braids blown across her breast, gazes upward, optimistic and compliant, as if about to break into "I Cain't Say No." The figure of the groom is more complicated. His body faces her slightly, but his upward gaze takes him completely out of the moment at hand, his mouth a thin line. He could be calculating freight tonnage or the finer points of an oil and gas sublease. The Oklahoma wind blows his tie aslant. He has taken off his hat and holds it behind his back, baring his head before his God. But the gesture is also inescapably and literally behind-the-back, with all its connotations of double-dealing. We, the viewers and museum-goers, have the advantage of perspective. We can, if we so desire, see most, if not all, of what the past has come to mean here.

The legacy of conquest haunts American place-names from Seattle to Seneca Falls, and when Elmer McCurdy rode into Pawhuska, Oklahoma, in September 1911, the work of conquest had long since shifted from the battlefield to the subtler, invisible realms over which the Dawes Severalty Act held sway. Indeed, land allotment had become the principal strategy by which Indian lands had fallen to non-Indian ownership, and the Dawes Act had become the government's main instrument, its prime remover. Yet the Osages, under the leadership of James Bigheart, had held out the longest against such bureaucratic measures, becoming the last tribe in the country to succumb to the allotment maneuver. Bigheart and the Osage leadership held out so long, in fact—with boomers for Oklahoma Statehood breathing down the necks of the territorial representatives in Washington—that the Osages gained substantial leverage in negotiating the niceties of law that finally broke up their land.

The single most important feature of allotment was that the Osages maintained communal ownership of subsurface mineral rights, a fact that would launch the tribe into stratospheric wealth.

It was, indeed, a strange and unlikely concatenation of historical events—of bogus treaties, removals, outright swindles, and assorted nefarious land giveaways, all designed to rob the tribe blind—that had, instead, left the Osages in the first three decades of the twentieth century with more money than they knew how to spend. Not all of the Osages were landowners with thousand-acre tracts of grazing land and white sharecroppers working their fields from dawn to dusk. Not every Osage was in a position to display what John Joseph Matthews called an "Olympian disregard for money," but so many were well off that the rich Osage Indian became an instant caricature, a target of scorn for some, a target of opportunity for many others. For McCurdy, the Osages would become both, and in this he would not be alone. Indeed, scorn and opportunism with regard to the Osages had a long and distinguished provenance.

Pawhuska, from *Paw-Hiu-Skah*, or White Hair, was the name of an Osage chief favored by the Chouteau brothers, Auguste and Pierre, pioneers of the fur trade in the 1800s, a group the Osages referred to as *"I'n-Shta-Heh,"* or "Heavy Eyebrows," because of their hairy faces. The fur traders were middlemen who brought something people would need on the frontier and planted themselves in a likely spot near the mouth of a river, say, or a deep harbor port, then made a killing supplying the horde passing through. Sheer numbers supported their business strategy. A few years after the Klondike gold rush, Jack London estimated that $220 million had been spent extracting $22 million in gold from the ground.

Middlemen stayed put and founded cities. When Meriwether Lewis and William Clark entered the Spanish-held city of St. Louis on the beginning of their journey of discovery, the Chouteau brothers were the first people they sought for intelligence about the tribes upriver. The news was disquieting. For generations, the Osages had maintained complete military control over a region that would today encompass the states of Missouri, Arkansas, and the eastern portions of Oklahoma and Kansas. They were a mid-continental people, occupying, as they called it, "the center of the earth." Their hunting range, which extended west into present-day Colorado and New Mexico, prefigured by hundreds of years the latter-day westward migration of European settlers that would uproot and change them beyond recognition. The Osages figured large in the mind of President Thomas Jefferson. "The truth is," he wrote to his secretary of war, "they are the great nation South of the Missouri, their possession extending from thence to the Red River, as the Sioux are great North of that river. With these two powerful nations we must stand well, because in their quarter we are miserably weak."

Locally, everyone who ventured into their territory paid tribute to the Osages, who controlled over three-quarters of the total St. Louis fur and hide trade before 1803, much to the annoyance of the Chouteaus, who sought any number of ways to undermine their strength. They had built Fort Carondelet in 1795 in an attempt to quell Osage raiding, and they had taken to meddling in tribal politics, with indifferent results. In 1804, in a power play at Jefferson's request, the Chouteaus helped organized the journey of a delegation of Osages to the east where they were shown glittering cities—Philadelphia, New York, Boston—showered with gifts, bedazzled by military parades and artillery displays, and introduced to President Jefferson himself. It was—and remains—an awkward moment in American history. For starters, the territory of Louisiana had been purchased at a fire-sale price from the French, who had no legitimate claim to sell land occupied, annexed, and administered by the government of Spain. In any case, if the United States was the new "owner" of Louisiana, who were the Osages, standing in their robes before Jefferson? They were, in the guiding metaphor of the time, "children," that is, dependents, with Jefferson the new "father" and protector. His speech to the Osages was filled with airy metaphors and foggy notions of unity, friendship, and trust. He concluded by saying, "No wrong will ever be done you by our nation." Yet Jefferson, who had inherited a particularly difficult situation, made more difficult by his penchant for giving away Osage land without their knowledge or consent, would, with the Treaty of 1808, set the tone and tenor of the imperial directive.

The treaty that year was one of the most inequitable land deals in American history. Attending the meeting, along with Pierre Chouteau, was a man whose very life had only recently hung upon the good will of people like the Osages. William Clark, newly appointed Indian superintendent under Meriwether Lewis, the governor of Louisiana Territory, spoke for Jefferson, making the American position clear: The Osages had to either sign the treaty or be declared enemies. Paw-Hiu-Skah, the enfeebled chief, spoke for the Osages, decrying for posterity the strong-arm tactics of the United States. "If the American father wanted a part of their land, he must have it. . . . He was strong and powerful and they were weak and pitiful. . . . [The Osages] had no choice." Thus, for $2,700 in goods and trinkets, the Osages ceded to the Heavy Eyebrows seven-eighths of modern Missouri and half of Arkansas north of the Arkansas River. So disgusted was he by his role in this and subsequent swindles that Clark, whom the Osages affectionately called *Paw Shu Tze*, "Red Head," vowed after 1825 never again to make another treaty for the United States.

*Pawhuska*, then, would come to stand as an anglicized and inflected form of *shell game*, which continued for seventeen years, with all the earnest trappings of diplomacy fully deployed on the national stage between the most powerful men on either side of a cultural, technological, and political chasm. But the tide began to turn in favor of the Osages, on paper anyway, in 1871, when they were paid millions of dollars as compensation for land in Kansas that they owned and occupied but that had been promised, without their knowledge, to the Cherokees. In a final round of musical chairs, the Osages bought back from the Cherokees land that had once been their southern hunting range in the hilly region of what is now present-day Osage County, with Pawhuska becoming its capital. Money from this and other land sales was put into a government trust, which, after 1879, was delivered in cash by express train, earning at the outset $40 for each Osage man, woman, and child. Amounts of $500 or more a year for an average family were common, and the rate increased over time. By 1898, with careful shepherding of grass leases and other revenues, the Osages had quietly ascended into an unlikely aristocracy that became the subject of magazine and newspaper articles and prompted Commissioner William J. Pollack to describe the tribe as "probably the wealthiest people per capita on earth."

The quarterly cash-payment system was, from the very beginning, a mixed blessing that would haunt the Osages far into the twentieth century. Cash money attracted a host of mercenary characters to Pawhuska—whiskey peddlers, gamblers, prostitutes, and every variety of snake oil salesman and con-artist. The influx of money, moreover, attracted outside businessmen and merchants who hoped to capitalize on the wealth of the Osage. In 1909, just two years before McCurdy's arrival, an advertisement in the *Hominy News-Republican* sought to attract business to a community of "1,000 white people and 900 Osage Indians drawing thousands of dollars yearly."

It is a moment of candor that bluntly describes a dividing line of race and the anomalous inversion of class structure that helped sustain the institutionalized fraud visited upon the Osages. Business owners overcharged Indian customers or extended credit at extortionist rates. After they'd been fleeced and sent home, highwaymen would take whatever was left. By 1889, Osage agent Laban J. Miles declared that "the presence of numerous vagabond white people on the reservation is a detriment to the welfare of the Indian. Many of them prove to be gamblers or whisky-peddlers . . . who succeed in evading officers until an opportunity offers itself for them to steal a horse or rob an Indian." By law, any Osage with half or more Indian blood quantum was deemed "incompetent," that is, liable to be reluctant to adopt white ways. Lawyers hired to serve as "guardians" for these "blanket Indians" skimmed money from their charges and often left them helplessly in debt. State and county courts turned a blind eye to such fraud and often overcharged the Osages for court fees. The promise of Osage money attracted another sort of non-Indian interloper who, by marrying into the tribe, acquired shares of land, and later, shares—or "headrights"—for the oil that lay beneath the land. It was a quiet rush for land and oil, gained by matrimony and perpetrated by any number of cads, gold diggers, and assorted scoundrels, including one celebrated serial murderer. The attitude seemed to be that "honest people could honorably cheat the Osages," and so it was that for most white settlers, merchants, lawyers, judges, ranchers, and chiefs of police, from the highest-ranking citizen of Pawhuska to the lowest vagabond, every move, every transaction they made, to their everlasting shame, was fueled by a spirit of larceny.

The discovery of oil in the Osage further served to attract outside intruders, with upwards of 5,000 non-Indian settlers arriving on the reservation in 1894. By 1904, that figure had at least doubled, with between 10,000 and 15,000 non-Indians outnumbering the 2,200 Osages. The Burbank Field, along with other discoveries in Osage County, contained more than a billion barrels of oil and would make a colossus of Frank Phillips, J. Paul Getty, and Harry Sinclair. By McCurdy's time, oil production in the Osage reached 20,000 barrels of oil per day, helping to make Oklahoma second only to California and representing over a quarter of the entire U.S. domestic production. Drilling crews clambered all over the county and struck oil nine out of every ten times they sunk a hole. Nearly 500 such holes were drilled in Osage County alone in 1911, doubling the number from the previous year and producing almost 12 million barrels of crude. Auctions were held under the shade of Pawhuska's "Million Dollar Elm," where huge sums were paid just for the right to drill for Osage oil. Soon the royalties began pouring in. By 1925, they peaked at $13,200 for each Osage family member. At a time when the annual salary of the Indian superintendent himself was a respectable $3,000, an average Osage family of five received an astonishing $66,000 in cash. Such sums lofted the Osage into an instant elite class whose ready cash and innate generosity fueled a micro-economy that quickly became the stuff of legend, attracting even more outsiders from near and far.

When McCurdy rode into town, his horse, assuming he still had one, or hadn't lost it, or traded it for whiskey—or blown it up—would have negotiated streets of downtown Pawhuska that were in busy transition. Horses with buggies were still hitched to street rails, but Model Ts and Packards sputtered by with increasing frequency. Pawhuska was modernizing itself and had embarked on that signature modern American rite of passage: improving its streets with cobblestones, paving them with concrete, or laying down steaming coats of tar. Here McCurdy and many otherwise unemployed whites found work digging ditches for a construction company hired for street improvements. As they looked around, they noted the occasional, chauffeur-driven Pierce Arrow, owned by a wealthy Osage, and wondered about this town and its strange reversal in the usual order of things.

McCurdy, who was a great frequenter of bars and speakeasies, could not have helped but notice how, like the coming of a full moon, or like the advent of some unannounced local holiday, Pawhuska would suddenly swell with people, the bars spilling over with lawyers, itinerant salesmen, and other smooth-talking agents circulating among the Osages, working the big and the small con. On Kiheka Street, Osages were on the promenade, buying household supplies, buying presents, having a good time. The shop owners treated them with special deference, dropped everything to attend their needs, directed them to the front of any line. Had McCurdy been in such a line—say, in a hardware store—he would have noticed this, perhaps with some irritation. Perhaps in a bar he would have noticed how the  unassuming Osage sitting next to him would become expansive, buying rounds for the house. Another Osage might wander in wearing an ensemble of store-bought clothes, or perhaps a new tuxedo, to lampoon the white man's newest style craze. And there'd be a few fistfights, and somebody might get the idea to enter the joint on horseback, and there'd be some pretty quick footwork getting out of the way lest people get stomped to death, and, of course, there'd be no calling the sheriff, because the man at the bar buying a drink for his horse *was* the sheriff.

These were payment days. McCurdy would have considered himself lucky to have been born an Osage, suddenly flush with cash, comfortable in the knowledge that it would ever be so. For McCurdy, the Osage payments must have shone the light on his own hard, ditch-digging luck. No matter what McCurdy did, it seemed, he ended up with a shovel in his hands and another yard of earth to move.

In Pawhuska, McCurdy met the men who would steer his resentments toward action. Amos Hays and his cousin, Elijah Higgins, were from families who had listed themselves in the most recent census as laborers and renters. The two may have met McCurdy while working to pave Pawhuska's streets. Hays and Higgins would have given McCurdy, their new-found compatriot, the lay of the land—the rich Osage lording it over the poor whites like themselves, sharpening McCurdy's bitterness. Hays, a small, wiry local boy from Chautauqua, Kansas, just across the border, was drifting and drinking his way into deep trouble. He'd killed—and been acquitted of killing—an Osage rancher from Elgin, Kansas, who himself had killed Hays's brother a few years earlier in a drunken argument in Kansas City.

Somehow, probably in a bar after a hard day's work, McCurdy and Hays met and found in each other a sympathetic audience. Hays and Higgins would have known about the Osage payment train, arriving every quarter, loaded with cash. Robbing that train would be a quicker, less circuitous way of doing what everyone else seemed to be doing under the guise of legitimate business—the piecemeal nipping and chiseling and defrauding of the Osages. How the idle talk of these disaffected men in a faraway town smoldered away, like a banked fire, until a plan emerged is anyone's guess. But it could be that McCurdy provided a needed catalyst, his recent bandit experience arousing in the men a desire to make more money in a single night of work than they could imagine.

Southward on Highway 99, at high speed, I blew past Chautauqua, Kansas, and had to circle back. East of the highway I found a handful of gravel streets, wind-worn old houses, trailers, propane tanks, and clusters of old tires lying around with tall grass poking through. You could hit a softball to the south end of town. Wind rattled the street signs at the north end where I stopped to admire a pair of handmade signs, weathered 2 x 6s nailed together, barking a lesson straight from the Enlightenment. "If you Sacrifice a little bit of Freedom to Attain more Law & Order, you deserve Neither." I wondered about the crank who lived there, quoting Thomas Jefferson to the bluestem and the crickets. Another sign quoted Voltaire: "ALL history is Little else than a Succession of useless cruelties."

It was an odd half-acre pocket of free thought located smack dab in the Bible-thumping heart of a republic rivaled only in its scope and influence by Augustan Rome. The vastness of the Kansas sky, and the unstoppable wind, and the little, hand-painted slogans of the philosophers broadcast to a town slowly being reclaimed by the prairie, brought to mind a poem, Thomas Hardy's "The Darkling Thrush," composed in a different time and a different season—a hundred years ago on a blustery New Year's Eve, 1900:

> *I leant upon a coppice gate*
> *When Frost was specter-gray,*
> *And Winter's dregs made desolate*
> *The weakening eye of day.*

Thomas Hardy could knock off a poem of lugubrious darkness like nobody's business, and this was one of his bleakest. He had given up on poetry, and much else, it seemed, dispatching an entire era with a bracing image:

> *The land's sharp features seemed to be*
> *The Century's corpse outleant,*

*His crypt the cloudy canopy,*
*The wind his death-lament.*

I thought of Hardy and the simple country folk of his novels, marginal characters set alongside some temporal abyss so that the present moment appears as an extended sleepwalk through the oceanic reaches of the past, the voices of his characters, like his most famous dairymaid, the simple, ignorant waif, Tess, echoing deep into the tombs of the ancient D'Urbervilles.

I had come to Chautauqua that morning to find a bit of history concerning a marginal character that nobody cared about, who seemed more distant to me there in southern Kansas at the dawn of a second millennium than the runic scratchings of Ptolomaic kings or the Parthian porphyry of Hadrian. This was odd because McCurdy had been dead, after all, a mere ninety years, well within reach of historical inquiry. Yet a steamroller seemed to have crushed and ground his remarkable story, and most of the world he'd inhabited, into oblivion. In his life, McCurdy was one of the silent majority who lived small lives, then vanished from the earth; not a great king, but a screw-up and ne'er-do-well bandit bungler who had accidentally achieved fame long after death. He hadn't exactly won immortality, for as soon as the spectacle of his discovery became old news, his story sank back into obscurity. His was rather an exemption, a temporary stay from the oblivion that awaits us all. He was an Everyman, our Everyman—a century's corpse—snatched out of the abyss for us to ponder. Coming here to Chautauqua to conjure him, then, was a way of coming up alongside the wonder of my own obscure and likely fate.

The Citizens State Bank was a diminutive, single-story red brick box with a large, Palladian storefront window, boarded up. I knew it was the bank because it said so, B-A-N-K inlaid in foot-high sandstone, right on the front entrance, with the date of construction, 1-9-0-5. It was the only structure in any direction that suggested a past older than the dish antenna, and it had held up well. I got out of the van and walked around to the rear of the building, where Elmer McCurdy, Amos Hays, and Lige Higgins had tried to take advantage of the trusting people of Chautauqua and deliver unto themselves, by nightfall and with pickaxes and high explosives, that which belonged to Caesar. The very hole they made with pickaxes and crowbars was still there, neither roped off nor sealed behind a museum's glass case, but patched up with a bit of mortar and iron across the opening, a few free bricks scattered on the ground. I walked to the front and looked through a transom window.

On September 21, 1911, around midnight, Hays, Higgins, and McCurdy walked up to the bank from a back alley. The bandits cut the electricity to the building, then took turns swinging at the brick wall, with Lige Higgins standing lookout. It was tough work. Two hours went by before they busted through. Inside, Amos Hays held a torch for McCurdy, who sealed the door with soap then carefully poured the nitroglycerin charge. The pair of them stepped backward, unspooling a length of wick fuse through the hole into the alley. Then they struck a match, and they set the match to the fuse.

McCurdy had prepared a charge that would do in a single blast what three successive detonations had failed to do to the safe on the Iron Mountain train a few weeks previously. Again,

McCurdy's work lacked a certain finesse. The explosion blew the outer vault off its hinges and it plowed through the building's interior like a freight train, crushing everything in its path. The concussion of the blast cracked a plate glass window across the street from the bank, yet this spectacular explosion failed to open the safe. Amazingly, the town slumbered on. Some had heard the explosion but apparently thought it was thunder. McCurdy set to work with a second charge, but for some reason the men failed to detonate it. It may be that Higgins, their lookout, became spooked and ran off early, which in turn panicked McCurdy and Hays inside, who scooped up what few coins they could from a tray outside the safe before fleeing themselves.

It was another fiasco, another big risk for such a small take—only $150 divided between three of them, and again McCurdy seemed flummoxed by the subtleties of nitroglycerin work. To his credit, nitroglycerin could trouble even professional "shooters," one of whom, after nearly thirty years of work in the oil fields of Oklahoma, confessed, "You can't tell what nitro's gonna do, which way it's gonna hit when it goes off." That certainly seemed true for McCurdy in Chautauqua. The charge had completely demolished the interior of the bank but left the safe sealed shut.

The trio rode south through the night across the Kansas line. At the Caney River ford they all split up, with McCurdy, perhaps at Hays's suggestion, heading to the ranch of Charles Revard a few miles away. He arrived just after dawn, giving his name as Frank Amos, riding on a borrowed horse and looking pale and older than his years, "like an unknown tramp," Frank Revard, Charlie's brother, would recall.

Charlie Revard was an original allottee, a mixed-blood member of a prominent Osage family whose name can be found on a city street in Pawhuska. His French-Canadian ancestor, Joseph Revard III, had married an Osage and been a full partner with Pierre Chouteau in a trading post near present-day Saline, *? Not scalped.* Oklahoma, until he was scalped by a Cherokee raiding party in what became known as the "Three Forks Massacre," part of a protracted border war with the Osages, in 1821.

Charlie Revard had been educated with his brothers and cousins at the mission school in Pawhuska and maintained throughout his long life a taste for literature and conversation. He could speak Osage, quote Shakespeare, and liked to drink. He had, moreover, a soft spot for the kind of rough-hewn but good-natured brigand that one associates with Falstaff and his milieu, and which were always moving through the country-side. He was, in some respects, an eccentric who passed his years in bemused detachment up on the Caney River as a kind of gentleman farmer and rancher. He had nothing that anyone wanted to steal, but he did have a place where someone, cross-ing the state line under an assumed name, might rest for a while.

McCurdy was told he could stay in the hayshed. The first thing he asked for was whiskey, which he used in the days to come to wash down meals of smoked pork. He spent the re-maining weeks of September in a sustained, drunken binge, sometimes rambling incoherently to those who wandered near.

*Sept. 21*      *Only a day less than 2 weeks*

The Chautauqua bank robbery was prelude by a number of weeks to a much more ambitious job, the robbery of the Osage *Oct. 4* payment train. As it turns out, the upcoming delivery would be twice as large as usual, approaching $400,000, because a previous and long-delayed royalty payment had finally come through some bureaucratic quagmire and been lumped together with the current installment for delivery in early October on the M, K, & T express.

All of this was common knowledge, reported in the local papers with moderate interest in a few editorials as the payment date approached. Anyone who could read a train schedule would know when and where to meet the M, K, & T in Pawhuska. A few men, however, planned to meet the train earlier than that. Had they accomplished their goal, it would probably stand, to this day, as one of the largest train heists in American history.

It offered a chance for McCurdy to redeem himself after the bungled robbery in Chautauqua. Here McCurdy would make his attempt to stop what even a generous soul would have described as a slide—to reverse his bad luck, to intercept the riotous wealth of the Osage and thereby enter into legend himself. By pulling off the job that awaited him here, McCurdy's name might have become synonymous with James, Younger, and Doolin. He would have arrived, characteristically a little late in the outlaw game, but he would have arrived, nonetheless. To my mind, then, this place, somewhere on the Oklahoma prairie, where McCurdy made his bid for fame, seemed worthy of a visit.

And so on a calm spring day I headed for Okesa, a wide spot in the road in southern Osage County. From there I headed southwest along a ridge roughly parallel to the old M, K, & T track, the bed of which lay a mile or so off to my left, concealed by dense post oak and black jack. When my trip meter clicked off three miles, I pulled over in the van and reached back for the Nelagoney quadrangle, finding my position on the 7.5-minute topographic map. Sometime after 1 A.M. on the morning of October 4, 1911, like something out of a silent movie, three masked bandits flagged down the southbound train #29. To the north the land fell away and buckled into deep hollers and heavily timbered draws, the fabled hills from which the common phrase synonymous for "escape" is said to derive, and here they were, Exhibit A, the very hills one headed for when it was time to *head for the hills*, the ancient southernmost extreme of the Osage hunting grounds. In the tribe's cosmology, they are the scene of a mythic escape from the floodwaters of creation.

The draws and gullies of the Osage remained a last pocket of remove for other castaways—a place of refuge for the outlaw and bootlegger of the nineteenth and twentieth centuries. The hills were the hideout and point of rendezvous for countless cattle rustlers, small-time brigands, and whiskey runners, but more famous outlaws, such as the Daltons, Henry Starr, and Kid Wilson, also took refuge here, where U.S. marshals simply declined to follow them. Now they are part of Osage Hills State Park, where park rangers bearing 9-mm Glock semiautomatic pistols walk calmly among the tattooed spillover from the biker convention in Pawhuska, filling out overnight receipts for RV campers of brontosauran stature with hookups and portable satellite dishes so that here, in this former shelter for the long rider, the dreamer of quick and dubious fortune, one could watch *Who Wants to Be a Millionaire?*

I looked down at the topographic map. A mile ahead, the county road dipped straight south and converged with the southwest-trending Missouri, Kansas & Texas railroad line. At that point I would stop and hike along the old line to survey the landscape.

By all reports, the robbery took place at some point directly south of where I sat, but there were at least two contradictory descriptions of the actual site itself. The *Oklahoma City Times* reported that "The robbers flagged the train in a deep cut near the canyon of Verdigris River." The only problem was that the Verdigris was in the wrong part of the state, about fifty miles east of where I was. Still, the essence of the situation may have involved a strategically chosen deep cut of some sort, so I circled two likely spots where the contour lines of the topographic map narrowed along the old track roughly three miles from Okesa.

The other report, published two days later in the *Dewey (Okla.) Sentinel,* said that "the men had chosen a spot near a long fill in which to commit the robbery." The phrase "a long fill," was, I'm ashamed to say, a mystery to me sitting there in northeastern Oklahoma with one or two ticks working their way north up my trousers. In any case, the *Sentinel* report had an eyewitness, a Mr. B. A. Lewis, whose description of the robbery scene—"as dreary and lonesome a place as one could find in the whole of Osage county," at least seemed to suggest a view, a prospect of land and sky from which one could derive the uniquely western, and not altogether unpleasant, sensation that the word "lonesome" evokes. This was helpful. The lonesome vista and the "deep cut" could not be one and the same. One of them was wrong.

Armed with these vagaries, I made two more circles on the map just to make myself feel better and pulled the Windstar back onto the macadam. Driving with one hand and following my progress on the map with the other, I looked in vain for the old railroad line and began to fear that I'd passed it. The timbered hills gave way to prairie, and I knew I was very close. I stopped the van and got out to scan the horizon. According to my estimate, I was within yards of the old track, but I could see nothing. Then, suddenly, I saw it, about 200 yards away, right in front of me, camouflaged by decades of overgrowth. Not the track itself, which had been ripped out years ago, but the old rail bed, a lineation like nothing in nature, the manmade signature, subtle but unmistakable, cutting its way through the rolling grassland.

I took my satchel and water bottle and began walking northeast, up the old rail bed, which looked like an ordinary rutted gravel road leading to a farm. I was on a patch of prairie several square miles in size that fed into the Osage. Recent rains had left it green and blooming with wildflowers under a blue dome with wisps of cirrus. A gradual, mile-long bend to the north led into a range of hills named Strike Axe, after the great chief of the Osage, and to the first cut I'd circled on the map, a right-turn bend to the east through red sandstone walls about 20 feet high. This could have been the place, but I'd grown doubtful of the "deep cut" theory. The bandits had signaled the train to stop with a lantern—some reports say they built a bonfire across the track. Either way, it would have made more sense to give the engineer time to notice and react to a signal of any sort, which he could not have done chugging through a red sandstone cut around a blind bend. Onward, then, to the long fill.

In another quarter mile the gravel deepened, and I noticed rusty rail spikes strewn about and old railroad ties decaying in the ditches. At the second site that I had circled, the track crossed a shallow draw, like a dip in a scallop shell, about a hundred feet long and forty feet deep. The railroad builders, instead of building a bridge, had filled the draw with gravel across the narrow span to maintain the grade—a short fill. A creek ran under the fill, burbling out the downhill side. In another quarter mile the same topographical dip occurred over a much longer gap between hills—a long fill—where a herd of cattle suddenly spooked itself and went crashing and rumbling through the woods. From here, moreover, with the land sloping away on either side of the track, one could see in both directions for miles. Here was the aforementioned lonesome vista. This was my best guess to establish the setting. Here, in all likelihood, three men waited in the dark for a train, so long ago.

I had the setting, but I wondered about the *dramatis personae*—and I still do, in fact. For the history here is anything but clear. There are too many conflicting points, details that simply don't add up to a single view of what happened on the night of October 4, 1911.

There seemed to be four potential players. The first three—Hays, Higgins, and the apprentice safe-blower McCurdy—seemed reasonable and likely candidates. Hays was eventually convicted for the robbery, after all, and Higgins knew enough about it to appear as a prosecution witness, for which testimony he may have received clemency. McCurdy's decision to fight a

last, desperate gun battle with the authorities in pursuit of the
M, K, & T bandits did not strike me, to say the very least, as
the act of an innocent man. The newspapers and other accounts
mentioned these three, and they also mentioned a fourth man,
Dave Sears. Sears was the man who led the sheriff's posse to
McCurdy. He was subsequently arrested as a coconspirator in
the M, K, & T robbery, stood trial, and was eventually acquitted. From my perspective, Sears was the biggest mystery, and
the closer I got to him, the harder he was to explain.

George David Sears, Jr., had grown up on his father's cattle
ranch, and later the family moved to the town of Chautauqua,
where his father opened a general store and conducted weekly
services at the Baptist church. The younger Sears, with his
brothers and sisters, watched his father's star rise and benefited
from his successes. Each sibling was set up on a tract of land
upon marriage, and when Dave Sears married Irene Anna Belle
Beason, in 1887 (Dave's father officiating at the ceremony), the
young couple moved into a farmhouse on Pond Creek, Osage
County, near the Kansas border.

At the time, it was almost impossible for a non-Indian to
own land in the Osage, so it seems likely that the arrangement
Dave's father made for his son involved a land lease, which made
Sears, whether he liked it or not, a renter, with Osage Indians
his landlords. The rent or lease payment may have involved a
portion of any crop or herd that Sears successfully raised, which
would have made him, in effect, a sharecropper. How Sears felt
about all of this is difficult to know. But we do know, as the
many land rushes in Oklahoma demonstrated over the years,
that for westward-settling Euro-Americans, the promise and the

quest for land ownership was a universally understood spiritual axiom of the time that required, in the Osage, at any rate, a period of tribulation, through which many whites voluntarily passed, remaining on land they could not legally own. And there they sat, waiting for the law of the land to change in their favor.

Until then, they laid claim to the next best thing. They formed the business bureaus and civic-minded booster associations and fraternal orders that spoke the language of development, and they published the *Osage Journal*, which became the voice of those who felt themselves part of a disenfranchised non-Indian majority. They incorporated the city of Pawhuska, elected its mayor and sheriff, improved its streets, and built its firehouse and schools all to teach the Osages a thing or two about civilizing the frontier. Yet somehow, Dave Sears, school builder and good citizen of Pond Creek, got himself tangled up with some very bad men.

One scenario casts Sears as an innocent victim. Sears was well liked, the kind of man people trusted with the keys to locked storage compartments containing the nitroglycerin that McCurdy needed. In later years, Sears was made superintendent of oil leases in the district where he lived. Prior to that, it seems likely that he would have had some supervisory role on any number of drilling crews, which would have meant access to equipment, including explosives. It is possible that Hays and Higgins viewed Sears, the model citizen, as a useful pawn, and, in the days prior to the Chautauqua and M, K, & T robberies, perhaps by some ruse, some neighborly request, asked Sears to take some nitroglycerin from the company supply—in order

that they might blow up a stubborn stump in a field, for example. By this means, Hays and Higgins may have ensnared
Sears, making him an unwitting, unwilling conspirator. Indeed,
the robbery of the Chautauqua bank, weeks before the M, K, &
T, may have been intended to intimidate Sears, the son of
Chautauqua's Baptist minister and Chautauqua town leader, into
silent complicity with Hays and Higgins, who, if they needed
to, could claim that Sears had supplied them with the explosives
to rob the bank.

A second scenario casts Dave Sears as a willing conspirator,
perhaps at first remaining at some cool remove, providing the
explosives and other tools for robbing the M, K, & T in exchange for a share of the swag. After the holdup, the word
around Chautauqua suggested that Sears was involved. The
*Sedan Times-Star* reported, in fact, that people had seen McCurdy,
Sears, and Higgins together "with dynamite in their possession"
on the eve of the Chautauqua bank robbery, and again the night
before the holdup of the M, K, & T. But this could have been
idle gossip. It was the robbery itself, and the strange behavior of
Sears in the days following the robbery, that spoke most clearly
against him.

Whoever they were, they came on horseback to the lonesome
vista and hid in a clump of trees as the rain began to fall. One of
the men held in his hands a pint beer bottle containing enough
nitroglycerin to blow all of them, including their horses, to a
fine, pink mist. Along with the bottle, deputies later found a sy-
ringe, soap, fuses, and assorted dynamite, which, taken together,

are like a calling card left by Elmer McCurdy. It is possible the items point to Dave Sears, who must have had some experience with explosives. Dynamite, nitroglycerin's successor, was the tool of a generalist like Sears. Anyone could use it, but nitro was something else all together.

In the oil fields of Oklahoma, long pipes, or "torpedoes," filled with nitroglycerin "soup" were lowered down wells and exploded, shattering the rock formations below to increase the flow of oil. These "production shots," as they were called, temporarily stopped all work on the derricks. Drillers, mudders, roustabouts, they all vanished when the man responsible for placing and setting off the nitroglycerin charge arrived. He was called a "shooter," he was uninsurable, and he worked alone.

Sometimes a drilling crew would try to get by without the aid of a professional shooter. Once, in Chandler, Oklahoma, a man tried to make a production shot on his own to save himself a little money. But the torpedo charge got jammed down in the hole, and he made the mistake of trying to dislodge it with a pipe. The ensuing blast destroyed the derrick, killed the man and his son, and decapitated a roughneck hiding 200 feet away behind a tree. When a nitroglycerin storage magazine blew up north of Tulsa, the force of the blast sent a steel door flying over a mile of prairie. It plowed through the entire length of a house when it landed, where a baby sat in a highchair eating Post Toasties. The projectile door knocked the box of cereal off the baby's highchair. The baby was untouched.

Nitroglycerin was a substance that required training, attention, and caution even when used under controlled circumstances, and it was difficult and extremely dangerous in less sanguine situations such as train robberies. Using it for such a purpose was like using a howitzer in a dart game, but McCurdy seemed strangely loyal to nitroglycerin, perhaps because whatever training he may have had in the army made him something of a specialist—and therefore more valuable to others, never mind that it seemed to keep blowing up in his face.

Hours passed in the rain. Someone, perhaps McCurdy, placed the bottle of nitroglycerin off to the side of the track behind a rock, so that the others would not trip over it. Then suddenly, much sooner than they had guessed, a train was coming down the track, slowing to their signal fire.

As soon as the train came to a stop, the men opened fire with rifles and revolvers and boarded the locomotive, taking control of the crew. One of the bandits walked the fireman at gunpoint past the baggage and the express car, which contained the safe. He then ordered the fireman to uncouple the passenger section from the train, which he did. This bandit then entered the express car, which happened to contain the Jim Crow section, where, according to one witness, he found "three negroes, two men and a woman, . . . and a tramp riding the blind baggage," all of whom were forced off the train at gunpoint. The woman was terrified, praying loudly, and had to be physically lifted off the train. The bandit forced everyone out of the express car and then fired a signal shot to his compatriots ahead in the locomotive. The locomotive, with its newly foreshortened section, pulled away from the passenger cars, which were left behind in the darkness.

The locomotive ran down the track a short distance, "about a mile," that is, out of the hills and onto the prairie, back near where I'd parked the van. There they began the search for the Osage payment, their big payday, the stacks of greenbacks that represented their early retirement. Things were going right on schedule. One report has them forcing the mail messenger to open the safe. In another, the messenger tells the bandits that he doesn't have a key or combination, which would not have been a problem since they were now out of earshot of anyone and could have blasted away to their hearts' content until the safe relinquished its treasure.

The bandits did not blow the safe. They did not blow the safe because there was no money in it, and there was no money in it because, as it soon began to dawn on them, the Osage payment—all $400,000 of it—was riding on a different train, an express train running a few hours behind #29. The bandits had robbed the wrong train.

They yanked mail out of sacks and scattered it everywhere. They walked through the Jim Crow coach, barking orders to the messenger, and, one imagines, yelling at each other. It couldn't have gotten much worse—but in small ways it did. They wasted time overturning every single seat cushion except for the one under which the auditor had stuffed $250.00. The conductor discreetly tossed his wallet in the cuspidor, which they also overlooked. Then, as every newspaper reported the next day, they discovered jugs of whiskey and several kegs of beer. They stopped, "broke in the head of one of the beer kegs and spent considerable time drinking it." This last detail drew me up short. It sounded so much like the trio of ne'er-do-wells—McCurdy, Higgins, and Hays—and so little like something Dave Sears would do, that it fairly convinced me that

Sears was not among the robbers that night. But other details would change my mind.

At some point, the beer-fest ceased and the besotted bandits turned their attention to filching what they could from the train crew, lifting a watch from the mail clerk, a pistol from the train auditor, a cravanette coat from the conductor, and about $46 in cash. Then they slung several jugs of whiskey across their horses and galloped southwest into the hills.

Behind them, a train stood on the prairie, the express car ransacked. A mile down the track, passengers waited for a good long while before it seemed safe to come out. The conductor walked the two miles back to Okesa to report the robbery, and the next train following was delayed until a posse could be formed in Bartlesville. At 4 A.M., a second train and a large posse of fifty men and bloodhounds were on their way to Okesa in full pursuit.

The bandits galloped through the hills. They were not gallant brigands stealing from the rich, abstracted companies of the east who would not feel the sting. They had aimed, instead, and in their own backyard, to take a portion from the Osage Nation, for whom the last century had been a sad and shabby procession of theft and deceit. What had bound them together was greed and a sense that they had nothing to lose, or, at any rate, that the payoff would be so colossal that it would be worth the risk. But all of that was now finished.

Having failed so miserably, the bandits set to covering their tracks, but even here they were inept. Recent rains had softened the sandy ground. Their departure to the southwest was meant as a decoy, but it was easy to follow the tracks of their horses as the bandits circled back upon themselves and headed north. It was equally clear to the pursuers that, when the riders had split up, a pair of them had gone north, where Hays and Higgins had a family farm, and a single man had gone west, toward the farm of Dave Sears. Who that single rider was may never be known, but it was either McCurdy or Sears. Either way, the rider was leading the law directly to Dave Sears, a most inconvenient fact, if Sears had something to hide. All of the men involved that night seem to have sought protection at home. Had they made their big haul, perhaps they would have abandoned hearth and home, fled south into Texas, and then to Mexico. But they'd come up empty-handed, and now for each man, home, it seems, was where the alibis were. Now each of the men who robbed the M, K, & T was a liability to the other, and as they rode their separate ways, leaving tracks for others to follow, their allegiances dissolved into the mist and rain of the deepest part of the night, and already the net was closing in around them faster than a horse could run.

The haul was, in the words of the *Bartlesville Enterprise*, "one of the smallest in the history of train robbery." The *Bartlesville Morning Examiner* gave a withering assessment, based on witness reports, of the manner and style of the robbers themselves. "Throughout the entire time the men were in possession of the train," the paper said, "they gave every evidence of having never before been in an express car or baggage car." "From further evidence," the paper continued, "it is thought that [the robbers] have never before engaged in a similar transaction." The paper suggested, as clearly and as delicately as it could be phrased, that the robbery had been committed by local amateurs "familiar with the surrounding country." The story had the effect of a Wanted poster, narrowing the field of suspicion to neighbors or family members in the county who couldn't account for themselves the night before.

Harve Freas, the thickset, no-nonsense sheriff of Osage County, set watch on a few likely spots and waited for word to come in. He let the network of fifty deputy marshals, two postal inspectors, plus railroad detectives, agency police, and a jumpy community, energized in part by reward money, work in his fa-vor, dispatching deputies to pursue any leads. On the night of the holdup, some had seen an automobile traveling at a high rate of speed near the site of the robbery. The bandits were said to be surrounded in Nelagoney, but then they seemed to vapor-ize into thin air. Some tried to draw the bandits out of the ether by using a clairvoyant to track them down, but the seer "strained his constitution," and the highwaymen escaped cap-ture. Amid all the searching and prying about, an opium den was uncovered and a cache of explosives was found in an old broom factory, but the bandits remained at large.

On the afternoon of October 6, two days after the holdup, deputies had followed tracks back to Dave Sears's farm, and Sheriff Freas arrived there with a posse to ask a few questions. Had Sears been present, he would have been arrested on the spot, for here the sheriff found a Savage 30-30 rifle whose shells matched those at the site of the robbery, and the stolen whiskey jugs taken from the express car. Indeed, Dave Sears had some explaining to do, but he was nowhere to be found, so Sheriff Freas, in a way that speaks so much of his time, left Sears a note demanding an explanation, then rode on to pay a visit to Lige Higgins, ten miles away.

Assuming it was Elmer McCurdy who helped rob the M, K, & T, and who then rode from the train back to Dave Sears's farm, perhaps hiding himself away for two days in a barn until October 6, why then, I couldn't help wondering, would Sears, upon reading the sheriff's note, load McCurdy that same night into his buggy—as he acknowledged that he did at his trial—and then drive McCurdy to the farm of Charlie Revard? Why did Sears, moreover, send his own son, Charles Preston Sears, through the rainy evening to the farm of Lige Higgins to deliver a note to Sheriff Freas? The note did not, apparently, direct Freas to Revard's ranch, where Sears had taken McCurdy, but instead—and even more perplexingly—called Freas back to the Sears farm, where, only then, protesting his innocence, did Sears direct the posse to the Revard ranch. A man with nothing to hide, it seemed to me, would have spared himself two trips to the Revard place and simply called the authorities back to his farm to arrest McCurdy where he lay, in all likelihood, too drunk to ride on horseback. How else to explain Sears's decision to drive McCurdy in his buggy in the first place, unless McCurdy was near to toppling over with every step? It was all very, very suspicious, and Sheriff Freas, to his credit, was having none of it. He arrested Sears and had him thrown in jail.

I folded my map and took a swig from the water bottle, which, in the glinting silence of a prairie afternoon, sounded like a wave crashing over my head. I walked a few miles back on the old track, my feet crunching the gravel. Finally I saw the glare of the van's windshield in the distance. I hadn't seen a soul for hours. No one had been this way for quite some time, nor would anyone come this way again—at least not to poke around for clues to a robbery now lost to history. Aside from a few notes on a topographic map and some photographs, meaningless to anyone who found them, there would be no marker to indicate what had happened down this road, no trace under this sky, nothing to remember it by.

My thoughts kept returning to Dave Sears, who had done everything he could—short of murder—to rid himself of McCurdy, his sodden coconspirator. Hays and Higgins may have found a way to strong-arm Sears into the conspiracy, but any version of events that cast Dave Sears as a hapless victim would have to contend with Sears's own inexplicable movements on the eve of McCurdy's death. The explanation he gave at his trial for giving McCurdy a late-night buggy ride to the Revard ranch (he said he had some oil-drilling business to attend to the first thing the next morning) seems particularly feeble. At the very least, the note left by Sheriff Freas on the afternoon of October 6, two days after a widely publicized train robbery, should have prompted Sears to report the appearance of a stranger like McCurdy to the authorities. According to witnesses, McCurdy arrived at the Revard ranch at night, openly bragging that the whiskey he was drinking had "come off the train which was held up down below Okesa." It seems unlikely that McCurdy, deep in his cups, would have withheld this same information from Sears. Why, then, would Sears knowingly transport a fugitive from one farm to another?

The most likely explanation is that, as the authorities began closing in, Elmer McCurdy began to seem more attractive to

Sears as a dead man. To that end, Sears supplied the desperate McCurdy, inclined to belligerence when drunk, with a gun and more whiskey, and then betrayed him to a posse. Some have argued that Sears and Hays acted in concert, Sears stalling Sheriff Freas long enough for Hays to put a bullet into Elmer McCurdy, thus guaranteeing his silence. Whatever happened that evening in the small triangle of miles that separated the ranches of Dave Sears, Lige Higgins, and Charlie Revard, what seems inescapable was that the machinery of betrayal was fully engaged and that Dave Sears and everyone else involved had sold the stranger, the outsider, the drifter McCurdy down the river. The intent was clear: They wanted McCurdy dead.

The Revard ranch revealed itself dimly in the slant light of a spring afternoon—saplings poking up through bare foundations, brick steps going nowhere—as Joe Kirshner, Jr., and I walked in deepening shadows through a grove of poplar, ash, and chest-high bluestem. Joe's father, Joe, Sr., had been one of the dozens of ranchers to hear the sound of the gunfight between McCurdy and the sheriff's posse so many years ago. Joe, Sr., had passed away a few years earlier, but his son had offered to show me what was left of Revard's place, and here we were.

The land, reclaimed by flood-tolerant trees, was now owned by the federal government as part of the Hula Lake Wildlife Management Area, where muskrats worked the banks and herons swooped away from our approach. It sloped gently to the south toward what in McCurdy's time would have been the Caney River ford, an ancient crossing on the Black Dog Trail

known by the Osages as White Swan Crossing. We were wad-
ing, aimlessly, it seemed, through tall grass, amid swirls of gnats
and the watery song of a redwing blackbird. Then Joe stopped
suddenly to point out a large rectangular stone foundation,
which he explained was once used as stalls for livestock or for
storing grain. At the foundation's midpoint, the span widened
enough to accommodate a wagon. Here, he said, was a kind of
breezeway where you could drive through to load or unload
grain or supplies.

We were standing, it seemed, on what remained of Charlie
Revard's barn. Somewhere near this spot, Revard had situated
his hayshed, a free-standing, roofed storage bin or shed with
slatted walls that allowed air to circulate through the hay,
which, in the harvest season of 1911, would have been piled up
close to the roof. The hayshed would have recommended itself
to McCurdy as a defensible position, offering concealment and
commanding at least a partial view of the farmyard. It was less
obvious as a place to hide than the barn was, and it was comfortable, so McCurdy climbed its ladder with his shotgun and
his jug of whiskey. The choice suggests at least an awareness of
the immanent possibility that the law was closing in. He drank
like there was no tomorrow, in any case, and he was right. Just
before dawn, Sheriff Freas and his men, including Robert Fenton, Richard ("Dick") Wallace, a marksman of some reputation,
and Robert's brother "Stringer" Fenton, surrounded the hayshed
where McCurdy lay dozing.

Around 7 A.M., Sheriff Freas yelled out to McCurdy, order-
ing him to surrender. His response was an oath strong enough
in caliber to be glossed, later, by the papers. Perhaps his oath

was a measure of his fatigue. He was a physical wreck, exhausted and gaunt from riding and heavy drinking. He was down to his last and only set of clothes, a borrowed horse, and a gun his compatriot had handed him hours before to defend himself with. There, through the slats of the hayshed, with nowhere else to run, he may have seen Sears, his betrayer.

According to one report, McCurdy continued to curse the men surrounding him for an hour. There were, after all, a few last slugs still remaining from the stolen whiskey cask, and if there was ever an occasion for an oath and a general cursing, surely this was it. Whatever else was going to happen that morning, there was no need to hurry it along, and so the standoff continued. Most accounts state that Charlie Revard was prevailed upon several times to enter the barn and talk some sense into McCurdy, but Revard returned saying there would be no surrender.

There are several different accounts of what happened next. In one, Charlie Revard and Elmer McCurdy have a last drink alone, after which McCurdy sends Charlie out to tell the posse that he will come out firing, which he does, dying in a fusillade of bullets. In another version, McCurdy, still hiding in the hayshed, opens fire on the approaching posse, whose return fire kills him. In still another version, McCurdy is killed, unarmed, in an ambush. This last version, in some ways, has the cold ring of truth about it, insofar as it refuses our penchant for western dramaturgy—the wily outlaw, cornered at last, going out in a blaze of gunfire in the manner of *Butch Cassidy and the Sundance Kid*—but it doesn't explain why the posse, in killing McCurdy, would throw away the substantial reward, which stipulated both his capture and conviction. The first version is the most moving, McCurdy and his erstwhile ranch boss getting snockered together in the hayshed before McCurdy dies in a hail of bullets. The second version, with McCurdy as the aggressor firing from a hidden position, while the men of the posse are exposed, challenges our sense of fair play, making it harder for us to view McCurdy as a victim. But the firsthand accounts, reported the day of the shooting, by telephone from the men immediately involved in McCurdy's last stand, strongly support this version.

"He took a shot at me first," Bob Fenton told reporters. "Then he took a shot at Stringer. After that, he took three shots at Wallace before we opened up." The fusillade of return fire was impressive enough to rouse the attention of neighbors who came and stood out of range to watch the gun battle. The shooting continued for about an hour, until, at one point, all was quiet from the hayshed. The deputies held their fire. Some later recalled that a young boy was first sent in to investigate. Then William Floyd Davis, the Pawhuska chief of police, recalled climbing slowly up the ladder, the guns of the posse trained on the top rung. Davis put his hat on his rifle barrel and poked it up into the loft. Nothing.

Inside, they found McCurdy dead, with a bullet wound to the chest. Everyone within a few miles had gathered to get a good look at the body, including Joe Kirshner, Sr., then still a young boy. All the shouting and the gunfire had created a kind of parenthesis, a suspension in the natural order of things. It was still early, and a dead man was stretched out on the ground, and the men around him were busy with their talk, perhaps pointing out where they'd stood and trading accounts of what had just transpired, passing the story between them the way people do. A man had been shooting at them, after all, trying to kill them. Now it was done. Eventually someone thought to bring a buckboard wagon around, and then there was nothing left to do with the morning but load the body and take it to Pawhuska.

# 5

# Of Cadavers, Their Care and Disposition

Late May is tornado season in Oklahoma, which meant I had the whole tenting area of Osage Hills State Park to myself. I strolled around, picking up two handfuls of trash, which I emptied into a Dumpster. Every now and then I could hear the far-off rumble of bikers barreling down the streets of Pawhuska, or roaring along Highway 60. With their deep tans, wallet chains, and creaking leather, they seemed to embody a loud if diminished vestige of the outlaw tradition. Earlier, at the grocery store in Pawhuska, I had watched as a tough-looking hombre sporting the full ensemble—scruffy beard, bandana, and tattoos—said thank you to the cashier making change for his purchase—a couple of cases of Coca Cola—then made his high-decibel, dangerously effervescent way back to the road rally at the county fairgrounds.

I chose a spot in the growing dusk, fending off a mild wave of melancholy, and assembled The Tent of the Future, with its flexed exoskeleton of poles, to which one clipped the tent itself, and— *voilà*—home on the range. The sun had set over the western hills, and I could hear the rustling of armadillos nearby in the under-brush. If only I had a guitar, I thought, I'd sing a song of armadil-los, their armature the color and sheen of abalone shell, how they scooted past me shyly as I sat at a picnic table, thinking about the violent death of Elmer McCurdy, the beam of my headlamp play-ing on the pages of Percival E. Jackson's *Law of Cadavers.*

It was slow going but not without its bright moments. The heading for the chapter on disinterment, for instance, which read, "Disinterment Generally Abhorred," was a knee-slapper. But I was interested more in the rights of the dead, and the duties and obligations of those entrusted with the care and disposition of the body of Elmer McCurdy. For as life drained from him on that distant day in the fall of 1911, a number of legal considera-tions came to bear of the sort that inevitably affect us all, whether we want to think about them or not. It was here in Pawhuska, after all, at the Johnson Funeral Home, that the pro-tections guaranteed us in the event of our passing somehow went strangely awry. The first involved the abrogation, or shall we say, the egregious delay, of the right to decent burial that made McCurdy's story what it is—a kind of gasping, grotesque defer-ment of something so basic we seldom inquire of its origins.

The eighteenth-century marmoreal historian John Weever observed that in the time of Tacitus, old Saxons "covered dead bodies . . . slaine in the field . . . with turfes, clods, or sods of earth," from which, Weever reminds us, the *burgh* suffix of cities and towns is derived; "Places first so called, having beene with walls of turfe or clods of earth, fenced about for men to bee shrouded in, as in forts or castles." Weever noted another, per-haps more pressing, practical origin for burial and segregation of the dead from the living in the "noysome savour and contagious stinke of . . . dead carkases," which the ancients solved by enacting laws "that all burials should bee without Townes and Cities." Thus Abraham purchases the cave of Machpelah, and the body of Lazarus is yarded out to the suburbs of Bethania.

The right to a decent burial reaches across the gulf of time—tens of thousands of years—to Neolithic funereal rites and procedures meant to propitiate departed spirits. From these customs came codified rules regarding the rights of the dead, and the obligations of the living, that found dramatic expression 500 years before the birth of Christ in Sophocles's *Antigone*. In that play, two brothers of Antigone are slain in the battle of Thebes. Creon, the Theban king and thick-headed father-in-law of Antigone, declares that Eteocles, who died defending the capital, will be buried with full military honors, whereas Polyneices, the traitor who returned from exile to attack Thebes, should be left unburied, upon pain of death. Antigone breaks the king's law, invoking a higher code, "the immortal, unrecorded law of God," the modes and obligations of the living toward the dead. Creon defends his decree against the outlaw Polyneices:

Creon: He made war on his country. Eteocles defended it.
Antigone: Nevertheless. There are honors due all the
    dead.
Creon: But not the same for the wicked as for the just.
Antigone: Ah, Creon, Creon, which of us can say what
    the gods hold wicked?
Creon: An enemy is an enemy, even dead.

In a moment earlier in the play that might have served as re-joinder to the king above, Antigone says to her wavering sister, "It is the dead, not the living, who make the longest demands. We die forever."

Once, I heard a story about a girl who drowned in the Chattooga River in Georgia, where the movie *Deliverance* was filmed. The girl's body had for two months been pinned down in what searchers called a "keeper hydraulic," a jaw of rock eight feet beneath the surface of a tumbling stretch of rapids called Raven's Chute. Three attempts by divers to retrieve the body had failed. Joseph Trois, the girl's father, had arranged to have a construction company build a temporary dam to lower the downstream water enough to reach the body, but the dam collapsed, nearly killing rescue workers. Undeterred, Mr. Trois enlisted the help of a senator in order to build a bigger dam, but the proposal was stopped by the U.S. Forest Service. "It's pretty simple," Mr. Trois told a reporter for the *Atlanta Journal Constitution*. "I want that daughter of mine. I want her out of the river."

However much we may have progressed as a civilization, we have a primitive desire to assert dominion over that which is beyond our control, to claim the deceased, to inter them on our terms rather than the terms imposed by the river, or the mountain, or the sea of which we are a part in the natural scheme of things. Nature sometimes conspires against us, choosing some rather than others, sometimes in ways that remind us, sometimes perversely, of our helplessness before its power. The body of a girl, pinned down in the rocks a few feet from the shore. To bury her on our terms is an act of completion, of closure, as they say. It's something we rehearse in our childhood with dead pets. It's our way of addressing the mystery of death through ritual place-ment—a planting, as James George Frazer's *Golden Bough* insists again and again—in a site we've named and dug and ennobled, raised above the grim biological processes. As Abraham for 400 shekels of silver bought the cave of Machpelah, so we with our $2,000 might purchase a coffin lined with steel. It's a choice we feel entitled to. It's one we fantasize about in our low moments; all our loved ones filing past us as we look up from our cushioned casket, noting the degrees of suffering among survivors. When nature takes that choice away from us, as happened with Rachel Trois, we are twice aggrieved—both the life and the body stolen by a roaring column of water crashing down Raven's Chute, the force of the Chattooga ripping the diving masks from the faces of men powerless to pull a body from its freakish dance at the bottom of a river.

Rachel Trois had her father to look after her body, and her father had a senator to insure that the time-honored obligation of the community to bury the dead would prevail. And Polyne-ices had his Antigone. But the outlaw Elmer McCurdy had no family to watch over him, only the men who drove the dusty road back to Pawhuska on a buckboard carrying his corpse— probably Stringer Fenton and possibly William Floyd Davis, the chief of police at Pawhuska. They themselves were not particu-larly focused upon thoughts that transcended their own press-ing concerns, which tended toward the mercenary.

They were perhaps the first in a long series of mercenaries who sought to transform the stiff in the back of the wagon into cash, although to Fenton and his men, unlike everyone else who would follow them, McCurdy was worth nothing dead—the

$2,000 reward was good only for McCurdy's capture, alive. Hence, one imagines their preoccupation. The automobiles that passed them by on the way to Pawhuska, if any, were probably driven by Osage Indians made rich by oil and grazing leases. The members of the posse had risked their lives in a gun battle with an outlaw who had tried to steal from the Osages, and Stringer Fenton felt so strongly about the justness of his case that he petitioned the U.S. Senate. The bill, S4669, "for the relief of S. W. Fenton, R. L. Fenton, and Richard Wallace," which sought reward "for their services in capturing a robber," that is, for shooting and killing McCurdy, was itself killed in committee at the close of the 62nd Congress. Not even Congress could bring McCurdy back.

There were laws on the books in Oklahoma protecting the rights of the anonymous and unclaimed dead. In the most general sense, there was, as Percival Jackson noted, "a duty imposed by the universal feelings of mankind . . . to protect [the dead] from violation; and a duty on the part of others to abstain from violation." They included laws that grappled with the enigmatic quality of the body itself.

William Blackstone, the eighteenth-century jurist, philosopher, and grand Enlightenment systematizer, was perhaps the first to puzzle over the problem. From the eleventh century, the church had claimed control of the body after death. But in commentaries that deeply influenced the shape of American legal thought and covered nearly every aspect of common law, including laws affecting cadavers, Blackstone came to define the dead as *nullius in bonis*, that is, "no person's property." When alive, he reasoned, we cast a net of human agency over things. Our language, our very grammar, parses up the world into objects and subjects, into things and their owners. Our dominion over things extends to our own bodies, until we die. Of course, when dead, we cannot own anything, but neither can the living lay claim of ownership upon our bodies. Blackstone created, in effect, a special category of objects in the world—the dead—that no one could possess. As Justice Joseph Henry Lumpkin of the Georgia Supreme Court wrote in 1905, "A corpse in some respects is the strangest thing on earth. . . . It is not surprising that the law relating to this mystery of what death leaves behind cannot be precisely brought within the letter of all the rules regarding corn, lumber and pig iron."

Other laws established how bodies were to be transported—in a decent manner, covered—and who, in the absence of next-of-kin, bore responsibility for them. In McCurdy's case, it was Charlie Revard, the householder under whose roof McCurdy had died. Revard's obligations were relinquished, however, when the body was taken into custody by Deputy U.S. Marshal Stringer Fenton, who in turn passed his responsibilities on to the Pawhuska funeral director, Joseph L. Johnson. And it is here, it seems, that the trouble began.

The law defined the obligations of men like Johnson, who normally served as trustees for the next of kin. But, as in McCurdy's case, when there was no next of kin, the law was nevertheless unequivocal about duty: The community was to assert its rights or assume its obligations. In this case, the community of Pawhuska, by laws of stare decisis that reached back to the civil law of ancient Rome, had an obligation to bury the body of Elmer McCurdy at public expense. There was a duty on these strangers to bury a man they did not know, killed so far from home.

This, of course, was never done. Johnson later claimed that he'd held the body in lieu of payment for services performed—cleaning and caring for it, performing an autopsy, embalming, and so forth. While this may have been English custom up until 1804, when creditors had been known to arrest a dead body for debt—John Dryden in 1700 was a celebrated case—in the United States, a body could not be held as security for funeral costs. Oklahoma's own case law made it a misdemeanor, in fact, to "arrest, attach, detain or claim to detain a dead body upon a debt, demand, lien or charge." To be fair, the singular feature of McCurdy's death made the case unique. He was an outlaw, not somebody's dead grandmother, so his body was treated differently. Like Creon of Thebes, the people of Pawhuska felt the honors normally due the dead were not the same for the wicked as for the just. Cast beyond the law, the bodies of dead outlaws were often prominently displayed, photographed, and otherwise publicly exhibited in contravention of laws protecting cadavers from such mistreatment. McCurdy's misconduct in life made a difference, it seems, for Joseph L. Johnson. But other factors came to bear as well.

The news of the shoot-out traveled quickly ahead of the wagon, though the bandit's identity remained for a time in doubt. Behind him, McCurdy left a string of aliases that led nowhere. He was "Frank Davis." He was "Frank Curtis." He was "Charles Davis." He was "Frank Amos." Newspaper renderings of his real surname—"Missouri McCurdy" or "McCarty" or "McUrdy" or "McAurdy"—seem to grasp, typographically, after a secret that kept slipping away. He was "Elmer Curtis." He was "Frank Davidson." He may have killed a man in Colorado, or Kentucky, or some other state.

The earliest report of the incident appeared in the *Iola Daily Register* later that evening. The paper spoke of "Frank Amos" and his "hour's running revolver fight" and said that Dave Sears was being questioned by authorities. On October 8, the *Bartlesville Morning Examiner* reported that officers had positively identified the dead bandit as McCurdy, and that Amos Hays had turned himself in. That same day the *Daily Oklahoman* named conspirators Sears and Hays and linked McCurdy to the Iron Mountain train robbery near Lenapah.

Although he was hunted down and killed, and his compatriots rounded up with a swiftness and a determination that spoke of a new era's boosterish pride in law and order, one can find in the regional newspapers a tone of tacit admiration for McCurdy's daring that was a signature mode of reportage for so many "social bandits" who predated McCurdy by several decades. In truth, the authorities had apprehended a handful of local, bungling, part-time felons, but by October 9, one year into the second decade of the twentieth century, the urge to bump the story a notch higher, to engage the machinery of western mythopoeia, to remind the fenced-in, automobile-driving merchants and farmers of a vanished outlaw past, became irresistible. The *Fort Scott (Kans.) Tribune* called McCurdy, whose three failed robberies amounted to a pathetic, nine-month crime spree, a "notable criminal" and claimed that McCurdy was "the leader of a gang of outlaws who have held up and robbed trains and banks and committed much of the outlawry of the past few years." Other papers followed suit, and the body of McCurdy, laid out in Johnson's funeral home for all to see, became an object of considerable public interest—became, strangely, an upwardly mobile celebrity corpse to which Joseph Johnson would hitch his wagon.

Twain, again: "Well, pretty soon the whole town was there, squirming and scrouging and pushing and shoving to get at the window and have a look," Huck Finn says of the crowd pressing around a drugstore window to view the body of Boggs, shot dead by Colonel Sherburn in *Huckleberry Finn*. "But people that had the places wouldn't give them up, and folks behind them was saying all the time, 'Say, now, you've looked enough, you fellows; 'tain't right and 'tain't fair, for you to stay thar all the time, and never give nobody a chance; other folks has their rights as well as you.'"

It is a fictional scene set in a Mississippi River hamlet, but it could just as easily have been on the quai de L'Archeveche, on the Right Bank, just behind Notre-Dame. The Paris Morgue was a public attraction, "a show," described by Émile Zola, "that was affordable to all" and listed in Thomas Cook's guidebook. Twain himself visited it during his tour that became *The Innocents Abroad*. It was a place where as many as 40,000 people in a day, up to a million visitors a year, in the words of a local observer, "came to see, just to see, just as they read a serial novel. . . . At the door, calling out to each other and demanding the program: 'What have they got in there?'" Built in 1804 in the rational, positivist spirit of public good, in which citizens could perform a civic duty by identifying anonymous bodies, the morgue—a term itself derived from *morguer*, to stare—became a "spectacle of the real," where each visitor came, as the morgue's registrar dryly noted, "to exercise his retina at the window." By 1907, the year it was closed to the public, it had come to be described by an English visitor as "a forlorn sideshow."

But for a few minor details, the idle flaneurs of Paris shuffling past the sealed glass of the morgue, or the Mississippi towns-people of *Huckleberry Finn*, viewing the body of Boggs through a drugstore window, beg comparison to the jostling citizens of Pawhuska after McCurdy's death. "Many citizens viewed the dead man at the Johnson undertaking rooms," the *Pawhuska Capital* stated less than a week after the shoot-out. A few days later the paper suggested that "thousands have visited this man in his exclusive quarters." *Thousands?* One wonders at the figure. If it were half that many, the event would have been a sensation in sparsely populated northeastern Oklahoma. For many months, according to another account, "hoards of people viewed the em-balmed remains. People from all parts of the United States . . . visited the Johnson undertaking establishment and anxiously gazed upon the inanimate form—with the fear and horror that they might recognize a long lost son, a wayward brother, or a truant husband."

Seventeen years after the fact, in an article published in the *Pawhuska Journal-Capital*, Joseph Johnson himself remembered "thousands viewing [the body] but no one identifying it." He added that "every showman or street carnival that came to town tried to buy the body for show purposes but they were advised it was . . . being held in the hope that relatives would claim it." But this is the sincerity of a crocodile rebuffing the competition, which arrived, seasonally, in the form of carnival operators offering cash for the stiff. Johnson, the local businessman, was, of course, enjoying the windfall of free advertising, an opportunity too good to miss. He may have begun with the best of intentions, perhaps in the civic-minded spirit of the Paris Morgue, but his decision to continue to display the body devolved into spectacle. For Johnson, Elmer McCurdy was better off above ground.

Johnson photographed McCurdy, dead in his clothes, lying in a wicker basket. This surviving photograph shows a gaunt, bedraggled figure, diminished by disease and exposure to the elements. He looks more like a hobo than an outlaw. Perhaps guessing that McCurdy's relatives might be long in coming, Johnson added a quantity of arsenic into the embalming fluid sufficient to preserve McCurdy deep into the century. After William Root, McCurdy's old employer from Iola, Kansas, identified McCurdy, Johnson dressed him in formal wear, combed his hair, and took a second photograph of the deceased, this time lying in profile. Sheriff Freas inscribed this photograph with Elmer's name, several aliases, and a brief encapsulation—"Shot by sheriff Posse near Pawhuska, Okl, 10–7–1911"—and officially closed the case.

A year later, McCurdy's old friend Walter Jarrett, shot after robbing a bank in Prue, Oklahoma, lay dead beside him in the Johnson Funeral Home, until the Jarrett family claimed Walter's body for burial beside his outlaw brothers. A third photograph of McCurdy, perhaps taken around this time, shows that the funereal clothing had been replaced by the rag-tag clothes in which he died. He wears a gray work shirt buttoned at the cuffs and the chin, black trousers, and suspenders. Somebody has put a high-crowned, soft-brimmed hat on his head, cocked rakishly to the left. In the photograph, the body and head lists slightly to the left, as if he'd just dropped his keys on the pavement in front of him. A rifle is propped between his legs. It is a striking transformation that Joseph L. Johnson's son, Luke, later recalled in a mortuary trade publication. Six months after the shoot-out, he said, they "saw that [the body] could be stood on its feet. And, as 'The Embalmed Bandit' had already become an object of local interest, we dressed him in the clothes he had worn at his last fight, and stood him in the corner of our Mortuary."

It is a moment worth pausing over, a moment of whimsy that took place in the back of a mortuary amid storage shelves and bottles of embalming fluid. It was perhaps no more than a lapse in taste, but, for the purposes of our story, it marks a particular and profound moment of metamorphosis—the rising up, Lazarus-like, of a new thing. Few of us, even professional morticians like the Johnsons, would so mishandle a cadaver. Yet in propping up the body, in breaking the plane of the horizontal, it ceased to be, in effect, a *cadaver*, a word derived from *cadendo*, which means "one who cannot stand." By standing, or being stood, McCurdy's body was understood differently and drastically by those who were charged with its care, and then, in turn, by the people of Pawhuska. Some say that Joseph Johnson charged the public a nickel to view McCurdy's body. Local memory has the younger Johnson boys mounting the body on roller skates, as a kind of spook-house exhibit to scare younger kids. Others recall a teenage ritual of sneaking into the funeral parlor to view the body after a late-night movie.

Even if these stories are apocryphal, and the Johnson Funeral Home vehemently denies them, McCurdy's body after 1912 seems to have entered a new ontological and taxonomic order. For him, the change from cadaver to curiosity was now complete. He was transformed by the refracting lens of a nostalgic public mind into an object that could be lampooned or cuddled safely with the kind of affectionate condescension reserved for high-school mascots. He became "a desperado who refused to surrender," according to the *Daily Oklahoman*, and a "notable criminal," according to the *Fort Scott (Kans.) Tribune*, "a leader of a gang of outlaws who have held up and robbed trains and banks and committed much of the outlawry of the past few years." If in life he was a wayward, pathetic figure, in death he became an up-wardly mobile historical artifact, drafted backwards in time into a Wild West league to which he'd never properly belonged, but to which he was now connected by the slenderest of threads.

## ≈ 6 ≈

# **Exeunt**

*Commerce defies every wind, outrides every*
*tempest, and invades every zone.*
                                    —George Bancroft

In 1881, the Pre-Raphaelite painter Edward Burne-Jones was enjoying a Sunday luncheon in the garden with his friend, colleague and companion –in hyphenation– Lawrence Alma–Tadema. The two had been discussing the finer points of paint, the grinding down of substances into fine powders, the blending of oils to form pigment. Alma–Tadema had recently visited the studio of his own colorist, who had been busy making a batch of Egyptian Brown, a type of paint known also as Mummy. The process Alma–Tadema described, however, so shocked Burne-Jones that he walked immediately to his studio, returned to the garden, then gathered his family and friends around him for an impromptu memorial service. "A hole was bored into the grass at our feet," Georgiana Burne-Jones recalled, and the deceased interred. "We all watched it put safely in," she remembered, "and the spot was marked by one of the girls planting a daisy root above it."

What Burne-Jones had dropped into the hole was a tube of paint, the selfsame Egyptian Brown, coveted by painters of the period for its versatility and silky sensuality and made, it seemed, with ground and pulverized mummy parts. The ad hoc funeral service, completed, one imagines, with a brief moment of silence, during which the scruples of an era fell ever so softly into alignment, was Burne-Jones's attempt to redeem the sacrilege visited upon a body that had been stolen, smuggled, emulsified, and tubed, so that now, in the words of a breathless decadent enthusiast of Egyptian Brown, it "flow[ed] from the brush with delightful freedom and evenness."

At the business end of this process of manufacture were those who specialized in the filching of mummies—the grave robbers and tomb defilers who made up a profitable niche market for human remains. Mummy theft represented the high end of the market. The low end, the disinterment and the selling of cadavers for anatomical study, burgeoned in the 1700s, and when the demand for bodies in the form of executed convicts, foundlings, and paupers outpaced the officially sanctioned sources of supply, startling scenes of violence occurred between the families of executed criminals and the men hired to procure medical cadavers. "As soon as the poor creatures were half dead," Henry Fielding reported of a mass hanging in London, "I was much surprised . . . to see the populace fall to hauling and pulling the carcasses . . . with so much earnestness as to occasion several warm encounters and broken heads. [Some] were friends of the persons executed . . . and some [were] persons sent by private surgeons to obtain bodies for dissection. The contests between these were fierce and bloody and frightful to look at." Anatomy professors had long sent their students roaming the countryside to acquire fresh corpses, taking advantage of the legal limbo of the dead. Yet such theft, while repugnant, was not deemed a crime until 1788, when Lord Kenyon, with recourse to no known legal precedent, simply made it so. The result of this new sanction drove up the price per corpse, ushering in a generation of professional body snatchers that would persist, in England, until 1832, when the passage of the Anatomy Act, which turned the unclaimed dead over to medical schools, put grave robbers out of business. Yet as late as 1850, when 700 bodies were stolen from graveyards in New York City alone, there seemed enough rogue anatomists and ambitious young researchers trolling American cemeteries to find a place in Ambrose Bierce's dictionary, published in 1911, the year McCurdy was shot, wherein "grave" is defined as "a place in which the dead are laid to await the coming of the medical student."

Professional thieves generally worked in teams of two or three, under cover of darkness. For protection from locals, who were extraordinarily touchy about their stock in trade, and to consolidate territory and intimidate competition, they formed gangs. In England, the Ben Crouch gang was the most powerful cadaver cartel of the period prior to the Anatomy Act, supplying all the trade to the United Borough Hospitals and St. Bartholome's. Citizens retaliated against these depredations by hiring cemetery watchmen, by constructing graveyard watch houses, some with gun ports, or by rigging elaborate tombstone alarms, bombs, and *mortsafes* to foil Crouch's men. You wouldn't have thought it to look at him, patrolling the halls of hospitals, making deals, setting the terms for the continued supply of bodies, but Crouch was on the advance guard of Enlightenment anatomical research. He and his companions were universally despised. One of their best customers described them as "the lowest dregs of degradation." Their object was to unearth what had for centuries been under the purview of the church, as stated in ecclesiastical law, watched over and cared for against the coming day of judgment. They were called Resurrectionists.

They are—or should be—the patron saints of all biographers, of all who profit, in one way or another, from raising the dead. Ezra Pound recognized this uncomfortable ambiguity between artistry and robbery. One of his persona poems, "Sestina: Altaforte," written a few years before McCurdy was killed, brings to life a twelfth-century warrior, Bertran de Born. "Judge ye!" Pound asks, in his own voice, at the poem's outset, "Have I dug him up again?" While the question urges us to consider how well Pound has pulled off his performance as de Born, it is put so crudely, in terms the Resurrectionists themselves might have used, that one cannot fail to feel the shadow of their passing, the pressure of the question, *Why, indeed, dig him up again?* Hemingway felt that biographers were in the same league as grave robbers and morticians: Their work, after all, involved theft and exposure, with a little touching-up thrown in for good measure.

All of this began to trouble me the more I pursued the story of Elmer McCurdy. Hadn't I, after all, dug him up again? That I wasn't alone in the matter was little comfort. There were the assorted articles about McCurdy in magazines, newspapers, and on the Internet. Richard Basgall's book, *The Career of Elmer McCurdy, Deceased,* and the BBC documentary, *Oklahoma Outlaw,* had cut a deep groove in the freak-show story line. Sometimes I felt like a late arrival, trotting out this macabre tale. Other times I felt as though the story contained some secret that kept skidding off the edge of things, just beyond vision, and for this reason the story kept resurfacing, like some reoccurring dream whose sheer strangeness of detail—the head-scratching weirdness of it all—distracts us from its meaning. McCurdy was, in many senses of the word, a cipher: a fringe character, a loser, an easy-to-dismiss zero bearing a coded message that we kept missing.

But even a cipher, it seemed, had first to make its way in the world. And in 1916, two dapper gentlemen stepped off a train in Pawhuska and strolled from the train station to the first of several appointments in town. They were two latter-day Resurrectionists about to help a dead outlaw get himself down the road.

McCurdy's body had lain unclaimed in the Johnson Funeral Home for five years, during which time thousands of people had come to view his mummified remains, making McCurdy something of a regional celebrity. Johnson himself reported that over the years many carnival operators had offered him money for the body but had been refused. In October 1916, The Great Patterson Carnival Shows were in residence forty-five miles away in Arkansas City, Kansas, where the cotton candy butchers, and the carnival rides, and the thirty carloads of equipment, including a sideshow containing a number of human curiosities, cranked and ground and wheezed its way through the Arkansas City Annual Fall Jubilee and Trade Week. Arkansas City happened to be the home of Charles Patterson, a traveling salesman whose brother James owned and managed The Great Patterson Shows. It seems likely that Charles, the salesman, knew of Elmer McCurdy down in Pawhuska, and knew, also, that his carny brother James would be interested in the body of a mummified outlaw.

One day during the Fall Jubilee and Trade Week, Johnson received a call from a man claiming to be the brother of Elmer McCurdy and informing Johnson that he and a friend would arrive to claim the body. In a way that now seems, in hindsight, like the signature flourish of a seasoned confidence man, the name he gave was Aver, Mr. Aver, as in *to affirm with confidence, to declare in a manner that precludes or does not admit of debate; in law, to allege as a fact.* He arrived in Pawhuska with a Mr. Wayne, both well-dressed gentlemen.

According to Joseph Johnson's son Johnny, Aver and Wayne met first with the sheriff and the county attorney, a shrewd, peremptory move. In this meeting, Aver either convinced the two officials that he was the long-lost brother of Elmer McCurdy, that he'd come to honor the dying last request of McCurdy's mother to find her wayward son and bring him home to California for burial, or offered a sum of money sufficient to momentarily suspend official disbelief. Advance agents for carnivals, known as "legal adjusters," commonly bribed local authorities to pave the way for grift shows and other unlawful games and exhibitions. Aver and Wayne may have been two smoothies of this sort, sent by Patterson on an errand to secure a stiff for his sideshow. Either way, the men emerged from their meeting with the approval of the sheriff and the county attorney, and there was nothing Joseph Johnson could do but relinquish McCurdy.

The following day, October 7, a casket containing the body of Elmer McCurdy was loaded onto the Midland Valley railway, which made a station stop in Arkansas City. The next morning, The Great Patterson Shows left Arkansas City for the Texas panhandle. Within two weeks, word came back to Pawhuska that "Johnson's outlaw" was being exhibited in a street carnival show in West Texas.

*[handwritten annotation:] Almost 5 years to the day from the death of McCurdy, Oct 9, 1911*

# The Bally

$A$ *corpse,* some wit once observed, *is a human with no problems.* No agenda, one imagines, no itinerary, no promises to keep, nor miles to go. To this we might add the lines of the poet Jules Laforgue, who declared that *the dead, under ground, hardly ever get around.* But Elmer McCurdy had never been buried, had, in fact, been snatched from the rubes of Pawhuska and pressed into service as a new and valuable conscript, whence he entered an afterlife existence as a carnival exhibit. From West Texas, The Great Patterson Carnival Shows, a caravan of rides and human curiosities with McCurdy its newest acquisition, billed now as the Oklahoma Outlaw, crossed and recrossed the continent on a route now forgotten but which in all likelihood covered about 6,000 miles each season. In the six years from the time Elmer McCurdy left Pawhuska until 1922 when he resurfaced in Washington State at Louis Sonney's Wax Museum of Crime, he traveled the equivalent of one and a half times around the globe, was viewed, at least momentarily, by tens of thousands of people, yet seems to have been just as quickly forgotten.

For McCurdy had vanished into the *demos*, into an unwashed realm of public entertainment that included at its upper limit that great leviathan, the circus—"the show that smells." This realm also included the Wild West show, the chautauqua lecture, the lyceum, the camp revival with its evangelical sky grifters, and, perhaps as remedy for the above, the soap-selling, laxative-dispensing, catarrh-vanquishing medicine show, known also as the Physic Opera. Yet even these lowbrow forms of entertainment bore the stamp of genteel respectability. The circus, by and large, was machinelike and all business and did not suffer hanky-panky or chicanery. The chautauqua offered culture, and the traveling revival offered salvation to the beat of a tambourine. Even the vaudeville sketches and songs of the medicine show were tempered and tailored for the ears of ladies and young children. But at the lower register, on the other side of the tracks, in a field strewn with sawdust, there existed—usually for an entire week—a netherworld of gaudy, grotesque, gas-lit images that momentarily distracted people from their lives and their wallets. This was the world of the traveling carnival, viewed by turn-of-the-century genteel America the way some pedants talk about movies or television today. It was a blight on the cultural landscape where the delicate moral balance of the universe was tipped in Satan's favor.

The carnival hadn't always been so closely linked with the work of the archfiend. Eleventh-century Norman prelates, in fact, took great pains to fit the feast days of the Christian saints to the preexisting pagan fairs of the conquered Saxons. It was and remains an uneasy alliance from which the word *carnival* derives its potent ambiguity. The pagan tradition suggests that *carnival* comes from a phrase meaning the *solace of the flesh*, from which we get the yearly conflagration of Mardi Gras and Spring Break—undergraduate women exposing their breasts *en mass* to intoxicated mobs. However, *The Oxford English Dictionary* points us, chastely, to the eleventh-century Latin, *carnem levare*, the putting away or removal of meat, as in pre-Lenten austerities, leaving us with a word that seems to smuggle in the flesh, only to forsake it.

With desire thus subsumed, it is no surprise that prelates of one sort or another have been grumbling about carnivals ever since. A royal mandate issued for the 1604 Stourbridge Fair seems targeted specifically to shutting down the carnival, listing among the prohibited activities "bull-baiting, bear-baiting, . . . games at loggets, nine-holes, and all other sports and games where throngs concourse or multitudes are drawn together." The Bartholomew Fair became the target of suppression in the 1670s and was successfully shut down in 1855. At best, the carnival was tolerated from a distance, but when it moved too close, it made the papers. "Some famous bonehead plays have been pulled in this city," a Lincoln, Nebraska, editorial complained in 1915, "but no council ever equaled the record of the present commissioners in turning loose a crowd of tent show freaks and ballyhoo artists and popcorn sellers on the principal street, only a short distance from the retail business center, and inviting them to do their worst." Such condemnation, of course, protests too much, the shrill note of opprobrium belying a desire to partake of the feast, a desire that few would countenance, acknowledge, or admit to.

Many regard the 1893 Columbian Exposition in Chicago as the watershed for the traveling carnival, for while the carnival had existed for centuries, attaching itself lampreylike to the margins of fairs and festivals everywhere, the Columbian Exposition marked the first time that carnival exhibits had been integrated into the overall program of attractions. At the Columbian Exposition, the connecting boulevard between Washington and Jackson Parks, called the grand Midway Plaisance, legitimized for no-nonsense America the idea of *flaneurie,* the idle, aimless Parisian stroll, the embrace of the urban scene with its noises and smells, its oddities and mysteries. The Midway Plaisance was a great success, and fortunately so, for the fair took a percentage from exhibitors along the great Midway, without which the Columbian Exposition, which opened as the nation pitched headlong into the biggest economic crash of the century, would have gone bankrupt. It was a galvanizing moment as well for the independent showmen of the time, who began to form themselves into large, train-bound, traveling caravans.

The layout of every carnival thereafter was designed to evoke the flashy, disorienting atmosphere of that first grand concourse, to bring to small-town America the illusion of urban congestion with its whiff of danger and discovery. At a typical carnival, the concessionaires would pitch their tents in a great inward-facing U-shape, in the center of which were the amusement rides. The open end of the U was the entrance, bedecked with loud banners and signs, and stationed with ticket takers. Once inside, the point was not to get anywhere but to dawdle, half-lost, amid the blinking, winking midway, which beckoned with its games of skill and chance, food vendors, amusement rides, fortune tellers, sideshow exhibits, and sellers of gewgaws and gimcrack. If it were the 1938 Johnny J. Jones Mighty

Exposition—"The Show Beautiful"—you might see the Royal Russian Midgets, or the Fat Girl Twins. You might find ten wondrous attractions all gathered under one tent—a 10-in1. There were tents that contained a single human oddity or freak—an alligator woman, a human skeleton; and shows with novelty acts—sword swallowers and contortionists. Each of these individual exhibits was called a *Single-O*, derived, some say, from *Single-O-traction*, but which, in any case, seems to take the proper measure of whatever was behind the curtain— nakedness, say, or disfigurement, or someone shoving a ten-penny nail up his nose, to which a single, measured "Oh," may have been the best response, the viewer shaping his mouth not in awe or fear or wonder, but in mild recognition of the part he has played in a small-time swindle. For the midway's aim and essence was to offer as many people as possible the benign pleasure of being taken for a ride. The midway, in other words, was like other kinds of flashy, trashy experience. It was some-thing people did, but few were willing to discuss it, and it slipped along beneath report or record. And so Elmer McCurdy slipped along, too, back and forth across the conti-nent, unrecorded, unremembered, seemingly beneath com-ment. Indeed, in his new afterlife, McCurdy seems to vanish from history altogether, subsumed within an itinerant form of the collective unconscious—the sideshow—offering America a glimpse of its own troubled dreamscape with its freighted cargo of freakery and wonder.

*Paradoxography*, originally the study and compilation of wonders and marvels in antiquity, stemmed from Aristotle's de-scriptive histories of the natural world. *Wonder* was used by St.

Augustine in the fourth century as a term for astonishment in the face of something rare, abnormal, awful, horrifying, or destructive that led to moral or spiritual contemplation. With the emergence of the traveling sideshow in seventeenth-century Europe, the more spontaneous quality of wonder, its sheer unpredictability, its rarity, its innately didactic function, gave way entirely to the taste for surprise for its own sake—manufactured wonder, arriving seasonally with the carnival or circus. A banner in 1818 features an "African Bison" on display in Charleston, South Carolina, that was probably part of what were then called "outside shows," which camped on the fringes of traveling circuses, menageries, fairs, and other events that attracted the paying public. By 1841, with the advent of P. T. Barnum's American Museum featuring "mysterious deviations from nature's usual course," the sideshow had become an integral part of the circus experience.

The completion of the transcontinental railroad in 1869 helped the circus and traveling sideshow flourish throughout America, and by the end of the nineteenth century the popularity of the sideshow was at its peak. The Buffalo Bill Wild West Congress of Rough Riders of 1907 featured twenty-three attractions above and beyond the usual cast of freaks and oddities, including glass blowers, comedians, snake charmers, tattooed men and women, mind readers, a Punch and Judy show, and a mysterious blue man. The sideshow remained the realm of peripheral entertainment, with its racy, provocative brand of amusement. If you were old enough, for instance, you might wander into the Style Review, the showcase for bathing beauties, or you might pay to see the tattooed lady. As a song of the period coyly says of one particularly famous tattooed lady, Lydia is an *en-cyclo-pe-dia*. *You can learn a lot from Lydia.* The song's chorus winks, and if you were there, watching, you'd get the joke. Educational instruction was just a veil in the service of the baser motivation to stare, without compunction, at the naked female form, to gawk without embarrassment at a tattooed lady, a made freak, someone who had, moreover, made herself available to you, visually anyway, after the manner of the oldest profession. The sideshow was the place where, for the price of admission, you could temporarily leave your qualms about the transaction behind.

Every such glimpse delivers less than what one hoped. What fueled the hope in the first place, and the carnival in general, yet gave it an air of respectability and joined it to the other forms of itinerant public entertainment, was the *bally*, the voice of the outside talker rising above the heads of passersby, promising everything, promising edification, promising the miraculous, the never-before seen.

*Bally*, short for *ballyhoo*, is a word, like the peripatetic carnival itself, of unfixed origin. H. L. Mencken suggested a tenuous link between *ballyhoo* and the rough and tumble village of Ballyhooly in County Cork, Ireland, though later he sensibly recanted. Others point to a type of West Indian sailing vessel, the *ballahou*, which was fast but awkward-looking to European eyes, but nobody can explain how this nautical term, which Melville uses in *Omoo*, joined the carnival.

Only one explanation for *ballyhoo* seems likely: the aforementioned Midway Plaisance at Chicago's 1893 Columbian Exposition. According to Charles Wolverton, in an article published in

*American Speech* in 1935, ballyhoo was born in front of the Turkish Theater at the fair's Oriental Village. Here a man named W. O. Taylor, press agent and pitch man at the fair, lowered the ticket price for a whirling dervish act that was receiving scant attention. According to Taylor, the dancers were offended and took their act outside, spinning and dervishing in full regalia in front of the tent. As they danced, they chanted, sang, and shouted their praise heavenward: "He is God! Through God it is! and Thou art God!" which to Taylor's ears sounded like "B'Allah hoo!" With his dancers attracting the curious stares of passersby, Taylor began his spiel, behaving as if the dance and the talk were all part of a plan, and a crowd began to gather. Afterwards, the dancers asked Taylor to "make B'Allah hoo" again for them, and he did, and the ballyhoo—or bally—was born.

It's such a good story, perhaps too good, too convenient, too full of the bally itself to be believed. Mencken didn't buy it, at any rate, nor do the editors of the *Random House Historical Dictionary of American Slang*, or of the *Oxford English Dictionary*, who express their doubt about Taylor's Turks with the lexicographically abbreviated equivalent of a well-informed, bespectacled shrug: *orig. unkn.* It hardly matters. How much better, in fact, as a portrait of an era that the primordial ballyhoo conflates the quest of the soul with the quest for the sale, prophet seeking with profit taking, god *in Allah!* with the almighty greenback; and how apt that ballyhoo would have as a defining moment a story, apocryphal or not, that featured W. O. Taylor, archetypal showman, clever and quick on his feet, making a sucker of Wolverton, the gullible lexicographer of *American Speech.*

The bally worked like this. Sideshow performers would strut onto a stage outside the sideshow tent—a sword swallower, a fire eater, a strong man, a woman with a snake, all meant to tease, to entice—while an outside "talker" gave his spiel about the further attractions within the tent, working the crowd into a lather of mild hysteria sufficient to lead it, against its better judgment, to the ticket booth. The talker first had to "build the tip," attract from the amorphous, milling passersby on the midway a group of sufficient density to warrant a show. The art of building the tip was to get people to step right up close. Bobby Reynolds was known to hold up a dollar bill and begin a kind of hypnotic incantation: "Watch the dollar, watch the dollar. Move in close, ladies and gentlemen, watch the dollar. Every move a work of art." He worked the dollar left and right, up and down, as if he were about to perform a magic trick. As an object, it was small enough to require the crowd to inch closer to the stage, encouraged by the patter of his repeated phrase. But the dollar as a phrase and the dollar as a visual cue worked together in a powerfully suggestive overture to the act that was to come—for beneath the level of speech, his spiel was about the redistribution of wealth, about how a controlling voice and a controlling hand were going to move a dollar bill from one place to another, from their pockets to his. What one witnessed with Bobby Reynolds, or any first-rate talker, was, in fact, a single man controlling the gathering crowd as if it were a large but skittish beast, shyly but obediently compelled by the steadying voice of the talker, disarmed by cheeky charm and cajolery. "Watch these fabulous moves of prestidigitation," Reynolds would say, setting up the gag. "You will notice that at no time do my fingers leave my hand. Watch the dollar."

Next, the talker needed to give the crowd a reason to stay a while and listen. Among the thousands of distractions at the carnival, a thousand reasons to move along, a crowd would watch and wait, given the proper inducement. To "freeze the tip," the talker might strike a deal with the crowd. A talker for the James E. Straits shows called out one of his showgirls, for instance, and asked her to stand on a pair of coins, one foot on each. "Notice," he said to his audience, "she has nothing in her hands and she's going to clench her fists. Now the object of the trick is this—before she leaves this platform, those two coins that she is now standing on will be in her hands. If she fails to have those coins in her hands before she leaves the platform, then I'm going to invite every one of you to come in here and see the show as my guest." This, of course, seemed an impossibility. Thus, with the tip frozen, happily awaiting a free ride, the next phase, the actual bally, could begin.

It was all about language, and of sonic patterning, alliteration, and vivid imagery. The bally was the rise of diction to the top of the tent post, its main purpose to point the mind of the listener to what one could not see, to what lay just beyond the tent flaps. The bally made whatever was behind the curtain—a pig with five legs, say—seem grand, the talker dressing up the truth, spreading it out, and building to a fevered climax, which coincided with a sudden, dramatic, precipitous drop in the price of admission. The enticement that had frozen the crowd—the girl standing on the coins—would be seen for what it was, a clever trick: The girl would simply bend over and pick up the coins, then enter the tent. All other acts followed her, hoping to "turn the tip." There were as many different ways to turn the tip as there were talkers. "The best bally spiel I ever witnessed was for a girl show," said one observer of the craft. "At the end of the spiel the talker said . . .

'Now, there are some men who are not interested in normal sexual activity, and those men know who they are. They can stay outside while the rest of the men come in to see our show."'

After this came the moment of truth for the bally—"the grind," the driving cadences of repeated phrases now filled the air, removing gaps of doubt, filling the silence where better judgment lurked, removing volition, triggering synapses, feet, hands unhinging wallets. The crowd, like a school of fish, would be funneled into a narrowing passageway. Here was the reeling in of the net.

The bally is the Siren's call to Odysseus across the waters, directing his attention away from the wreckage on the shore. It is Moses turning his staff into a serpent, wowing the children of Israel. The bally, the big buildup of rhetorical embellishment, is Marco Polo, changing the title of his thirteenth-century book of travels from the prosaic *Description of the World* to something that would be at home on any carnival banner: *Million's Book of the Great Wonders of the World*. Bally rhymes with rally and has in common with inflated stock prices and political campaign promises the simple key to any con—that all such games depend upon willing victims to suspend their disbelief, to forget that at the heart of the exchange is an emptiness that needs puffing up. The bally is the promise driving a sentence the way vacuum propels an engine. It is the booming voice of Oz—*child, look not behind the curtain!* It is father to the ad man. It is the promise and the sham at the heart of the world.

Look up from the page, reader—you've paid retail all your life—and tell me you don't prefer the bally. It looms over the century. It hops from medium to medium, from carnival talker to typesetter to teleprompter. Its first, best-known artisan, P. T. Barnum, caught the bally in mid-metamorphosis and made millions, whereupon President Ulysses S. Grant, on their first meeting, teased, "You are better known than I am." Barnum's modest reply spoke oceans about the world that was to come. "Advertising made me," P. T. Barnum said.

In 1922, while with the Craft Carnival in eastern Washington State, Louis Sonney acquired the body of Elmer McCurdy from another sideshow operator who had left it as collateral on a defaulted loan. Sonney was a big bear of a man who spent his youth in the coal mines of central Pennsylvania before moving to the West Coast, where he worked as a policeman in the rough logging town of Centralia, Washington. In 1921, while on his regular police beat, he stumbled upon the notorious train robber Roy Gardner and used the $5,000 reward he received to launch himself into the carnival business. He put down his police baton, picked up the bally horn, and became a road showman. He made a short film, *I Captured Roy Gardner,* and acquired distribution rights to other "crime doesn't pay" films. But the pet project he nurtured simultaneously with his film interests was a collection of 150 life-sized wax figures that made up the Louis Sonney Wax Museum of Crime. If Sonney wasn't traveling with a larger carnival, he would rent an unused store or theater, a practice that carnies called "four-walling." Along one wall of Sonney's museum, wax figures of infamous criminals would be displayed, while on the opposing wall, staring grimly across the space between them, stood all of the U.S. presidents. "I never understood why he did that," his son Dan later recalled, "but that was just the way his mind worked."

As part of his bally, Sonney would stand outside wearing an
ersatz western outfit, handcuff passersby, and drag them into the
lobby. Once inside, he would fire blanks from his pistol into
nervous theater patrons, who were asked to wear a special bullet-
proof vest in which Sonney had planted a gun slug. In a film clip
from the 1920s, Sonney demonstrates his handcuff technique
upon an unwitting friend. The two men face each other chatting
amiably, then comes a quick flourish, too fast for the eye to see,
and the friend finds himself bound by the wrist. He tugs against
the handcuff but quickly sees there is nothing he can do until the
smiling Louis Sonney decides to release him, a school-yard
prank carried over into adult life. The friend makes a nervous,
uncomfortable noise, teetering between annoyance and helplessness, like a giggle but empty of mirth. It says *ha-ha, let me go, you
jerk*. It was pure, lowbrow carnival come-on, for which Sonney
displayed an innate inclination, a *jerkitude*, which in carnival circles must have seemed a genuine gift.

After McCurdy came into his possession, Sonney bought a
casket and displayed the Oklahoma outlaw. Now, in addition to
infamous criminals—Bill Doolin, Jesse James, Billy the Kid—
people who robbed and murdered as a matter of course, Sonney
could offer for inspection at close range no mere visage of an
outlaw, not some waxen simulacrum, but the real McCoy—
Elmer McCurdy himself, in a back room devoted to the Oklahoma Bandit. Sonney, wearing a six-gun, chaps, and ten-gallon
cowboy hat, would declaim in his booming voice how McCurdy
had been a man who, when alive, might have spat and killed you
right there in your boots. Sonney addressed McCurdy's great
feats of derring-do—the trains stopped, the banks robbed,
the men murdered in cold blood, the money, the whores, the

whiskey, capture, and escape, then the bloody shoot-out somewhere in the knuckled hills and draws of the Indian Territories.

McCurdy was an instant success. Sonney quickly recouped
his initial investment and soon found that McCurdy, as an extra
attraction, or "blow off," brought in more money than the entire
Museum of Crime altogether. Up and down the West Coast,
Sonney toured his multimedia spectacle, which utilized the new
medium of film but also embraced an older form of entertainment that was in every respect, albeit unwittingly, a direct de-
scendant of the late eighteenth-century Parisian crime dioramas
of Philippe Curtius and Marie Grosholtz, more famously known
as Madame Tussaud. That few could resist the urge to watch a
short crime film and then ogle the body of a real bandit spoke
to the enduring draw of the western outlaw in the mind of the
American public.

Sonney was by no means the first to trade upon the American outlaw past in the new medium of film. Indeed, *I Captured
Roy Gardner* may have been inspired by similar movies made by
some of the last surviving outlaws themselves. In 1907, when
Emmett Dalton was released from prison, he began a lecture
and film career, and later he promoted at least three films: *The
Last Stand of the Dalton Boys*, in which he played himself in the
Dalton gang's disastrous raid in Coffeyville; *Beyond the Law*, a
1918 epic in which he starred, playing the roles of his brothers
Frank and Bob; and, in 1940, *When the Daltons Rode*, his autobiog-
raphy. Throughout the period, he based himself in Hollywood,
where, between films, lectures, and appearances in the Pawnee
Bill Show, he vigorously campaigned against pirated versions of
his own life story.

Tri-state Mining District contemporaries of McCurdy, wearing felt hats and sunshine lamps, circa 1910. (Photo credit: Joplin Mineral Museum)

Lieutenant Douglas MacArthur, military demolition expert, during one of his annual demonstrations in the use of high explosives, Fort Riley, Kansas, circa 1908. MacArthur and Elmer McCurdy were exact contemporaries, both born in 1880, and were stationed together at Fort Leavenworth, Kansas. McCurdy left the army with a decided interest in the use of nitroglycerin. (Photo credit: The Combined Arms Research Library)

Frank James as outlaw relic and quasi-side sideshow curiosity, 1911. (Photo credit: The State Historical Society of Missouri, Columbia)

The only known photograph of McCurdy in life, taken after his arrest in St. Joseph, MO, for possession of burglary tools, 1910. (Photo credit: Newspaper Archives, Oklahoma Historical Society)

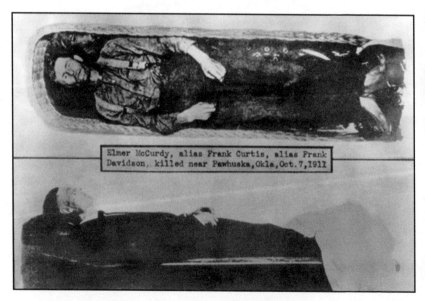

Elmer McCurdy, alias Frank Curtis, alias Frank Davidson, killed near Pawhuska, Okla, Oct. 7, 1911

McCurdy in death, Johnson Funeral Home, October, 1911. "Thousands came to view the body," Joseph Johnson recalled of an outlaw throwback whose criminal career lasted barely six months. (Photo credit: The University of Oklahoma, Western History Collection)

Citizen's State Bank, Chautauqua, Kansas, site of McCurdy's only bank robbery, a fiasco netting he and his accomplices a handful of coins. A visitor in 1999 could still see evidence of their handiwork which, because they robbed the bank at night, required busting through a brick wall. (Photo credit: Mark Svenvold)

The most successful bandit of his era, bearded, bedraggled Bill Doolin in death, killed by an eight-gauge shotgun blast, August, 1896. Thousands came to Guthrie, OK, to view the body. (Photo credit: Glenn Shirley Western Collection)

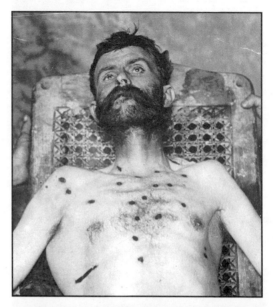

One of the original "Forty Thieves" of exploitation film, mummy and wax figure custodian Louis Sonney with his Crime Doesn't Pay roadshow, circa 1928. (Photo credit: Something Weird video collection)

Exploitation film makers used advertising methods of the traditional sideshow. By 1933, with the *Narcotic* roadshow, seen here in Indianapolis, the emphasis had clearly shifted from the display of physical abnormality, a common sideshow staple, to a spectacle of a different sort. (Photo credit: Something Weird video collection)

ONE OF THE MOST READ ABOUT ATTRACTIONS IN THE WORLD — THE NEW SHOW PIT ATTRACTION

## An Old King Tut-ankh-amen

EGYPTIAN MUMMY

Wrapped in cloth Egyptian style supposed to be 3000 Years Old

A WHOLE SHOW ALONE

LOOKS LIKE THE REAL THING

LECTURE

Price With 8x10 Banner
$40.00 Cash or
$45.00 C. O. D.
on $15.00 Deposit

THE NEW LATEST LIST No. 10

# The Nelson Supply House

SOUTH BOSTON, 27, MASS., U. S. A.

BILLY NELSON, Manager

— Manufacturer Of —

## MUMMIFIED CURIOSITIES

Price List of Strange, Remarkable, Curiosities and Monstrosities, both Animal and Human, Mummified Reproductions of the World's Greatest Side Show Wonders who once lived and were exhibited alive. As well as Wonderful Imaginary Wonders conceived by the mind of man.

I Sell only Main Features, Star Attractions for Museums, Side Shows, Five, Ten, Twenty and Thirty in One Show and Supply Shows, Parks and Carnivals in all parts of the world and will Ship Goods to any Civilized Clime on Earth that a Transportation Company will Reach.

ALL GOODS ARE SHIPPED WELL PACKED, READY FOR THE ROAD, IN GOOD STRONG BOXES MADE EXPRESSLY FOR THEM.

Mummy manufacture. The demand for authentic-looking sideshow mummies was enough to support the Nelson Supply Company of Boston for two generations, beginning in the late nineteenth century. This catalog, from the 1920s, included marvels such as the Egyptian mummy, left, which came with its own suggested "lecture." (Photo credit: Warren Raymond Collection)

C. C. Pyle's publicity machine, the "Land Yacht" with its fancy appointments, high-tech gear, including a portable dark room, and celebrity passenger Harold "Red" Grange leaning out the window as a few racers gamely pose for a publicity shot. Transcontinental Footrace, 1928. (Photo credit: Underwood & Underwood)

Elmer McCurdy: the later years, as *objet du storage* (note waxed figure heads in the background) on the E.V.I warehouse lot, circa 1960. (Photo credit: Something Weird video collection)

Long Beach, California amusement ride where John Doe #255 was discovered in December of 1976. (Photo credit: circa 1955, from the collection of Ken Larkey, Long Beach Heritage Museum)

Crime scene photograph inside the Laff-in-the-Dark amusement ride, December 1976. (Photo credit: Daniel P. Sallmen)

Storyteller and bed and breakfast owner Rebecca Luker, whose "Elmer McCurdy Murder Mystery Weekend" in 1991 touched off a First Amendment firestorm that focused the brief attention of the national media once again upon McCurdy and the town of Guthrie. (Photo credit: Mark Svenvold)

The long delayed burial of Elmer McCurdy, April 22, 1977. "There were crews from all the major networks, wire service writers, and reporters from all over. I couldn't begin to guess how many people were there."—Glenn Jordan, delivering the eulogy, and, counterclockwise, hats off, Bill Lehmann and Ralph McCalmont. (Photo credit: Gene Lehmann)

"Then a young girl—nobody knows who she was, a sort of flower child—dropped a single rose onto his coffin." —Bill Lehmann (Photo credit: Gene Lehmann)

Left to right (on horseback): state Senator John Dahl; Sheriff of Osage County George Wayman (with chewing tobacco in both sides of his mouth); State Representative Jim Cummings. Standing left to right: unknown; Fred Olds (with pipe); Max Warren; Leland Warren (of the Warren Monument Company); Bill Lehmann; Don Odom (with his tongue in the left side of his mouth); Truman Moody (in top hat, driving hearse); Glenn Jordan; Leroy Fischer, "sheriff" of the Indian Territory Posse of Oklahoma Westerners. Kneeling in front: Ralph McCalmont, Glenn Shirley. (Photo credit: Ralph McCalmont)

It was a pattern that other outlaws would follow. Al Jennings, who was pardoned in 1907 by Theodore Roosevelt, made impressive if unsuccessful bids for, of all things, Oklahoma County attorney, then later for the governorship of the State of Oklahoma. In 1914, Jennings, inspired by the literary success of his former prison inmate William S. Porter—O. Henry—coauthored an account of his life that was published in the *Saturday Evening Post* and later made into a feature film called *Beating Back*, which depicted Jennings as a social bandit heroically overcoming the attempts of cowardly lawmen to arrest him.

The following year, incensed by the flagrant inaccuracies of *Beating Back*, former lawman Bill Tilghman produced his own movie, *The Passing of the Oklahoma Outlaws*, for which he enlisted the lone survivor of the Bill Doolin gang, Arkansas Tom Daugherty, who played himself in the film and traveled around the country on a promotional tour. By chance, during the filming, seventeen miles away in Stroud, Oklahoma, the outlaw Henry Starr attempted to rob two banks at the same time in an apparent effort to outdo the Dalton Brothers' disastrous Coffeyville raid of 1892. Starr was wounded and captured, and Tilghman, seeing an unprecedented opportunity to document the moment, raced to the scene and included Starr in his film.

If the days of the Oklahoma outlaw had passed, the paroled, "rehabilitated" former outlaws themselves capitalized on the burgeoning mythography of the west and discovered, in the deep fund of public nostalgia for outlaws, a kind of ad hoc retirement plan for reformed brigands. Ed Morrell, former member of the Evans-Sontag gang, toured with the film *The Folly of a Life of Crime*, produced in 1914 by the ex-con George Sontag. Even Cole

Younger, who seemed truly to repent of his former lawless career, shrewdly understood the market value of his dangerous past. Though restricted by the terms of his parole to travel within Minnesota, he went from town to town as a traveling salesman, selling tombstones.

What were people buying when they bought a tombstone from an old outlaw? What were people watching in the nickelodeons that featured former outlaws playacting at the men they used to be? A photograph taken in 1911 shows an aging Frank James in a suit and bowler hat standing in front of the family farm. You know it's the family farm because a sign on the front gate says so: "Home of the James [sic]," it proclaims boldly, adding on the next line, in smaller lettering, "Jesse and Frank James," and, beneath that, "Admission 50 cents." His brother Jesse was long dead. So was Frank's long-suffering mother, who had nearly been killed years earlier by a bomb tossed into the house. "James Farm," another sign says in the upper left of the picture, "Kodaks Bared." (Frank would bet people five dollars the word was not misspelled. He'd take their money then reveal that a second "r" had been penciled in faintly.) It's curious, that last injunction against the camera, caught by a camera. It makes me wonder what Frank James may have thought people were getting away with by snapping a free photograph of him. What else would they be taking when they aimed and shot their Brownies at Frank James if not a kind of photographic tombstone? Not the man, but the relic, a stand-in James which, it seems, had so changed, had become so diminished, as to need a helpful identifying sign. Perhaps Frank James sensed that the literal-minded photo would print the sad fact, whereas the momentary, face-to-face encounter with the man gave some breathing room for the legend to live on.

The west was as gone as gone could be, except for such anachronistic figures as James, who was both attraction and ticket taker, or McCurdy, the traveling mummy propped in a coffin, each authentic in his way, yet both seeming to require the bally to assuage in their respective audiences a growing sense of hollowness at the center of things. At night the stars still shone above the James house, fixed in their places, but the world, with all its new gadgetry, at 16 frames per second, had clearly moved on. *Let it move,* Frank seems to say, and in the few months that were left to him he seems to have decided to stay put, to let the crowds come to him, fifty cents a time.

McCurdy, the "stiff," the dead guy, was, by comparison, strangely all go. But he was by no means the only itinerant corpse on the carnival circuit. By 1922 there were hundreds of traveling carnivals crisscrossing the country, many of them exhibiting mummies. Whether part of a 10-in-1 sideshow or a Single-O, a mummy, after all, was a potentially lucrative asset for a showman. There was no overhead, no upkeep, no complaints about food or work. With a mummy on board plus other acts, a carnival operator attained a certain prestige and sent a positive message to would-be performers and to the public. It said the outfit was prosperous. And when mummy exhibitors, like other acts in the free-wheeling carny world, left for greener pastures, the exigencies of each touring season being what they were, operators hurried to the pages of *The Billboard,* the trade magazine for outdoor showmen, where mummy ads were placed and found.

Those who make it their business to know about such things
estimate that there were probably dozens of mummies traveling
with carnivals, some real, some fake. There was enough demand
for the manufactured sort to support a Boston business—the
Nelson Supply Company, which turned out realistic-looking
mummies to the carnival trade from the turn of the century to
the 1930s. Many authentic mummies in circulation attained a
certain fame because of the known circumstances of their deaths.
Outlaws like McCurdy, for instance, or James Davis, known as
Gold-tooth Jimmy, a member of Detroit's notorious 1920s-era
Purple Gang, toured the carnival circuit for decades. The scan-
dalous demise of Marie Oday, a dance-hall girl killed by a jealous
lover then purportedly dumped into the preserving waters of the
Great Salt Lake, would also attract a paying crowd. There were,
without a doubt, many more touring mummies of uncertain
provenance, to which carnival operators, with a characteristically tangential relationship to the truth, would simply attach an
outrageous story. Thus, Dave Friedman, who went into business
with Louis Sonney's son Dan and is regarded by many as an expert in sideshow history, recalls a sideshow in his boyhood home
of Anniston, Alabama, that exhibited the body of Jesse James.
Never mind that James had been buried fifty years earlier. There
may have been several Jesse Jameses in circulation, several Billy
the Kids, several John Wilkes Booths, numerous Sitting Bulls.
According to a nineteenth-century broadside, there was at least
one genuine, authentic skeleton of Don Quixote working the
southern and northern carnival routes.

To these bogus bodies, to the fabricated stiffs from the Nelson Supply Company, and to the several dozen mummies of

relatively authentic origin we must add a number of unclaimed bodies lying in state, slowly petrifying in funeral homes across America. It was an era that produced many an unclaimed body, after all, the early part of the century churning out and consuming a steady supply of the working poor, many of whom, as we have seen, died far from home. Even country morticians like Joseph L. Johnson, moreover, knew how to arrest the process of decay using embalming fluids containing arsenic compounds. Dozens of stories suggest that, as an increase in the number of unclaimed dead across the country coincided with improved and widespread use of embalming techniques, mummies began to emerge in the back rooms of funeral homes and mortuaries, sometimes by happenstance, other times by a process that now seems guided less by chance than by design.

Such was the case with Cancetto Farmica, an itinerant musician murdered the same year McCurdy was killed; or Anderson McCrew, a hobo who died in 1913 after falling off a train and was immortalized in a song by Don Maclean; or Charles Henry Atkins, who fell into the Tennessee River in 1928; or William Lee, who in 1915 died in a poorhouse in Madison County, Illinois. Funeral directors in possession of such unexpected inventory held bodies, often for decades. Joseph L. Johnson, we recall, injected enough arsenic into McCurdy's body—several hundred times more than was ever used to preserve an Egyptian mummy—to make McCurdy's body toxic to handle nearly sixty years after his death. Farmica, McCrew, Atkins, and Lee, to name only a few, were all similarly embalmed and held.

These mummies-in-waiting were kept for a certain period of time—most often entire decades passed—with the funeral home quietly displaying the body, almost always without charge, to the many hundreds, if not thousands, of the morbidly curious who inquired after it. The free publicity became irresistible. Sometimes, as in McCrew's case, carnival operators purchased the body—occasionally for as much as $10,000—but most often the funeral parlor could not afford to lose their draw. The community would adopt the body in any number of ways as a public figure, usually giving it a nickname—Farmica's was "Spaghetti"; William Lee was "The Alton Mummy"; and Charles Henry Atkins's nickname in life was "Speedy," which no doubt took an ironic turn in the sixty-six years he was kept in the Hammock funeral home of Paducah, Kentucky. Anderson McCrew was purchased by a sideshow and billed as "Sam, the Amazing Petrified Man"; a Chicago mortuary mummy named George Stein, who after 100 years remains unburied, is to this day called "The Stone Man."

Their stories are remarkably similar to McCurdy's in all the salient details, and their numbers suggest that in a country born of transport, one in which the open road would become a trope of potent mythic self-identification, we must add the figure of not one, nor a handful, but perhaps dozens of mummified bodies—real or manufactured—roaming the earth, wandering the continent, or propped up and poised for their moment to light out for the territories.

By 1927, McCurdy had been on the road for over a decade. Louis Sonney, perhaps tiring of the yearly grind, established more permanent digs for his wax museum in Los Angeles—on

Main Street between Fifth and Sixth Streets next to the Burbank
Theater, where McCurdy was used in a backroom blow off. On
occasion, if the money seemed right, McCurdy traveled inde-
pendently from his waxen brethren. Such was the case with the
1928 Transcontinental Footrace.

Predating extreme sports and ultra-marathons by about sev-
enty years, but sharing much of the malarkey of these more recent adventures in product promotion and self-dramatization,
the Transcontinental Footrace of 1928 was the brainchild of a
sports promoter named Charles C. Pyle, sometimes known as
"Cash and Carry" Pyle, who used the completion of the first
federally funded transcontinental highway, Route 66, to sponsor a footrace from Los Angeles to New York City. That such a
footrace would seem worth doing in the first place speaks to the
period from which the idea sprung, a period in which marathons of one sort or another popped up with such frequency as
to suggest that an entire country had gone a bit soft in the head.
There were walking marathons and talking marathons (a "Noun
and Verb Rodeo" in 1928 lasted 81 hours) and dance marathons,
in which some contestants literally danced themselves to death
or went crazy from fatigue. The Dance Derby of the Century,
in Madison Square Garden, was shut down after three weeks by
the New York City commissioner of health after people started
going berserk on the floor.

The Roaring Twenties coincided with a period of radical
change in the U.S. economy, a profound shift from an industrial-
based to a consumer-based economy of mass-produced gizmos,
gadgets, and gollywogs designed to increase one's sense of comfort and status. People had more free time to worry about things

like status, for one thing, and as retailers began to offer revolving credit, more Americans embraced debt as the price one paid, in the pursuit of happiness, for the latest refrigerators and the newest cars. It was a shift from an economy of manufacture to an economy of manufactured desire, an economy fueled, in other words, by the bally.

The word *ballyhoo* was used to refer to advertising as early as 1901 when newspaper advertisements began to carry banner headlines and ad copy appeared in the same type style and column width as the regular newspaper stories beside it. The bally had hopped from one medium to the next, from the pitchman's platform to pages of print. Thus came the weird juxtaposition of train wrecks with testimonials for WARNER'S SAFE CURE FOR KIDNEY STONES, the conflation of headlines about bank robberies with "headlines" and "stories" for tonics that read to the innocent eye like breaking news, SUFFERERS OF WOMANLY WEAKNESS TRY CARDUI. As the graphic revolution gathered momentum, the bally became more sophisticated, harder to spot. Politicians and press agents grew more skillful at manufacturing events that seemed like news but whose sole purpose was really the publicity such events would generate, what historian Daniel Boorstin famously called the pseudo-event.

Charles C. Pyle, master of the pseudo-event, timed his announcement of the Transcontinental Footrace during the off-season winter months of 1927, when sports reporters were hungry for news of any kind. The race, he announced, would start in Los Angeles, follow Highway 66 across the United States, and finish 3,400 miles later in Madison Square Garden. It was the longest and most ambitious test of human physical stamina that anyone had ever conceived. There seemed to be, moreover, no end to the money-making opportunities the Transcontinental Footrace afforded Pyle or its would-be sponsors, and there seemed to be nothing anyone could do to shut him up about it. Indeed, on this last point, Pyle showed a bottomless reserve. He lobbied and extolled and extorted and cajoled potential sponsors in the upper reaches of overblown prose. He was incapable of making a simple declarative statement. He hiccuped hyperbole. He burped the bally. And the most annoying thing of all was that his methods seemed to work.

Pyle was a kind of carnival talker for a modern age. So successful was his representation of Harold "Red" Grange, for instance, whose contract for the Chicago Bears football team included product endorsements for ink pens, shoes, a candy bar, and even a Red Grange Meat Loaf, that Pyle and "the Galloping Ghost" became rich and offered to buy a controlling interest in the entire Chicago Bears franchise. In managing the careers of *French* Grange and the British tennis champion Suzanne Lenglen, Pyle, more than anyone, ushered in the era of the super athlete, of appearance fees, product endorsements, and the sad phenomenon of the sports has-been—Grange, in later years, stooped to telling gridiron stories between burlesque acts at the Minnesota State Fair. In so doing, to many observers Pyle seemed to sully the realm of sport. After Pyle, there was no turning back. A terrible beauty—the celebrity-athlete, the walking pseudo-event—had been born. And now came his footrace, his wild gamble. With all his chips thrown into the pot, he hoped to usher in a new "era of the foot." Now, instead of representing a single athlete from a single sport, Pyle hoped to attract from around the world the very best athletes from an entire field of long-distance running.

Contestants were required to report no later than February 12 to Ascot Raceway, Los Angeles, where the renowned Finnish long-distance trainer Hugo Quist would supervise a three-week training regimen. Photographs from the official program show runners gamely speeding around the track, but the fact was that no amount of training could prepare anyone for the test that lay ahead. It was, quite simply, beyond any human sense of scale and remains to this day the longest official running contest in recorded history. At the time, previous records for distance running had been set by British endurance runner George Littlewood, who held all records above 200 miles, including a 500-mile grinder set in Sheffield, England, during a six-day race in 1882. The limit was six days, for on the seventh, He rested.

The Transcontinental Footrace, by comparison, dwarfed all previous races. It was more than five times longer than the course on which the official record for greatest distance run by any human being had been set—623 miles in just under six days—also by George Littlewood. More than this, however, the pace of the footrace boggled the mind. The average daily "lap" would exceed a staggering 41 miles over a period of 84 days, a course that would take the runners over mountain ranges, through snow blizzards, sandstorms, thunderstorms, and desert heat. As the field was open to both runners and walkers, considerable debate emerged about the efficacy of each. The runners, of course, had the clear advantage of speed, but many were convinced that they would be less durable, that the sheer length of the challenge would give the race to the walkers, whose style was less punishing on the body. The world record for the hundred-mile walk, set a year earlier in London, was just under 17.5 hours, only an hour and a half longer than the professional running record for the same distance.

Pyle worked every angle to make money from the event. He would make money even before the race began from the Highway 66 Association, which hoped that the race would help fund improvements to the road. There were product endorsement contracts for autographed shoes and other foot-care products, but also for roller skates, animal crackers, and hair slick, all of it amounting to nearly a quarter million dollars, according to Pyle. There were regional sponsors—cities, towns, boroughs, counties all along Highway 66, all of them bidding against each other for the right to host the racers for the night. "We'll run through hundreds of towns, cities, and villages," Pyle said to a reporter for *Life* magazine. "Spectators by the thousands will be attracted to these places to see the race pass through. That will mean money for the local merchants and advertising for the towns, especially where the race halts overnight. It will help the sale of everything from mouse-traps to grand pianos."

If a town failed to pony up the cash, Pyle decided he would resort to a more coercive measure and reroute his race through a rival town. "You know what that means," he said. "Local pride comes high. The smaller the town, the higher the pride and the price." Most of this, of course, was speculation and hyperbole, but a race such as this could not be run on hot air alone, so Pyle wisely hedged his bet and made arrangements for a traveling carnival to tour with the footrace. The carnival and its midway would become the focus point of each overnight stop, a place where townsfolk could gather to meet the racers and to spend enough of their money to cover the considerable overhead expenses: daily meals for the runners and salaries for the trainers, referees, and medical personnel. In the winter of 1927, Louis Sonney heard through the carny grapevine about the midway that would accompany the Transcontinental Footrace, which was to begin the following March. By joining the carnival, Sonney would start his season three months ahead of his competition, who would still be hunkered down in Gibsonton, Florida, or other parts south, awaiting the first of May. So it was that Louis Sonney sent his son Edward on the road as an independent operator to run a Single-O featuring Elmer McCurdy.

Meanwhile, Pyle strategized. His great insight into this cult of endurance was that in stretching his race across America itself, he made every city and town along the route an open and exploitable market. He who hired a flagpole sitter, after all, hired one man to remain in one spot, sitting above one building in one town, and a regular marathon made its course around a single city. But a race that spanned the continent changed everything, changed the scale of the harvest for anyone who could pull it off. While one could argue that the circus had long made the same use of American towns, only Pyle's Transcontinental Footrace made the route itself an integral part of the event. The route *was* the event. The route, moreover, was symbolic, from sea to shining sea. American isolationist sentiment of the late 1920s threw up barriers to trade and immigration, and foreign policy fell somewhere between listless noninvolvement to outright xenophobia. The scheme of the footrace thus aligned itself with a growing trend of political and cultural self-regard, with its fundamentally fragile insecurity. Pyle shrewdly played this for all it was worth, inviting an international cast of competitors, who represented, at least symbolically, the threat of conquest from outside. Thus, Pyle reasoned, Americans would watch Americans compete against foreigners in a race *for* America. It was unthinkable that American cities, American towns, American booster organizations and chambers of commerce, and plain old everyday Americans themselves would not rise to such a challenge *on* and *of* and *for* their own home soil and open up their checkbooks and purses and wallets to C. C. Pyle.

As the deadline for the race approached, Pyle, like an expectant bride, hoped for at least 100 entrants at the training camp. Anything less and the newspaper critics, smelling blood, would begin to howl. For Pyle and his footrace had met with a certain unambiguously worded skepticism, the press dubbing Pyle's "Titanic Struggle" the "Bunion Derby." John Kiern, a reporter for the *New York Times*, dryly noted that Pyle's method of regulating the race's daily progress along Route 66 depending on the money put up by each town amounted to "perpetual motion under another name." Will Rogers quipped, "If somebody had offered Pyle $5,000, he would have gone by way of St. Johns, Newfoundland." But this was the thing about Pyle. Nothing, no amount of adversity, no swarm of newspaper critics, no mountain of debt, no braying pack of creditors could stop him from dreaming up more ideas for making money. For now, however, the news was all good. By January, almost 300 men had arrived at Ascot Camp, where they lined up for physical examinations, were issued bedding and other amenities, and saw their first glimpse of the rigorous routine to come: By day they ran in the mountains surrounding Los Angeles; by night they slept outdoors in canvas tents. They were fed breakfast and dinner daily, as they would be on the road, in a commissary tent that would travel with them under supervision of "expert dieticians." A staff of doctors and nurses tended to their blisters, sprains, and other ailments.

The field of foreign competitors was, indeed, formidable. They included proven distance runners Niels Nielsen, a Danish marathon champion; Italian champion Uemk Guisto; and Finnish stars Nestor Erickson and the legendary Flying Finn, Paavo Nurmi. In the weeks before the race, dozens of record-holders from around the world signed up—Theodocio Rivera, the Philippine 100-mile champion; John Gober from Greece; and Kurt Peters from Germany.

Foremost among these, however, was the most famous distance runner in the world, South African Arthur Newton, holder of the world 100-mile record, whose presence added luster to the field. Newton was a scientist of ultra-distance running who analyzed his stride for maximum efficiency and minimum stress so that when he ran he seemed to glide a few inches from the ground. He invented his own drink to replace salt loss and other vital minerals, an early version of Gatorade, and he began and finished his 20-mile-a-day regimen by smoking a fine cigar.

The American entrants seemed to take Pyle's call for contestants at his word: "Open to Any Physically Fit Male Athlete," the announcement trumpeted. Most of the Americans were not scientists, nor professionals in any sense, nor were they particularly practiced at distance running. According to the official race program, Charles M. Gallena, of Miami Beach, Florida, for instance, held a record for skipping 11,000 times, standing in one place. Walter J. Grafski, of St. Paul, Minnesota, while having no running records, hoped his bowling skills would assist him in some way, and William C. Naftel of Alabama felt his experience as a rural letter carrier would see him through. Others had more likely claims to preparedness. Some used the North American continent as their personal training ground. Harold A. McNutt hiked the West Coast from Vancouver, B.C., to Los Angeles. Louis J. Perrella roamed thousands of miles with a backpack through forty-five states and parts of Canada and Mexico. Seth Gonzales ran from his hometown of Denver through Colorado, New Mexico, and Arizona, averaging 40 to 50 miles per day. Some racers, like Jose Torres, had marathoning in their blood. Torres was one of a number of Tarahumara Indians from northern New Mexico competing in the Transcontinental Footrace. They were members of a tribe whose very name, it was said, meant "foot runners," who had for centuries run after game in the deserts of Mexico, had captured Spanish horses by running them down to the point of exhaustion, and had engaged in epic hundred-mile running quests for sport. There were five black runners, including the Canadian walking champion Philip Granville and an American runner from Seattle, Washington, named Ed Gardner, nicknamed "The Sheik" because of the white bandanna he liked to wear on his head. There were also racers who seemed chosen to make good newspaper copy. They included a Hindu philosopher; a prolific young racer, Roy F. McMurtry, with one arm; a singing, ukulele-playing distance runner; several men who ran barefoot; several with long flowing beards, including an aging actor named Lucien "Jack" Frost, who had once played Moses in a movie; the tall and skinny "Wildfire" Thompson, who became known as the Bearded Skeleton, and a sixty-three-year-old British distancer, Charles Walter Hart, who had once defeated two horses in a six-day contest.

It was all wonderful material for a publicity hound like Pyle. To keep the story of the Transcontinental Footrace in newspaper headlines during the weeks to come, Pyle secured his very own publicity machine—a bus, a palatial land yacht, a double-decked leviathan of the open road with an observation roof above and living quarters below. The riding compartment had collapsible, double Pullman type seats, a collapsible table, writing desk, and, in a forward-thinking gesture to car audio, "a combination phonograph and radio receiving set." The center of the bus was equipped with a full galley, and the rear housed the sleeping quarters. It had hot and cold water, showers, and air conditioning and could glide down the pike at a mile a minute. It was a story in itself, meant to capture the attention of newsmen whose articles about its astonishing features—all the gizmos and fancy appointments, its mohair and mahogany and gold trim—would sound like the catalog of ships from the *Iliad*. The bus was meant to seduce its chroniclers and to supply them with the all-important images for the papers back home. To this end, Pyle included a custom-made darkroom car, where photographs of daily highlights were sold or mailed to newspapers around the world, and a car outfitted with a mobile radio station—KGGM—the only one of its kind in the United States, which announced the location of each nightly control station,

trumpeting the news of the Transcontinental Footrace, broad-
casting the bally in every direction for hundreds of miles.

Within this plush and pillowed vehicle, appointed like some
pharaoh's pleasure barge, rode the dapper "Red" Grange, whose
job was to wake up in the morning and fire a starting gun, to
make a few presentations at night, and, more or less like the
modern-day celebrity, to hang around and be famous, to cast his
aura along the route, to burnish the towns of Barstow and Lud-
low, to make Amarillo and Daggett and Stroud ring with excite-
ment, to bring to Canute and Elk City a luster they had somehow misplaced or never known.

Along with the caravan, in seeming counterpoint to the display of high-tech media gizmos, came the traveling carnival that
rode ahead of the racers and their support vehicles, stopping at
each control station to set up its concession stands, its games of
chance, its merry-go-round, and, of course, its sideshow, which
featured, among the human and animal wonders of the world,
the mummified body of the Oklahoma Outlaw.

The carnival would arrive in a town designated by Pyle with
trucks bearing tents and attractions, which were unpacked and
unfurled, and soon the broad enclosure of the midway was bedecked with banners advertising Kah-Ko, the trained police
dog, the Piu-poison girl, a tent featuring the Wonders of Hollywood, a menagerie of tropical birds, beasts, and reptiles, a fat
lady, the Oklahoma Outlaw, and other attractions. At noon,
Red Grange would arrive in his roadster as pamphleteers sold
Transcontinental Footrace programs for twenty-five cents each.
The programs were the only means by which people could
identify the racers. By the afternoon the town would be abuzz

with anticipation, as one reporter described it: "Small boys scurried around on bicycles, necks were craned, traffic patrolmen assumed a new dignity, and presently a sun-scorched figure in dusty running-trunks came trotting into town."

A typical daily leg or lap of the footrace was more than 40 miles, often closer to 50. Townsfolk gathered in the carnival midway to meet these amazing specimens, athletes capable of running such staggering distances. The athletes themselves, gaunt and dusty, some delirious with exhaustion, were pressed into service upon a bally stage after each race. Red Grange would step up and introduce the runners, who would autograph programs, give speeches, or tell jokes. Peter Gavuzzi would sometimes sing a song. Ed Gardner was known to imitate a steamboat whistle. Most, however, waved to the crowd then walked stiffly to the medical tent.

It was in this context that Elmer McCurdy came to the fore, dressed in "outlaw" garb and placed in an upright coffin alongside exhibits that included a five-legged pig and a dog that talked with its ears. Against this kind of competition, McCurdy stood out enough to make the papers and was described by *New York Times* reporter John Kieran as "one of the greatest attractions in the sideshow." The traditional critics of the midway, the small-town American editorial writers, many of whom felt the presence of the carnival tainted the footrace, were out in force. It didn't help matters that the carnival games of chance were apparently full of the grift and scorched enough of the locals along the route to pose a publicity problem for Pyle. To mollify the aggrieved rubes, Pyle conceded that his carnival was a "shillaber affair, in the world of showmanship . . . banal, faded stuff [that brought in] necessary revenue."

The first lap, a mere 16 miles to Puente, California, was the shortest distance the racers would see for a long while. Most of the contestants finished easily. The second day covered 34 miles. The third, a grueling 45 miles, half of which included an ascent of Cajon Pass before dropping to the sun-bleached floor of the Mojave Desert, the ancient seabed darkened with creosote bush and wolf bush. By the evening only 136 runners remained of the nearly 300 who had started out that morning.

The winners of each daily race were announced with a fanfare that sometimes seemed swallowed up by the sound of the wind and the emptiness of the landscape they were running through. At the control station at Mojave Wells, runners found a water hole but little else, and Pyle was forced to give his carnival workers the night off. The control stations were mostly little-known towns whose place-names—like Bagdad or Siberia—lent the race an air of heroic remoteness and isolation that was counterpoised by reports of runners being harassed by automobiles. In more populated towns, the celebration for the daily winners was always measured in proportion to the overall leaders, whose names began to appear like themes in an overture: Gardner and Gavuzzi, Newton and Payne, Wanttinen and Suominen, Granville, Umek, and Abramowitz.

Leaving the desert at Needles, the racers crossed the Black Mountains, running into 40-mile-per-hour headwinds on the northern plateaus of Arizona. Of the main contenders who emerged within the first 500 miles, few were more impressive than Arthur Newton, who could set a merciless pace or dog the leaders all day, breaking their resolve in the last few miles. But when the race reached Flagstaff, Arizona, Newton shocked everyone and called it quits. "My legs are gone," he said. It was a devastating early blow, and Pyle quickly hired Newton as a race adviser, hoping his legendary status would shore up the bad publicity.

Even to the most aggressively optimistic observer, the contest was soon showing ominous signs of trouble. The southwestern leg of the journey was proving, it seemed, too sparsely populated to support the carnival concessions that Pyle had hoped would pay for the food and accommodations for the racers, trainers, medical personnel, track officials, and countless others required to keep the show on the road. Instead of paying a quarter to enter the carnival fairgrounds, meet the racers, and spend more money on food and games, the thrifty citizens of the Republic lined Highway 66 for a free glimpse of the odd cavalcade. The cafeteria vendor had quit in a contractual dispute, leaving Pyle to make other plans for his hungry racers, plans which included meager rations of mulligan stew cooked over campfires. At least one desert campsite couldn't provide any water. As chambers of commerce proved less forthcoming with sponsorship fees, Pyle obliged his contestants to run off course through the American desert, around the offending cities, away from better sources of food and accommodation. Bypassed towns did not respond well to Pyle's punitive tactic. Racers were routinely run off the road, and residents of Carthage, Missouri, hurled rotten eggs at the Land Yacht in protest of Pyle's decision to stop in the rival town of Joplin. Soon, the racers, complaining of the wretched conditions, were ready to strike.

None of this would improve in the weeks to come, when Pyle, already strapped for cash, found himself dodging creditors, lawyers, and sheriff's marshals who waited with their padlocks and writs of attachment at the finish line of any number of Midwestern cities. For Pyle, it was becoming a footrace of another sort, no less a test of endurance, a coast-to-coast contest of creditors chasing after a comprehensive, heroically enabled debtor, a campaign of skipped payments, bounced checks, dissembling deferments, and defaulted loans, made all the more taxing for its coverage in the daily newspapers. It was perhaps history's first ultra-marathon in chicanery, spectacular in its own right. Yet so masterful was Pyle at the art of the bally that he was able in every crisis to slip beyond the sheriff's grasp, to outmaneuver the collection agent, to placate the repo man, leaving behind him a string of promises of better things to come.

In spite of these larger exigencies, despite the complaints of the runners and their eroding goodwill toward Pyle, an actual, authentic competition was taking shape between a British racer, Peter Gavuzzi, an Oklahoma Cherokee named Andrew Payne, and a Detroit doctor and massage therapist, Arne Souminen, who took a commanding lead of more than five hours in early April as the footrace moved across the Texas panhandle. The weather on the high plains was merciless, with freezing rain and snow. On April 7, Philip Granville became the first walker to win a daily race, covering almost 40 miles through a sleet storm to McLean. Here, as the front-runner Souminen quit the race with a pulled tendon, Payne and Gavuzzi began a daily battle for the lead that would last nearly five weeks and cover more than 1,300 miles across the states of Oklahoma, Missouri, Illinois, and Indiana, ending in Ohio. Payne entered his home state of Oklahoma in first place, with a two-hour lead over

Gavuzzi, who, in three days, would narrow Payne's lead to half an hour. Then, in Bristow, Oklahoma, Gavuzzi took the spoiler's role, capturing and holding a half-hour lead into Tulsa.

Tulsa, of course, was the de facto capital city of oil in northeastern Oklahoma in the boom year of 1928, the inland metropolis closest to the oil fields that lay to the north and west that had made the region world famous. Routing the footrace and its attendant money-making carnival through Tulsa made sense, and the carnival had set up shop before the racers made their evening entrance to the town. But Elmer McCurdy was nowhere to be seen. Indeed, ever since the race had crossed the Oklahoma state line, with Gavuzzi and Payne dueling every day on the road, a quieter bit of brinkmanship was under way in the sideshow. Louis Sonney's son Edward had quietly tucked the body out of sight and closed for business. It was a shrewd measure meant to protect Sonney's investment, in the off chance that an Oklahoma relative of McCurdy's would step forward to claim the body.

This fear was not unfounded. Long before the race reached Oklahoma, reporters from around the country had mentioned the "mummified Oklahoma bandit" in their stories, and the word had eventually reached Bob Fenton in Pawhuska. Fenton had been one of the original posse involved in the shoot-out at Revard's ranch. It had been determined that a bullet from Fenton's pistol had killed McCurdy. And so he traveled to Tulsa with something like a proprietary interest to see if the much-ballyhooed mummy was indeed the very man who had tried to kill him so many years ago. Making his way through the carnival grounds he found Edward Sonney, who gave Fenton a private viewing of the body inside his tent. Fenton stood and stared at McCurdy's body, then quietly went on his way.

The caravan continued through Oklahoma, passing near Lenapah, the sight of the Iron Mountain train robbery, and Bartlesville, the town closest to where McCurdy had died. Crossing into Missouri, the mummy blackout was lifted, and the Oklahoma Outlaw was again put on display at an evening stop in the mining town of Carterville, where, years earlier, and hundreds of feet below ground, McCurdy had shoveled ore by the ton.

As the Bunion Derby struggled through the Midwest, Gavuzzi stopped shaving, his beard taking on a life of its own in the minds of newspaper reporters. The *New York Times* called the hirsute Gavuzzi "the bearded French-Italian of England," and in the weeks to come, as Gavuzzi recaptured the lead across the Midwest, stretching it by as much as six hours over Payne, the "bristle-bearded Britisher." With the race a few days out of Chicago, Gavuzzi decided upon a shave in Normal, Illinois. Pyle's reaction plainly revealed the kind of event he thought he was running. "What the hell has come over you?" Pyle shouted at Gavuzzi. "Here I've been working like a dog getting things set for a swell Chicago ballyhoo and you spoil my best plans by getting your whiskers shaved just when they were getting nice and flowing and curly on the ends." The runners and their promoter, it seems, were showing signs of cracking up.

Pyle quickened the tempo of the race, increasing the distance between checkpoints to 50 and 60 miles. Louis Perrella of Albany, New York, won the lap out from Gary, Indiana, to Mishawaka, a distance of 66 miles. At such a pace, over such an extended period of time, the racers were at the limits of human metabolism. They simply could not eat enough for what their bodies were being asked to do, and so their bodies began to consume themselves. The racers slowly began to starve, and the daily sight of the increasingly sullen, emaciated figures, limping into each dusty control station, pitched the tone of the event headlong into the grotesque.

Here Pyle dropped all pretensions, and when he spoke to one newspaper, calling his racers "bearded freaks" and "human prodigies," there could no longer be any doubt that Pyle had finally assumed the role of the carnival talker that had been his all along. The Transcontinental Footrace had become his traveling sideshow. Gavuzzi, who had run halfway across the continent, who held the lead in the longest running duel in the history of footracing, had become its leading performer, its bearded wonder, its headline freak, and somewhere in all this mix of sun-blasted skeleton men, like a weird afterthought, came the gaunt and tanned remains of the Oklahoma Outlaw.

On May 11, in Fremont, Ohio, Gavuzzi did something that, for the last 2,689 miles, no one suspected might happen. He gave up. He stopped running, not because of a pulled tendon, or blisters and sores, or homesickness, but because of a bad tooth. More likely, the pace of holding the lead over five states had simply done in Gavuzzi, but a tooth infection was given as the official reason for his withdraw. As the bad teeth of the British gave way to robust American oral hygiene, Andy Payne, the Cherokee from Claremore, took a commanding lead, twenty hours ahead of his nearest competitor. With Gavuzzi gone, so went England's best chance of winning.

Within a few weeks, the runners were soldiering through the longest lap of the contest, a 74-mile stretch into Deposit, New York, with Andy Payne now sixteen hours ahead of John Salo, of Passaic, New Jersey. Salo was charging hard but had no real hope of catching up unless something happened to eliminate Payne. It said something about the tone and spirit of the contest that two days from the finish line Andy Payne's trainer asked for a police escort through John Salo's hometown. The community of Passaic was indignant but provided the escort, a motorcycle thumping quietly ahead of Payne as he entered the burgh where Salo and Payne were obliged for publicity purposes to share the same room overnight. A single day separated them from the finish line.

Shaved and showered, their trunks and jerseys freshly washed, their shoes repaired, the fifty-five surviving contestants of the Transcontinental Footrace left Passaic at 4 P.M. the next day and ran along the Paterson Plank Road to Union City, friends of John Salo driving in advance of their favorite, honking their car horns in encouragement as he passed, then speeding ahead of the pack again to cheer their man a little farther down the line. The evening brought the runners finally to the ferry docks at Weehawken, where, for the first time in nearly three months of continuous running, they could run no farther. A boat propelled them over this smallest fraction of the 3,400-mile route, the quarter mile across the Hudson River, through the wind and the wave wash toward the far shore, with its buildings cubed and stepped and lofted high above the humming traffic. How sweet it must have been.

Manhattan, however, seemed quite unaware of their arrival. As they made their way up 10th Avenue, there were no cheers, no waving crowds, no throngs of adoring girls seeking autographs, just neighborhood people going about their business, stopping for a moment to watch as policemen on motorcycles helped clear the thoroughfare. But word quickly spread, and by the time the runners reached Madison Square Garden, a crowd of several thousand had gathered outside the arena. Watching over it all, of course, was C. C. Pyle. The evening would bring to a conclusion an event that had failed to galvanize the public imagination, but he would give the public a finale. His race would end with a flourish, the crowds cheering the racers down the last stretch, the runners giving their all in a final kick to the finish line.

What Pyle saw inside Madison Square Garden, however, made him nervous: a sea of empty seats surrounding a thin crowd of a few hundred people. Despite Pyle's attempt the previous night to spruce them up a bit, the runners came limping in, some still wearing bandages and tape where dogs had bitten them, others tortured by shin splints from their long descent from the Adirondacks. They did not hurry along. Forty-five of the runners were out of the money, and nothing they could do would change that. For the top ten contestants, the outcome of the race was long settled: Andy Payne would win the $25,000 first prize; John Salo, fifteen hours behind, would come in second, earning $10,000; Philip Granville, twenty-five hours further adrift, would claim third place and $5,000; and Mike Joyce would earn $2,500 for fourth. The next six runners would earn $1,000 each.

The Madison Square Club had posted a $100 prize for the winner of the final leg, but only a handful made a go of it, the rest gimping and limping and taking their own sweet time around the quarter-mile track for 10 miles. Some of them could barely walk, and the sight of these being carried by their friends was enough to provoke in Pyle a dramaturgical crisis. He made his way down to the inside oval and began to shout, "Come on, you fellows. Streak it, boys, streak it. Show 'em what I've brought to New York." The runners would briefly quicken their pace, then fall back again. Some of the men began eating sandwiches. Others drank sodas in celebration. "The winner, if anybody cares, was Andrew Payne," wrote F. Raymond Daniell of the *Evening Post*.

The next day, to a reporter for the *New York Times*, Pyle brushed aside questions about the as yet unmaterialized prize money and began a bally that would serve as a model for any medicine-show spieler. "The human foot is going to come into its own," he proclaimed. "I have made such a study of the human walking mechanism as has never been equaled, and I claim to know more about toe trouble, heel trouble, instep trouble and ankle trouble than any man living. I can tell you exactly what to do for anything that goes wrong from the knee down." Whatever had become of Pyle's athletic competition had given way to advertising for a foot-care product, Pyle's Patent Foot Box, containing, he said, "remedies for every one of the 1,000 maladies of the human foot. I will make vast sums out of this because this country is going marathon mad," he said. "We are entering . . . the golden age of the foot. There are going to be more marathons, more twenty-six hour footraces, more six-day footraces, and more transcontinental footraces than anybody would have dreamed to be possible. All along our route," he said, "children who could hardly walk were out trying to keep up with my transcontinental runners. Schoolboys were organizing cross-country runs and marathons. We are going to have hundreds of thousands of distance runners in the country, and every one of them will naturally buy C. C. Pyle's Patent Foot Box."

On June 1, nearly a week after the completion of the race, Pyle failed to make good on his promise to hand the prize money over to Tex Rickard, who was to present the awards to the racers. The *New York Times* published a minute-by-minute record of the dispatches from Pyle's headquarters in the Vanderbilt hotel, which broadcast for all to see Pyle's manifold and manifest dissimulation.

5:35   Mr. Pyle just left the Hotel Vanderbilt with the $48,500 to give to Mr. Rickard.

5:45   Mr. Pyle is still at the Hotel Vanderbilt, but is just about to leave with $48,500 for Mr. Rickard.

5:55   Mr. Pyle has not been at his headquarters at the Hotel Vanderbilt for two hours and nobody knows where he is.

6:05   Mr. Pyle left his headquarters twenty minutes ago with a suitcase full of money to give to Mr. Rickard.

6:15   Mr. Pyle has not been here since early this morning and nobody knows where he is.

All anyone could do was wait and hope. Racers out of the money had spent the week making themselves available to the press. Wildfire Thompson, who could provoke a reporter into a fit of mythopoeia (he'd "won several day's runs when the winds were westerly by using his beard as a jib topsail"), took a room down the street from the Garden and ran up and down the block so as to keep feeling the pain in his aching feet.

"I believe in tapering off," he said. "When you've been through torture like this, it is a dangerous thing to stop the agony all at once. A little while ago I got kind of scared. I said to myself, 'I miss something.' Then I said, 'Oh, yes, I miss those stabbing pains.' When all the misery's gone you feel kind of lonesome and lost. A lot of the boys are feeling terrible and don't know what is the matter with them. . . . The thing they are suffering from is lack of pain."

The runners finally got their money before "The Smallest Crowd in History of Garden," as the *Times* declared, careful to note that a brass band blared "and the echoes rolled back like the voice of a small boy shouting in a tunnel." What could have been more hollow for the winner, Andy Payne, than the sight of this cavernous building, the sound of the speechifying superlatives "flung about recklessly," and the announcer booming praise for C. C. Pyle through amplifiers, as "row upon row of empty seats hurled back his voice?" It was telling that when Tex Rickard handed Payne his check for $25,000, then snatched it quickly away again, a brawl nearly broke out. A late-coming photographer had missed the moment and asked Rickard to repeat the gesture, but Andy Payne had seen enough and was ready to fight for what was his.

From New York City, the footracers dispersed, each using his $100 deposit to find his way back home. McCurdy also hit the road and two years later was spotted in Southern California by

Joseph Johnson's son Luke, who was on a business trip for the Hollywood Casket Company. McCurdy was playing a carnival in Ocean Park. Luke was enjoying a stroll on the boardwalk when a sideshow talker giving a spiel stopped him in his tracks. Inside the tent was a mummified Oklahoma outlaw whose story in every detail reminded Luke of McCurdy, with one exception: that in the shoot-out with deputies, the outlaw had drunk poison rather than been taken alive. The poison, according to the talker, had fused with the acids in the body and caused it to become mummified.

Luke paid the admission and entered the tent. He recognized McCurdy's body instantly and felt compelled to set the talker straight about a thing or two. Taking him aside, Luke showed the talker his embalmer's license and said: "What would you think if I told you my father embalmed that body, that it was just an ordinary process of embalming, and that the fellow never drank poison at all?"

"Well, I'd say you had made a darn fool out of me," the talker said. Then, without missing a beat, he made a flourishing gesture toward Luke Johnson and threw himself into a new story that enlisted Luke Johnson as an impromptu expert lecturer. It was, perhaps, a little too much for the young man from Pawhuska, who quickly slipped away without further comment, leaving the bally in his wake. "Hurry, folks," the talker bellowed, in front of a growing crowd. "The man who embalmed the body of the Oklahoma Outlaw is now inside and will tell you the first hand account of his spectacular death."

# ≈ 8 ≈

# King of the Dwarfs

I was headed through fog over the George Washington Bridge into New Jersey toward the Sheraton Meadowlands on the second to last day of the Chiller Theater Convention, a gathering of horror film industry players, horror film buffs, and the attendant, many-headed hydra of subindustries, each in support of, each seeking to extract its percentage share from the hearse-driving, cape-wearing, fang-bearing segment of the *demos*.

The Sheraton Meadowlands is situated right off the Jersey Turnpike in the no-man's-land that is the heart of the busiest transportation corridor in the country, where automobiles, trucks, freight and passenger trains, container ships, and all manner of commercial aircraft from Newark Airport converge in shrieking vectors over cattails and tamarisk. These are not the dulcet gardens of the Garden State, but the marshy wastes of a late-phase industrial apocalypse, the kind of non-place people think about when they think about dumping a body. And if all the dumped bodies came back to life, killing, torturing, and maiming everyone in their path, then the Chiller Theater Convention would be the place for them to take a load off,

perhaps mingle with the iconoclastic purchasers of Elvira fig-
urines, the lone wolf patrons of mail-order videos, the fiercely
independent collectors of celebrity ghoul autographs.

Inside, with the convention in full swing, a solid crush of
people milled along endless booths filled with horror-related
tchotchkes. There was a heavy Goth presence throughout, dark
clothing, pale smiles, fangs flashing amiably. People dressed in
black and wore T-shirts that said, "I Was Evil Before Evil Was
Cool," "I [heart] Eternal Damnation," and "You're Just Jealous
Because the Voices Talk to Me." Their cars, parked in the lot
outside, bore the stickers of the bands that spoke to them: Black
Sabbath, Sepultra, Faith No More, Marilyn Manson, Cannibal
Corpse. There were the usual ten-foot Martian monsters rising
above the crowd and folks walking around with axes buried in
their skulls. But it was in the celebrity tent that the scope of the
convention—or perhaps the width of its margins—seemed
most striking.

I wasn't prepared, for instance, to see June Lockhart, still
pretty at seventy-two, the same actress who appeared with Judy
Garland in *Meet Me in St. Louis*, signing autographs in an outdoor
tent, the sound of car mufflers clanking and dragging down the
interstate. Above her, a sign read, "June Lockhart, star of *Lost in
Space, Lassie,* and *Petticoat Junction*." To my relief, she was surrounded by admirers, chatting sweetly. Business was thinner a few
tables down, where a handsome man in his forties stood idly beneath a sign that read "Guy Williams, Jr., *representing* Guy Williams
from *Zorro* and *Lost in Space*." I felt sorry for Guy Williams, Jr., who
seemed ready and eager to talk, but nobody wanted to talk to
him. Farther down the line, Mark Goddard, who played *Lost in
Space's* Major West, sat beneath a sign that declared who he'd

been, in case you'd forgotten. I hadn't, of course. I remembered exactly where I'd been the evening the show premiered in 1965, thirty-four years earlier (on a slow-motion space walk, oxygen supply running low, pounding on the door of the Galaxy 500 parked in the carport, Newcumberland, Pennsylvania). Deanna Lund from *Land of the Giants* was doing brisk business, as was Gerard Christopher of *Adventures of Superboy* fame. Earlier I had noticed that his own personal website, which listed Gerard Christopher's television, film, and theater credits, also included a "Special Abilities" category—competitive triathlete racing, skiing, boxing, and a notice of graduation from the Skip Barber Race Car Driving School—all of which, while suitably rigorous in a Superboy sort of way, were strangely silent about the subject of time, about *when* any of these credits or abilities had been acquired. It was like reading a resume without any dates attached. The *Superboy* series, I was surprised to learn elsewhere, had lasted 104 episodes, from 1988 to 1992. And now, in what must have been difficult not to consider—increasingly, perhaps alarmingly—as a seven-year, post-Superboy slump, Gerard Christopher sat in a tent with the cast of *Lost in Space*, in a timeless parenthesis, in telegenic suspension, all of them as perfectly preserved as mummies.

I didn't have the heart to ask Gerard Christopher, June Lockhart, or Mark Goddard what had gone wrong, nor could I ask Bill Hinzman, who had a little sign that said, "Bill Hinzman, #1 Zombie in *Night of the Living Dead*," or Robert Vaughn (*The Man from U.N.C.L.E.*) what the hell they were doing here, in a parking lot in bleakest New Jersey. Yet even here they mustered an admirable *sprezzatura*, a lightness and ease composed, in part, by the celebrity dental and facial touch-up work, reinforced by the autograph tables themselves, which separated us from them, and their own celebrity chairs where they sat, while the rest of us stood before them like peasant petitioners. And they smiled and chatted amiably, allowed pictures to be taken of them, and signed their names in great, exaggerated script onto glossy photos of themselves, by which means they proffered a sign of authenticity, purchased at thirty dollars a pop, though what or whom these penned names were meant to authenticate was difficult to know.

Upstairs, in the far corner of another room, a man named Wes Shank seemed to have cornered the market on the authentic. He stood over a black bucket of red silicone goop next to a sign that read, "The Original Material Used to Make *The Blob*, Steve McQueen's Third Movie." Steve McQueen was paid $5,000 for work in an otherwise forgettable film made on a budget of $125,000 by Valley Forge Films and shot not in Hollywood but in small towns across central Pennsylvania. To McQueen's chagrin, *The Blob* did not go quietly but became a spectacular drive-in movie success for its producer Jack Harris, ultimately grossing nearly $8 million. And now, *The Blob*, or the actual stuff they used to make *The Blob*, was making a guest appearance on a table in a gallon bucket tipped slightly forward for better viewing and covered with a piece of clear Plexiglas. "It was made by Union Carbide," Wes Shank explained to anyone within earshot, "and it came naturally clear. Naturally clear silicone." In the movie, the Blob is also at first naturally clear, crashing to earth hidden inside a meteorite, making its oozing, ambling way to its first victim, a hapless farmer, then, like a tornado darkened by what it destroys, reddening on the blood of small-town America. It was this glistening, incarnadine glop that Wes Shank had purchased at great expense from Valley

Forge Films in November 1965 and had been shepherding around the country ever since. It was all breathtaking, in its way, but I had other matters to attend to.

I had an appointment with David F. Friedman, the man credited for directly influencing at least four different types of exploitation film. His coproduction, with Herschell Gordon Lewis, of *The Adventures of Lucky Pierre* (1959) shaped the genre of the nudie-cutie; *Nature's Playmates* (1960) broke new ground in the nudist camp volleyball epic, so I'd learned, by introducing a trampoline scene and a noir-type detective story line; *Scum of the Earth* (1961) was the first "roughie," or softcore sexploitation film; and *Blood Feast* (1963), along with its hard-core gore successors, *Two Thousand Maniacs* (1964) and *Color Me Blood Red* (1965), opened the gates for later films like Tobe Hooper's *Texas Chainsaw Massacre*. But I had come that afternoon to interview Friedman about his little-known role (along with business partner Dan Sonney) as de facto custodian and keeper of the body of the Oklahoma Outlaw, Elmer McCurdy, which, decades after its disappearance from Pawhuska in 1916, had become haplessly entangled in a Hollywood cinematic netherworld dedicated to the exploration of the bottomless American cultural obsession with sex, drugs, and violence—topics which, in their own twisted way, remain as definitively American as red, white, and blue.

Friedman sat at the far end of a long table belonging to Something Weird Video, one of several companies to discover a flourishing mail-order after-market in Friedman's films and other exploitation favorites with titles like *Confessions of a Psycho Cat* (1968) and *The Incredibly Strange Creatures Who Stopped Living and Became Mixed-Up Zombies* (1963). Sitting next to Friedman was Miss Playboy Playmate of 1968, Cynthia Myers, who was experiencing

something of an after-market comeback of her own, signing autographs and chatting with admirers, while Friedman surveyed the
milling crowd, some of whom stopped occasionally to talk to
trash film's *eminence gris*.

I introduced myself and he led me upstairs, away from the
clamor, to his hotel room, where he offered me the only seat in
the room and sat facing me on the corner of his bed, a stocky,
silver-haired gentleman in his seventies with dark, full eyebrows
and a neatly trimmed mustache. He wore a no-nonsense blue
blazer and tie, the Republican uniform of a man who had married
his childhood sweetheart and had voted seven times for Richard
Nixon. There was a shrewdness in his gaze that spoke to the old
carny's ability to size up a customer. It was the look of a man who
divided the world, as any carny would, between those who are
"with the show" and those who are not, between those who do
the taking and those who get taken, between the players and the
played. And I had a feeling, as I sat there with my tape recorder
and my notebook and my list of questions, that I was not
counted among the players of the world. Old carnies had a term
for people like me, and that term was, alas, my own given name.

He smiled and chuckled occasionally, folding his arms at
times or resting his hands comfortably on his knees. His voice
was pure, mid-continental American, lacking any trace of his
Alabama roots. In his left hand he held an unlit cigar. "My life,"
he began, "has been like a lot of American kids. I had more guts
than sense. I just sort of got out there and started doing things."

His was a story designed to evoke, along with a smile, the elements of a Horatio Alger tale. *Designed* was the key word, for
he'd told his story so many times, it seemed, to so many writers,
that it had acquired an impregnable gloss. People were interested

in David Friedman, all sorts of people, as the bustle in front of the Something Weird Video table attested. And it wasn't just offbeat film junkies anymore, but *people who taught film school*, or cultural studies types trolling the bottom of the cultural melange, burnishing their own academic hipster credentials. So many journalists, academicians, and filmmakers had come before him in an explosive, Foucaultian ecstasy of interest in marginal or "transgressive" culture, and Friedman had grown so used to providing the copy and framing the history of *Blood Feast* (1963), *The Ramrodder* (1969), and *Ilsa, She-Wolf of the S.S.* (1974) in the bracketing and unassailable quotation marks of irony and camp, that his career was experiencing an unexpected third or fourth wind. He'd become the genre's avuncular spokesman, speaking not only in documentary films and from the chapters of books in university libraries, but also from newspaper and magazine articles and from numerous interviews in fanzines like *Cult Video* and *Outré*, and of course, from the deep arcane of the Internet. As such, Friedman found himself in the charmed predicament of Bialystock and Bloom, the heroes of Mel Brooks's movie and Broadway musical *The Producers*, who—try as they might—find it impossible to make their brand of tasteless entertainment tasteless enough. By way of accounting for his rise from obscurity, Friedman had taken to quoting H. L. Mencken: "No one ever went broke," he said to a newspaper reporter, "by underestimating the taste of the American public."

"You see," Friedman said, "the whole exploitation film business had its origins in the carnival and circus. My friend Mike Ripps made a picture called *Poor White Trash*, which you could have played in a Sunday school and not gotten any beefs." But Ripps, using the old carnival ballyhoo, distributed fliers that promised something sensational. "Due to the abnormal matter shown in this picture," they read, "only those above the age of 18 will be admitted." Here Friedman's voice shifted easily into the mode of the bally. "Armed guards," he said, with emphasis on the assonant initial vowels in both words, his mouth opening as wide as a grouper under a rock—"*Armed guards* will check to make sure that no one under age is admitted."

The transition period in the history of the American pursuit of happiness began in the 1920s. Between 1890 and 1925, American workers enjoyed a 92 percent increase in annual earnings, accompanied by a nearly 20 percent reduction in working hours. By 1925, living expenses ate up only half of the average annual income, leaving the second half to be spent however one pleased. A new consumer middle class was emerging from factories offering high wages and a shortened workweek. Yet the older generation, still firmly entrenched and strong in the faith of the deferment of pleasure into some far-off Calvinistic future tense, looked on skeptically, sometimes aghast, as Americans contemplating a new sense of time—leisure time—responded favorably, enthusiastically, to a new mandate, fueled by corporate advertising, to eat of the tree of disposable income and the tree of revolving credit. In 1921, there were 9 million automobiles in America. A few years more would double that figure. By 1925, motion pictures were a half-billion dollar industry, second only to the automobile in recreational consumer expenditures.

The paradigm shift from prudence to profligacy was well under way during Friedman's boyhood in Anniston, Alabama, in the 1930s, and the ambiguities about the change made themselves felt in the forms of entertainment that he found there. He could spend every day on the show grounds of the Tom Mix Circus, for instance, which once wintered in Anniston, yet also sneak into movies like the hillbilly miscegenation feature *Child Bride* and the early sex-hygiene film *High School Girl*. His uncle worked on traveling carnivals, so he spent part of his school year on the winter carnival circuit, living the carny lifestyle, and part of it working as a movie house projectionist. It didn't take a genius to see that the two—the carnival and the medium of film—were not incompatible, and indeed many carnival operators sensed that an important change was already under way. They saw, in film, a tremendous opportunity to take a new kind of sideshow onto the open road.

It was called the exploitation film—a cheaply made movie that pandered to people's prurient interest in the sensational or the illicit, often under the pretense of offering an educational experience. Such covert appeals to prurience under the protective scrim of education, of course, predated film and could be found in any sideshow. In the 1850s, traveling wax museums in France exploited the popular interest in science and the titillation of anatomical display. According to film historian Eric Schaefer, the precursor to exploitation films appeared at the beginning of the century, when film was seen as a delicate way to educate people about the perils of modern, urbanized life. Short reels about venereal disease, drug abuse, and prostitution were produced by government agencies and distributed to the public, but initiatives of this sort backfired in 1918 when the release of three World War I films, *Fit to Fight* (1918), *Fit to Win* (1919), and *The End of the Road* (1918), produced by the U.S. Commission on Training Camp Activities, caused a public uproar. Intended to help stop the spread of venereal disease among army troops, they were also shown to the public at large, army doctors boldly training their cameras on the ravages of the disease in order to shock some sense into people.

Those who would become the first generation of exploitation filmmakers, the so-called "Forty Thieves"—Louis Sonney, Dwain Esper, and Kroger Babb, among many others—all took notice, in an admiring way, of the public scandal that ensued. Bad publicity, they observed, was still at least *free* publicity—and, anyhow, the uproar had not kept people away from the box offices. On the contrary, up and down the mid-Atlantic states, for weeks at a time, crowds lined up to see *The End of the Road*. If a subject like sex hygiene could pull in big crowds, what of other topics? The old carnies responded to this question with a spate of low-budget films covering a range of taboo topics—illicit love, nudity, drug and alcohol abuse. Prostitution or "white slave" films proliferated, and sex-hygiene films, or "clap operas," which focused on venereal disease and contraception—kept movie houses filled to capacity for weeks, often shown under the aegis of phony, blue-ribbon medical associations, which lent an air of propriety to the spectacle. Throughout the 1920s, the early exploiteers spread a kind of anti-gospel across America, touring their films from town to town in the old carnival tradition, profiting from the exploitation of ambiguities, tensions, and fears long associated with leisure, idleness, and the hazards of gratified desire.

Two carnival men in particular, Louis Sonney and Dwain Esper, made the leap from sideshow to exploitation film and in the process brought the body of Elmer McCurdy along with them. By the early 1930s, Sonney's museum, now located in downtown Los Angeles, went into a state of decline. The waxen heads of the American presidents began to sag and the heads of the American outlaws to nod this way and that in the Southern California heat. Sonney seemed to have lost touch with a culture now provoked not so much by the criminals that were his stock in trade as by the sins of the flesh. But if his career had revealed anything about him thus far, it was that he was adaptable. Indeed, Sonney was at another turning point in his career, but he would soon demonstrate a shrewdness, not to say courage, by entering into a world completely beyond his ken. Just down the street from his wax museum, a lurid film called *The Seventh Commandment* was playing, and people were lining up around the block to see it. Sonney wanted to meet the man who owned the film.

His name was Dwain Esper. A former motorcycle stuntman from Seattle who had performed under the name "The Fearless Chick," Esper moved to Los Angeles after breaking his hand and became a building contractor. When the owner of a film-processing lab defaulted on a loan, Esper seized the property and began experimenting with film production, developing a portable sound-recording system—Radiotone—around 1930. His business ethos was informed by his years on the carnival circuit. He was a hard-drinking, "fifth-of-Scotch-a-day man," with a penchant for spontaneous litigation. He sued big movie companies. He sued small operators. He sued, it seemed, as a way of conveying an emotional attachment to someone. As Friedman liked to joke, "He wouldn't answer the phone 'hello.' He just said, 'I'll sue.'" To many, including his closest associates, Esper was a chiseling, conniving paragon for whom a deal wasn't a deal unless someone was getting shafted, a man who, in his later years, would swindle his own grandson simply because it was in his nature to do so. It was Esper's instinct as an old carnival entertainer, and his appreciation for the cheap thrills that fed the lowest common denominator, that led him to the unseemly, marginalized, but often highly profitable realm of the exploitation film.

*The Seventh Commandment* was Esper's first feature film, and it drove the future head of Hollywood's Production Code Administration, Joseph I. Breen, into a state of comprehensive outrage. Breen called *The Seventh Commandment* "the most thoroughly vile and disgusting motion picture which the three members of this staff . . . [had] ever seen." It was "thoroughly reprehensible in all its details." It was "poorly produced and poorly photographed. The whole thing [was] very offensive and disgusting."

Breen's outcry was like a fusillade fired blindly toward a cunning, swiftly moving insurgent enemy that lay hidden and, indeed, seemed to flourish in the wilderness of the American landscape. For his part, Louis Sonney aligned himself with the partisans in the hills. He bought a half-interest in Esper's film. From that point onward, the figures from Sonney's Wax Museum of Crime were obsolete. Only McCurdy escaped the storage bin. Only McCurdy, it seemed, still had a role to play in the new age of film.

Esper's second full-length feature, *Narcotic* (1933), typified the exploitation genre. Written by Esper's wife, Hildegard, who used the facts of drug addiction within her own family as material for her script, *Narcotic*, according to the New York State censor board, portrayed "the mental, moral and physical degeneration of a physician who becomes addicted to the dope habit. He begins by smoking opium and ends his career with heroin, supplemented by pistol shot."

Esper took *Narcotic* on the road, and he brought Elmer McCurdy with him, where he was propped up in theater lobbies and sidewalk displays across the country in the manner of the old carnival come-on, the show before the show. He got his first break in film, as it were, in a "March of Crime" short subject produced by Louis Sonney and possibly distributed along with the *Narcotic* roadshow. The film was the kind of added attraction that was typically spliced onto longer features and sent by distributors to towns across America, where it eventually made its way to Pawhuska, Oklahoma. Here, in a small theater, the body once displayed in the local funeral parlor for a nickel and known locally as "Johnson's Outlaw" made its cinematic return engagement. Here, too, McCurdy seemed, more than ever, caught in a vortex as large as the country itself. Johnny Johnson, the son of the man who had embalmed McCurdy, recalled going into the local theater as a young man and watching in amazement as a familiar image from his boyhood, the old mummy that his dad had kept in the back room so many years ago, now captured in celluloid, turned grotesquely on the screen like a pig on a spit while a narrator harangued the audience against the perils of drug abuse.

As old carnies, Esper and Sonney recognized a fetish when it presented itself. Ever since McCurdy's death so many years ago, his body had become a site, a locus, a mirror of the fantasy life of an American public. As the century progressed, the reflection in the mirror changed—the original fantasy, with its nostalgic embrace of the anti-hero, of the outlaw as a rebel of commerce, gave way to internalized fears and anxieties of moral degeneracy and victimization, and McCurdy, the erstwhile Oklahoma Outlaw, was now thrust into a new role that spoke of a new age. Here was "Elmer McCready [sic], The Dope Addict, One of the Greatest Dope Addicts of All Time."

While McCurdy was being ogled on the exploitation circuit, Dave Friedman was getting his degree in electrical engineering at Cornell, a degree that would find no practical use in his life. Friedman joined the army during World War II, after which he worked for Paramount Pictures, moving up the ranks to head the publicity department in Paramount's Chicago offices, a dream job in which he spent a lot of time on the road, occasionally golfing with Hollywood stars like Bob Hope and Charlton Heston, while learning the landscape of American theater distribution and promotion. "I could tell you every town over 25,000," he told an interviewer for *Film Comment*, "whether it was a mainstreet or a courthouse square town, where the railroad went through, where the loading zones were, what highway it was on, if there was a movie house, how many and who owned them." Friedman learned the film business from the business end: at the level of the ticket taker and the popcorn vendor, and he knew the quirks and kinks in the great machinery of distribution.

Then, in the mid-1950s, he packed it all in—the Paramount expense account, the golfing with Bob Hope—and for the next seven years Friedman toured the country for the exploitation impresario Kroger Babb, road-showing the sex-hygiene hit *Mom and Dad*. The Paramount executive had, in effect, run off and joined the circus.

It wasn't half as crazy as it sounded. Friedman had tested the waters with Babb while still working for Paramount. In 1956, he and his wife, Carol, took *The Story of Bob and Sally*, a sex-hygiene film that Babb was distributing, for a limited engagement at a drive-in near Minneapolis, just to see what kind of business the film would bring. Babb had agreed to split the proceeds fifty-fifty. "People came from all over Minnesota to see this film," Friedman remembered. "They came from North Dakota. They came from Iowa. We opened on the Wednesday after Labor Day. I stayed through the weekend, then bought a gun for Carol and drove back to my job at Paramount. I told her to take the money to the bank each day, get a cashier's check, and to keep the pistol on the seat of the car. Every weekend I would go up there. We stayed until Thanksgiving. When it was all over, I had in my hand something like 18,000 dollars." Friedman had made in three weeks almost twice as much as he made all year at Paramount, and he could count on similar results in four or five other cities in the region Babb had promised him.

But what Babb really had to offer was something Freidman seems to have sought since childhood. Indeed, the early imprint of carnival life from his boyhood days in Anniston informed every major career decision Friedman would make. Something like a compass seemed to pivot inside him, pointing him toward an increasing association with people who were "with the show," who received their education on the road, the rough-hewn, quick-witted confidence men of exploitation film.

*The Story of Bob and Sally* was a spin-off of Kroger Babb's best-selling sex-hygiene film, *Mom and Dad*, which set the standard for success in the exploitation world. But *Mom and Dad* was also a spin-off of earlier films of a similar sort going as far back as the mid-1930s Brian Foy clap opera *High School Girl*, which Dave Friedman had seen as a young boy in Anniston. Lifted almost verbatim from *High School Girl*, *Mom and Dad* was produced for

$62,000—an extravagant sum for most exploitation films. Babb's timing couldn't have been better, for American soldiers had gone abroad and had come back changed, and *Mom and Dad* moved through America like a wildfire, fueled by Babb's sure-handed grasp of the bally.

Babb hired actors to pose as armed guards in front of theaters, blocking admittance to underage viewers. He segregated audiences by sex, the women seeing the film at different hours than the men. There was an inside lecturer, billed as the distinguished sex hygienist Elliot Forbes, who gave a talk at the half-way point of the film on *The Secrets of Sensible Sex*. And Babb hired "nurses" to stand inside his theaters and sell the sex-hygiene book—one for men and one for women—printed at Babb's own private printing facility in Ohio. At one point, Babb had twenty-five teams blanketing the country, twenty-five copies of *Mom and Dad* with twenty-five Elliot Forbeses giving the intermission lectures, dozens of nurses in attendance selling hundreds of thousands of copies of the sex-hygiene book that Babb had printed for pennies and sold for a dollar. Friedman was one of these Elliot Forbeses. Decades later, Friedman could still summon the old spiel as if it were a drink that he'd set down just a few minutes earlier.

"Ladies and gentlemen," he began,

I am not speaking about birth control. I do not advocate birth control in this book, in this lecture, or in this film. However, nature does operate in patterns. And every young girl upon reaching puberty starts on her own personal menstrual month. This means that once each menstrual month an egg is released. It travels *down* the oviduct, *through* the Fallopian tube, and settles in the uterus, or womb. This period lasts three days, and during that *three-day period,* and that *three-day period only,* that a woman is fertile, she can conceive and have a baby.

In its sonic patterning and imagery, its cadences, emphatic gestures, and repetitions, and its fantastic journey through the anatomy, Friedman's delivery revamped the old-fashioned nineteenth-century medicine-show pitch for a new era, substituting the twentieth century's fixation upon the reproductive cycle for the previous century's fixation upon the digestive tract. By showing the film and selling the sex-hygiene books—"Available to you, the great American public, at a slight fraction of the actual cost of printing, handling, and distribution"—Friedman, as Forbes, and all the other Elliot Forbeses across the country, claiming sponsorship and endorsement by a nonexistent "Women's Research Guild," presented themselves as frocked crusaders for a new era.

"In your windup," Friedman recalled, "you almost went into 'Onward Christian Soldiers.' . . . Most of the guys we had doing this were carnival sideshow talkers; they could bring tears to the eyes of those suckers."

After seven years of road-showing *Mom and Dad,* Friedman formed his own film distribution company, which he based in Chicago. Then he met Herschell Gordon Lewis, who had been a professor of English before venturing into exploitation film. Both he and Friedman fancied themselves adepts of the corporate marketing blarney. Each was a poet in his way. Friedman had the carnival talker's gift for the filigreed, hyper-alliterative line, for winking, elbow-swinging puns, and this jibed nicely with Lewis's own sort of annotated, heavily credentialed elbow-swinging.

"He had a command of the English language," Friedman recalled, "that I envied and a wit that wouldn't stop. We were simpatico."

With financial backing from regional grindhouse theater owners, Lewis and Friedman brought with them the intellectual capital that would make them major players in the exploitation world. They immersed themselves in that world, but they were not *of* it, unlike most of their contemporaries, such as Kroger Babb, who were content to work within the received parameters of the genre, happily cutting the boring parts out of Ingmar Bergman's *Summeren mit Monika* to get straight to the tits and ass. It was nothing for Friedman and Lewis to see beyond the narrow dog trot that was the genre's enclosure. In 1960 alone, they produced three movies—*Nature's Playmates*, the first nudist film noir, followed by the first nudist musical, *Goldilocks and the Three Bares*, followed by a parody of nudist colony movies entitled, *B-O-I-N-N-N-G!* You can almost feel them yawning, looking for something new to try.

The result was *Blood Feast* (1963). Based on a 14-page script written in one night, the film was shot in less than a week. The story involves a demented caterer who carves up the bodies of beautiful women and offers them to the Egyptian goddess Ishtar. Friedman and Lewis added a homemade musical score that consisted of a kettle drum rhythm section with Lewis playing the organ and Friedman on the triangle. They were both repulsed by the end product. Friedman's own wife called it "vomitous," but their financial backer, drive-in theater owner Stan Kohlberg, loved *Blood Feast* and planned to play it first, of all places, in Peoria, Illinois.

The night it premiered, traffic to Kohlberg's Bel Air Drive-In was backed up for five miles. Friedman, perhaps nervous about how bad his movie was, had shifted his publicity skills into high gear, stationing a phalanx of ambulances at the entrance, their lights twirling brightly, and distributing air-sickness bags on which were printed the slogan "You May Need This When You See *Blood Feast.*" Meanwhile, in Sarasota, Florida, he arranged to have a judge grant an injunction to prevent *Blood Feast* from being shown in local theaters. This planted "story," an old ploy he had learned from his days with Kroger Babb, was picked up on the wires, gaining the movie free nationwide publicity. Movie critics were stunned by what they saw, but the negative reviews of the film—the *Los Angeles Times* called it a "blot on the American film industry"—played right into Freidman's hand, fanning the publicity flames. Within months, the movie, which had cost $24,000 to make, had earned a quarter of a million dollars, prompting Friedman, who seemed chary of the project, to sell out his interest—a little too soon—for *Blood Feast* eventually went on to gross $6 million.

In a few years, the partnership was finished. Friedman and Lewis split acrimoniously over, of all things, quality control. When Friedman lobbied for a more polished product, warning Lewis that their production values were too poor, Lewis, according to Friedman, invoked the people lining up for *Two Thousand Maniacs* and *Color Me Blood Red,* saying, "They don't know any better." Lewis, the former professor of English literature, was unable to hide his contempt for his chosen realm ("No. I'm not a student of film," he once said when asked to name a favorite film or filmmaker) and harbored a palpable disdain for his audience, whom he described as yahoos and lab rats. Friedman, however, seems to have decided to get behind the camera and have some fun. In 1964 he quit Chicago and fell into a long-running business partnership with Dan Sonney, who had inherited his father Louis's business. Sonney Amusement Enterprises occupied an office block of single-story warehouses in east Los Angeles, once known as Film Row, where all of the big film companies had once located their distribution offices. In later years the Cordova Street address become better known as Exploitation Row. Here, in a new partnership called Entertainment Ventures Incorporated, Friedman began cranking out a string of successful low-rent skin flicks.

"When I first got out there it was more like the winter quarters of a carnival than a film company," Friedman recalled. "Dan had the wax figures, he had stuffed crocodiles, and he had Elmer . . . and Dan would have to show people that stiff. He'd have to show them Elmer."

In a storage room behind Friedman's office, Elmer McCurdy weathered the mid-1960s like a tuxedo growing dust on the shoulders. McCurdy had faced the hazards of the great American traveling sideshow, as one of its big attractions, with apparent equanimity. He had survived the industry's transition into film, first with publicity appearances for *Narcotic*, and in his crossover debut "March of Crime." But now, if he was used at all, it was for children's Halloween parties or for practical jokes around the office.

Then, in 1966, Friedman took his Ariflex hand-held camera out to the Sacramento State Fair in Bakersfield, California, where in seven days he shot most of *She-Freak*, his homage to Todd Browning's *Freaks* and his tribute to the American carnival that he'd known all his life. He arrived early as the West Coast Shows set up its rides and exhibits and crawled in and around everything. He stayed to film the crews tearing it all down. He cast himself in several cameo appearances—as a carnival talker, as ticket taker, as a poker-playing carny. Friedman spent three days on the Cordova lot in Los Angeles finishing *She-Freak*. At some point during this time, McCurdy, who had remained in the warehouse, was given a chance for a star turn. But the climactic shot in which McCurdy would have loomed for us all to see—as one of many creepy ghouls lurking in the background while Claire Brennen receives her ghastly comeuppance—was left on the cutting-room floor. Thereafter, McCurdy lingered, as Dan Sonney recalled, "like a piece of junk," washed up on the shore of the 1960s civil-rights era like some embarrassing throwback, some tobacco-store Indian or a Negro lawn jockey—part of an American century that had gotten tucked out of sight.

Meanwhile, on the margins of that era, in the back pages of the daily newspapers, *The Erotic Adventures of Zorro* (1971) and other films of Friedman's high sexploitation period were gamely fulfilling Alexis de Tocqueville's forecast, it seemed, that Americans would "habitually prefer the useful to the beautiful . . . and require that the beautiful be useful." And while there was little need to walk too far down the darkened, Lysol-disinfected theater aisle of male arousal and titillation to imagine in what particular way later films of Friedman's, such as *My Tale Is Hot (Pantie's Inferno)* (1965) and *Trader Hornee* (1970), had served the Republic, Mike Vraney, of Something Weird Video, had given me a copy of a dozen trailers, a Friedman sampler, of sorts, which I decided to watch in the spirit of casting a wide net. But the only thing worse than watching *Thar She Blows*, it seems, was watching the trailer for *Thar She Blows*, where the marginal world to which McCurdy had once belonged had been transformed beyond recognition, the bally replaced with a grinding verbal priapism, condensed to near toxic levels, which gave the effect of being trapped for the weekend in a pup tent filled with overheated thirteen-year-old boys. The language was a relentless juggernaut of the asinine, an empire of bathroom-stall humor, that left me feeling acutely, and for the first time in a life of mostly wasted time, that the minutes I'd spent with the trailer for *Thar She Blows*, or *The Lustful Turk*, or *The Ramrodder* were minutes I would never have back again.

Why then, I wondered, had Friedman's films become such a hot commodity in the new millennium? "Because of two words," he said, "One word being *camp*. The other word being *cult*. In the United States the fourteen- to twenty-four-year-old age group is one of the biggest segments of the population. These kids never saw this stuff. They never knew it existed. They never knew there were 750 little nudie houses around the country that every week played one of these things."

The resurgence of interest in his films was a turn of events that he relished and to which—as an old advertising copywriter—he was perfectly suited. While I was with him, Friedman did all he could to guide me to the Best of Friedman, the choicest, most quotable lines, but he soon seemed anxious to get back to the convention and offered to continue the discussion in the elevator, down which we rode in silence with a crowd of conventioneers. Soon I found myself watching him from a distance as he worked the floor again, glad handing, signing autographs. I was standing in front of Cynthia Myers, Miss Playboy Playmate of 1968, who smiled at me and asked if I wanted to sit down.

She motioned to an extra chair on her side of an autograph table neatly organized with photographs from her days at *Playboy*. In December 1968 she'd appeared on the magazine's Christmas cover, a five-foot-four bombshell—39DD–24–36—

who so resoundingly shocked the troops from Da Nang to Dien Bien Phu that she still receives fan mail from Vietnam veterans. Among the photographs she had for sale were a glossy of Santa's little helper dressing a Christmas tree and a movie still of her looking fabulous in the lesbian love scene with Erica Gavin in *Beyond the Valley of the Dolls*. I sat down.

"Will you watch my things?" Cynthia Myers asked me sweetly. "I've got to go to the little girls' room."

She walked away quickly and I spent a few moments assessing the situation. A crowd had formed at the other end of the table, where Mike Vraney and his wife, Lisa, were restocking videos as fast as they could, while Friedman, his cigar still unlit, leaned into a deep discussion with a cluster of fans. The interview was over.

Still, it felt good to be on the other side of the autograph table, although by comparison to the bustle elsewhere, the area now temporarily under my purview felt a trifle neglected. Before I could figure out what to say if anyone approached, two men in their forties materialized in front of me, their heads bowed in silent contemplation of Cynthia Myers floating on her back in a swimming pool, Cynthia Myers reclining voluptuously by a fireplace, Cynthia Myers kneeling on a white rug alongside a teddy bear. She had the big, turbulent hair of Brigitte Bardot, enough for two or three Bardots, it seemed, and it was tossed and teased in a carefully haphazard manner that Baldassari Castiglioni would have admired. *JBF hair*, I once heard it called: *Just Been Fucked*. Her eyes were darkened windows that put the masque back into mascara. A beauty mark added a final point to the matter. Here, in full glossy display, was the 1960s feminine baroque, the all-compliant and available goddess and Warhol object of obsession, the drag-queen ideal. It was the triumph of farce and artifice, of vamp and camp, and, like Friedman's films, it was having its own triumphalist revival on the margins of America.

As for the *real* Cynthia Myers, the one who had children and who traveled from trade show to trade show, for all I knew she had left the building. No matter. The two men stood over the photographs like connoisseurs in admiration of a particularly rare discovery—vintage 1968—one of the men pointing with his index finger to the most marketable part of Cynthia Myers, her bona fides, as it were, displayed in good faith, without deceit, to a world where the Blob, or the stuff they used to make the Blob, had made strange infiltrations.

"You better believe *those* are real," he said.

Just then a young man who looked like an enforcer for a hairspray commercial walked straight up to me and leaned over the table.

"Where's Cynthia?" he said.

"The little girls' room?" I shrugged, and off he went in a rush.

There was something going on here, and I was pretty sure that Cynthia Myers was misbehaving in some way and was about to get yelled at, which made me feel bad, so I tried to perk up a bit, and I sat there with an alert, attentive look on my face, as ready as I could be to inform anyone who cared to know that Miss Playboy Playmate of 1968 would be returning to sign autographs very shortly.

## ❧ 9 ❧

# Eternity, a List

The way a pair of window shades flutter through an afternoon. The little motorized office fan like the far-off purring from *The Spirit of Saint Louis*. The after-hours lives of coffee mugs and paper clips. Office machinery. Envelopes. The keys of a typewriter, poised like a silent orchestra at the rest or pause in the musical score of eternity's anthem, which was like the hum of fluorescent lights down the hallways of the hereafter. Like all these, McCurdy idled his way through that portion of eternity that blossomed inside the EVI warehouse on Exploitation Row's Cordova Street, Los Angeles. The only thing missing from the scene might have been a doleful, faraway trumpet solo warbling the theme from *Chinatown*. The warehouse was filled with film canisters and a half-century's worth of oddments from a road-showman's life: dusty tribal masks and shields used for an old Louis Sonney girl-and-gorilla movie; broadsides and posters and fold-up sideshow banners for films and attractions that had long come and gone; the wax figures of American outlaws and presidents; a menagerie of taxidermy—tropical birds, crocodiles, and, propped up in a corner, McCurdy himself. And all of it was for sale.

Dan Sonney had been trying to clean house for a long time, but he'd found no takers for the *disjecta membra* of a bygone time. To the few who came by to look at the junk, he would speak of the mummy with a mixture of affection and exasperation. "I grew up with this guy," he once told a visitor. "In fact, he was part of the family. Like I was."

This family feeling, of course, covered a lot of ground and included episodes of the sort that many families might choose to ignore or soften with the term *highjinks*—like the time Dan broke off McCurdy's arm and chased his secretary around the office with it, for instance. (He reattached the arm with electrician's tape.) In truth, McCurdy seemed a piece of his father's past that Dan Sonney was loath to keep, yet could not bring himself to destroy. Nor could he manage to sell him at any price. McCurdy was like a bothersome, ne'er-do-well uncle who had taken up residence in Sonney's youth, persisted unchanged through Sonney's adulthood, and now, in Sonney's early middle age, seemed like a sort of Egyptian curse of the garage-sale circuit, plying away the California afternoons.

Then came a sparkle and a stir. Two men strolled down the aisles of Sonney's warehouse, bargain hunting, eyeballing the bric-a-brac. They were Don Crysdale and E. D. ("Ed") Liersch, both from British Columbia, Canada. They arrived in a black Lincoln Continental, which Crysdale had bought new off the lot—in cash—six years earlier after a big success at the 1962 Seattle World's Fair.

Crysdale, Liersch, and another Canadian by the name of Ed Hicks occupied a subgenre of entrepreneurial enterprise, one long on ideas and perpetually short on capital. They were

drawn to money-making inventions of the sort one sees advertised at state fairs or in the back of magazines or during late-
night television commercials. They dreamed of discovering
their own version of the pocket-sized fishing rod or the kitchen
knife that can cut through steel plating or debone a shad, and
then sitting back and watching the money flow in. The idea to
rent wax figures second- or third-hand then display them in a
rented hall as close as one could possibly get to the disposable
income of World's Fair sightseers, for instance, was initially a
short-term scheme that meant no more or less to them than any
number of earlier ideas—but the wax museum just happened to
work out fantastically well.

The men traveled to Hollywood, where they rented a mot-
ley assortment of wax figures, castoffs, and extras, whatever
they could find. The exhibit that they pieced together had, at
one end, movie stars such as Clark Gable and Marilyn Monroe,
and, at the other end, an interesting taxonomic grouping of
criminals and heads of state—Jack the Ripper, Hitler, Stalin,
concluding with a grand religious tableaux called "Our Lord's
Last Supper." It was the kind of cheesy attraction that nobody
in their right mind would spend money on, but the Canadians
had three things working in their favor: location, location, and
location. Hicks had rented a hall outside the fairgrounds but
near the southern terminus of a wildly popular shuttle called
the Monorail, an elevated, futuristic train that took thousands
upon thousands of people from downtown Seattle to the heart
of the fair. They had bet that most of these people could be at
least temporarily distracted from their right mind by a beautiful young lady dancing a jig to a bagpipe blown as loudly as

possible near the museum entrance. And of course they were correct. The Monorail and the bagpipes and the beautiful girl got people fairly marching into the ticket booth, and for Crysdale, Liersch, and Hicks, in that glorious year of 1962, the money poured in—a daily river of cash flowing directly into their pockets.

Ever since their triumph in Seattle, the three Canadians had been trying to make a second successful foray in wax. In 1965, Hicks and Liersch helped another fellow Canadian named Spoony Singh hit the wax museum jackpot in Hollywood. By chance, Singh had recently sold out his interest in a logging business and was in the market for another business to buy. Singh did not identify himself with lumber, or timber, or the great outdoors, or the sundering thereof, but was first and foremost a businessman, which meant that, in some way, his heart of hearts belonged to the numbers, to the balance sheet, to making numbers dance to the tune of steady, measured growth. Whatever form the business took was almost a secondary concern, as long as the numbers did their mambo dance. And so, upon the urging of Crysdale and Liersch, Singh flew down to Los Angeles to investigate what may have seemed at first like a crazy idea.

The three men proceeded to Mann's Theater, which famously bore the imprint of fame and celebrity, and bore witness to one of the forms that mass hysteria had taken in late twentieth-century America, as thousands of tourists flocked to that particular block of Los Angeles, and stooped down at that particular stretch of sidewalk, to measure their hands against the hand of Mickey Rooney, say, or Charlton Heston, and maybe take a few pictures, and then wonder what to do next with their money. And *that* precise moment, that precise question, would happen hundreds of thousands of times in any given year. Crysdale and Liersch had brought Singh to inspect a vacant building just down the street from Mann's Theater that had made the eyes of Crysdale and Liersch widen, their palms sweat, and their hearts nearly palpitate in unison—*location, location, location*. Within months, Singh had signed a twenty-year lease, had gutted the space, and had brought it up to code, and the Hollywood Wax Museum had opened for business.

It would become one of the most spectacularly successful museums of its kind in the country, a shrine of sorts to the glamour kings and queens of twentieth-century celebrity. The Hollywood Wax Museum, with its lifelike replication, right down to the tinting of Mae West's arm hair, was a mausoleum of the immortals. One saw, as one walked its halls, not the real Sharon Stone, say, growing older year by year, but her immortal body double that made the franchise possible. Spoony Singh profited, in large part, because it was his money that kept the whole thing going. It would make enough money for Singh to retire to a house in Malibu, while Crysdale and Liersch, who had brought Singh to Southern California in the first place, were left with their idée fixe. It seemed to hover on the horizon, ever in front of them, like Brigadoon, or one of Coronado's seven golden cities.

Decades later, I caught up with Crysdale, over the phone, a few months after Ed Liersch had died, and Crysdale spoke, with bemused detachment, of the years following the 1962 fair and leading up to his encounter with the mummified body of Elmer McCurdy. For a short time after the Seattle Fair, Crysdale left Liersch behind with Spoony Singh in California and went out on his own with a small wax museum that toured the state fair circuit. His recollections of the time were those of a cultural outsider, familiar but also full of odd little holes:

"We had about twenty figures," Crysdale told me from his daughter's house, in Chico, California.

"We had Kennedy and Johnson, *and the guy who shot Kennedy. . . .*" Crysdale paused to think.

"Oswald?" I offered, helpfully.

"*Oswald,*" he said.

By 1968, when Crysdale and Liersch strolled into Sonney's warehouse, the vicissitudes of the wax museum trade had brought Crysdale and Liersch back together, perusing threadbare merchandise that was destined for the Dumpster. In truth, they were broke. Borrowing money from Singh, they purchased Sonney's inventory. Singh, of course, had little interest in the wax figures, which were too down market for his operation, and he showed even less interest in McCurdy, who was simply "too gross to display." McCurdy was too gross, even, for Crysdale and Liersch, who were busy preparing their next exhibit. Everything they'd done until now had taught them the importance of location, and so, leaving McCurdy behind, they grabbed a few wax presidents and a few western outlaws and in 1970 they hit the road, heading for their chosen spot.

The plan was to haul their collection to Mount Rushmore, South Dakota, and set up a small exhibit within the penumbra of the great figures of Washington, Jefferson, Roosevelt, and Lincoln carved into the granite mountainside. It was a pretty good idea, too, except that the Stubergh family, renowned suppliers of high-quality wax figures around the world, had already established an exhibit called "The Hall of Presidents" right at the base of Mount Rushmore. Blocked out by the Stubergh family's beachhead, Crysdale and Liersch set up shop about five miles *before* the entrance to the national monument. There they lived in a trailer by a road made busy with an endless stream of buses and cars and camper vans all gaily passing them by. After two dismal years, Crysdale and Liersch called it quits.

"We showed President Lincoln," Don Crysdale recalled, "getting shot by . . . *what's his name, the guy who shot Lincoln?*"

"John Wilkes Booth?" I said.

"It was a pretty good little scene. Lincoln and his wife were there. It all came from Sonney," he said.

Years later, after McCurdy's story broke, the published accounts of this last phase of McCurdy's afterlife incorrectly placed McCurdy in South Dakota with Crysdale and Liersch's wax exhibit. In another report, a thunderstorm flattened the infidel Canadian enterprise, knocking McCurdy's body around with enough force to break off fingers, toes, and the tips of his ears, these shattered bits carried away by the wind across the prairie. But nothing of the sort occurred. One can understand the impulse to send McCurdy into the Black Hills, to imagine his slight figure against the colossal backdrop of Washington, Jefferson, Roosevelt, and Lincoln. It's as if the chroniclers could not imagine much of a story in McCurdy being left behind in California, which was what happened. But the story hadn't reached its bottom, even though McCurdy had slipped beneath the regard of gypsies like Crysdale and Liersch, had been separated from Friedman and Sonney, the last people to know or care about who he had ever been.

The bottom for McCurdy was deeper still, and he had further to fall. Crysdale and Liersch returned from the Mount Rushmore debacle, and in the fall of 1971 they took out a year's

lease at the Nu-Pike in Long Beach, California, and cobbled together a haunted house of wax. Crysdale brought McCurdy
into his workshop, where he'd made a coffin, and began drilling
a hole in McCurdy's foot. He then drilled another hole in the
back of McCurdy's neck. Then he mounted the body on a rotat-
ing cam device that fit inside the coffin. The plan was to set the
coffin upright in front of the haunted house, so that when
people walked by the casket, the body inside appeared to suddenly twitch.

"When I drilled a hole in his foot," Crysdale said, "some yellow, almost *gooey* stuff came out on the drill, and of course at
that point I thought—*my god, what have we got here?*"

Judging from photographs taken of McCurdy's body at the
time, it's difficult to imagine how anyone could have mistaken
McCurdy for anything other than what he was. Crysdale was
either spectacularly unobservant about the mummy whose foot
he was drilling into, or his mind was focused on other things.
His qualms were easily shelved, in any case, and he placed
McCurdy on the boardwalk, where, twitching away in his coffin,
he was billed as the One Thousand Year Old Man, a final alias, a
last erasure of identity. Tended by two fly-by-night operators,
who, indeed, by September 1972 had fled in default of unpaid
rent on a wax museum that nobody wanted to see, McCurdy entered the threshold of oblivion.

The Long Beach Amusement Company confiscated the body
and put it in the closet of an electrician who worked for the Pike.
His name was Ray Scott, but everyone called him "Lucky," and
he shared his apartment on the Pike with Elmer McCurdy for
about a year until Long Beach Amusement Company decided to

revamp the Laff-in-the-Dark fun house, using McCurdy as a prop. Lucky hung him high near the ceiling, painting him Day-Glo red and installing a switch that triggered a blue light, and for the next four years, teenagers and young lovers and sailors on shore leave made their way through the darkened maze of the Laff-in-the-Dark, one after the other, triggering the blue light at a blind corner, where they would be spooked by the glowing body, and where, on a winter morning in 1976, under this same blue light, a number of men from the set-dressing crew of Universal Studios stood gaping at the mummy, wondering what to do. Chris Haynes was among them. So was a man named John Purvis, a distant relative of the famous FBI agent. Like so many before him, Purvis had drifted from the east and found himself blinking at the waters of the Pacific, hungry and homeless on a beach near the Pike.

"I come up here," Purvis told a reporter, "and the same guy I'm working for right now, he looked at me and says, 'You looking for a job?'"

I says, "Well, I'm gonna have to do something. I'm getting hungry."

He says, "You ever worked in a concession?"

I says, "No sir."

He says, "Would you like to try it?"

I says, "I'll try anything to eat."

"And he put me in. That was Jack Streiss and Kitty Flint, back in 1957."

Now Purvis managed a dozen concessions and had been asked to keep an eye on the Laff-in-the-Dark during the filming of the *Six Million Dollar Man* episode. Shortly after McCurdy's discovery, people had gathered around in wonder. First the fire-men, then Detective Sallmen, who took a few photographs of McCurdy hanging by the neck, then John Mossbrucker, the coroner's investigator.

Within hours, someone had spray-painted a sign at the Laff-in-the-Dark that read, "The Mummy's Hangout." Years later, in 1979, just before the Pike was closed for good, before it was sold, razed, and leveled forever beneath a steaming sheet of as-phalt, Purvis would point to a place where the sign had hung, the stenciled letters still visible beneath a fresh coat of paint.

"He was painted infrared and a blue light came on," Purvis said, "and you saw him hanging there. Then somebody said, 'Well, we can take him out now. Has anybody got a knife?' I had my buck knife on my side and I said, 'Well, hell yeah.' And I just reached around and got him, you know, cause Lucky didn't want to cut him down. When everybody found out he was real, they wouldn't cut him down. I just said, 'Hell, I've got one.' I was going to cut him down and Mossbrucker said, 'Oh, don't cut it yet—let somebody help you—he's gonna be heavier than you think.'

"Then we picked him up and laid him on a rubber stretcher, and the Coroner's Office wheeled him out to the county morgue car, a black, Chevrolet station wagon. Then they cov-ered him in a white sheet and hauled him out, just like they would anybody else."

## ∾ 10 ∾

# For Greater Guthrie

*The more you do anything that don't look*
*like advertising the better advertising it is.*
                                    —Will Rogers

Two representatives of the Indian Territorial Posse of Oklahoma Westerners moseyed down the corridor of the Los Angeles International Airport, weaving among the locals in the
warm, shirtsleeve weather of a Southern California evening in
mid-April 1977. The milling crowd, for its part, seemed accus-
tomed to occasional celebrity, arriving like a cruising barracuda
in a school of mackerel, the slice of a Masarati disappearing
down Sepulveda Boulevard. The crowd had grown used to visual oddity as well, the momentary displacement of its own
equilibrium by 1960s-era fallout, blending with the constant
flow of foreign nationals coming and going in the terminal, but
the two Okies walking side by side managed to turn a few heads
anyway.

The first wore his finest pair of stovepipe cowboy boots, his pants tucked into a pair of hand-tooled beauties that bore his own personal cattle brand and came nearly up to his knees. He wore pressed jeans and the kind of belt buckle that said or seemed to say "howdy," a soft leather vest, a ribbon tie, and a black hat with a rattlesnake hat band. His long, silver mustache depended from both sides of his mouth, which smiled, his head nodding to anyone who took notice. This was Fred Olds at his poking, jibing, head-turning best. It was an instance of the Okie put-on, a kind of aw-shucks anti-sophistication that Will Rogers, with his prominent cowlick, his rope tricks, and his sudden, laserlike wit, had used with such disarming success the year McCurdy was killed. "The peculiar thing about the cowboy, . . . " a Columbus, Ohio, paper said of Rogers's first solo act, "was that you couldn't make out whether he was in earnest or just kidding." Exactly. Unlike Rogers, however, who soon discovered that a dry tone of mock-puzzlement was the only western vestment one really needed as a cowboy Socrates, Fred Olds felt compelled to push his arrival in Los Angeles heavily toward a kind of cowboy burlesque.

The nation, still smarting from its humiliation in Southeast Asia, was in a full-blown recession, and its president, having given voice to a sense of national "malaise," was being vilified for his candor. What was needed, it seemed, was not the cloud of unknowing evoked by the term *malaise*, which sounded vaguely foreign, after all, inviting a mode of self-scrutiny that ran contrary to the American temperament, and seemed, therefore, almost seditious. What was needed, rather, was a good cowboy of the old-fashioned sort, and one was waiting in the wings. He was then governor of California, an ex–cowboy actor who would eventually lead the country through two presidencies, vanquish an "Evil Empire," and spend his dotage on a ranch, riding his horse under the California sun. But Ronald Reagan's time on the national stage had not yet come, and so it was, then, during an era of privations, as if in answer to an unheralded cowboy shortage, that Fred Olds arrived on a lesser errand, but one that relied no less heavily on a flourish of western regalia. Olds looked as if he'd wandered off a rodeo parade route, his howdy-dos like someone who'd stuck his face through a cowboy cut-out at the fair. And he was beaming, relishing the moment. Here was someone who offered an antidote to a spate of revisionist cowboy culture which had in recent times strayed dangerously into a *malaiselike territory*. The world knew from *Billy Jack*, for instance, from Jon Voight in *Midnight Cowboy*, from the movie *Nashville*, Robert Altman's parody of the Grand Ole Opry, and even from Glenn Campbell's popular hit "Rhinestone Cowboy," which, perhaps wafting even now along the airport corridor, added a baleful, self-conscious note to whatever the word *cowboy* had come to mean.

The other man, dark-haired and buttoned-down like a banker, was Ralph McCalmont, who betrayed no trace of the trail, no acquaintanceship with fences and cattle, no slight sartorial flourish of boot or belt. He was, in fact, a banker, the former president of City National Bank of Fort Worth, Texas, who had moved to Guthrie after purchasing the controlling interest of the First National Bank of Guthrie in 1974. That someone could put this on his resume—*purchased a $17 million bank*—said something about where the money was in that gloomy decade marked by oil shortages, widespread unemployment, and double-digit inflation. McCalmont flourished in the low-key, soft-spoken way that one comes to recognize in the wealthy when one has lived long enough in the world. In a room full of people, or in a crowded airport terminal, the eye was naturally drawn to Fred Olds, the outrageous character, dressed like a high roller, but the eye would be fooled, as it so often is, by appearances. Olds was the ceremonial goofball tethered to the straight man, McCalmont, who wore the unprepossessing uniform of the genuine article, the real high roller, who gambled with large sums every day and whose money had funded the present gambit to Los Angeles.

As Fred Olds basked in the attention his outfit drew toward him, howdy-doing and tipping his hat at passersby, McCalmont strode quietly beside him, a little out of sorts in the big city. For him this was the culmination of a quest that had been months in the making, one that had started out as a lark, borne on a puff of whimsy, a kind of joke, really, pursued, teased out, and nursed along with rigor, as far as the joke might be taken, in the best tradition of the Okie put-on—and it had landed them here in L.A. to try to prove beyond a reasonable doubt that the mummified body being held by the County Medical Examiner Thomas T. Noguchi was, in fact, the body of Elmer McCurdy.

It had all started months ago, over Saturday morning coffee, at the offices of the *Guthrie Daily Leader*, where McCalmont and a few others had gathered to talk about things far and near—the state of the world or the state of the weather, the here or the hereafter, whichever came first to mind. It was a gab session of no seeming purpose or foreseeable consequence, a gumbo of local business news, regional and national politics, and a fair amount of dime-store philosophizing—heavy on the Tabasco that men of a certain age allow themselves when they know they're alone together. Yet it was above all a conversation borne aloft by a shared natural curiosity and by a wide and, in some places, a deep reading of the world, the whole of it tempered by hard experience. If asked why they met, each would offer a variation of the same response: It was a reason to get out of the house on a cold January morning. There were no church deacons among them, nor members of the Chamber of Commerce, nor elected city officials, but what bound them and seemed to keep the conversation going from Saturday to Saturday was a certain low-grade sense of concern about the fate of the town in which they lived.

Guthrie had been born, famously, during the last land giveaway of the nineteenth century, the Oklahoma Land Rush of 1889, when at noon on a damp Monday, April 22, the sound of rifle shots sent more than 60,000 Boomers cascading over the pickets to lay claim to 2 million acres of land. Prior to the opening, the Santa Fe railroad had built a line extending into the Unassigned Lands as far as Cottonwood Creek, at which terminus an eastern regional land office had been built. There could be no clearer sign that a town was planned at this site, and there was much talk among the tens of thousands who waited Sunday behind the pickets that the fastest riders on Monday would stake for themselves entire city blocks of a future state capital. Little did they know that on the eve of the land rush the choicest parts of a future town had already been staked, in contravention of the law, by the very people entrusted to uphold and oversee the fair and equitable access for all homesteaders. Among those who took part in unlawful proceedings, the *Kansas City Daily Journal* reported, were U.S. marshals and dozens of deputies, including the U.S. attorney himself; the registrar of the regional land office, John I. Dille; and the man for whom the town would be named, Judge John Guthrie of Topeka, Kansas. By nightfall, campfires flickered in every direction around Guthrie and many other nascent towns across the prairie. "It was a great change for the cowpunchers," observed Evan G. Barnard, a cowboy who, along with a number of friends, had joined the land rush and staked claims along Turkey Creek valley near present-day Dover, Oklahoma, just west of Guthrie. These men saw, in a matter of hours, "the great cattle county transformed . . . from a region with thousands of cattle to one with thousands of people moving about. We wondered what they would do to make a living." It would not be the last time such a question would be asked.

Guthrie boomed for twenty years, lofting an impressive downtown district worthy of a state capital. Many of its buildings were designed by the Belgian architect Joseph Foucart—gorgeous brick structures built from dark red native sandstone in a decorative Victorian idiom with flourishes of the nineteenth-century penchant for middle-eastern exotica. Foucart, who arrived just after the land opening and lived in Guthrie throughout its boom, had a hand in nearly every important town structure, including the State Capital newspaper office, the Brooks Opera House, and his masterpiece, the Guthrie City Hall, with its clock tower, stone finials, and broad Palladian windows that drank up acres of prairie light. In the year of Oklahoma statehood, Foucart vanished out of sight, perhaps in anticipation of the deathblow Guthrie would receive, in 1910, when the state capital was removed to Oklahoma City, and most of the people who had a choice moved along with it. In the long period of decline that set in thereafter, Guthrie's architecture seemed a reminder of better times past, with dowdy old Victorian structures no one could afford to keep up. After World War II, people began tearing down the old buildings, and later, in a craze of urban renewal, covering everything in sight with aluminum siding.

Guthrie remained what McCalmont called "a sub-regional trading center" for the fairly prosperous agricultural community of Logan County, the place where farmers and ranchers went when it was time to "go into town." But the 1970s changed all of that, and Guthrie, along with the rest of the country, pitched headlong into a serious economic slide. The completion of Interstate 35 made shopping in Oklahoma City a mere thirty-minute drive, and vast shopping malls springing up outside Oklahoma City shortened the trip even further, draining business away from Guthrie. In McCalmont's view, the Guthrie Chamber of Commerce had spent most of its energy trying to attract large industry to the area, but "smokestack chasing," as McCalmont called it, would make Guthrie a corporate dependency.

Then in 1974 McCalmont took a walk around town with a bank trustee and local history buff named Lloyd Lentz, Sr., who pointed out the wealth of history in Guthrie's past: the building where Tom Mix had been a bartender; the only jail that had ever held the outlaw Bill Doolin; the bar that the combative, hatchet-wielding Carrie A. Nation, leader of the Women's Christian Temperance Union, had tried to close down; the hotel where Teddy

Roosevelt had organized the Rough Riders, and the building where a wholesale grocer named Wrigley had sold his first cinnamon-flavored paraffin squares. It all seemed fairly magical—and hard to believe—for aluminum siding covered most of the buildings, obscuring the past to such an extent that McCalmont had been planning to demolish some of them to make a parking lot. Now he suddenly saw *the value of history* for Guthrie, a phrase that had special meaning for a banker. Heritage tourism, as it came to be called, would put Guthrie back on the map. Working in cooperation with a number of regional historical societies, and aided by new tax laws that favored historical renovation, McCalmont used the considerable resources of his bank—a budget that exceeded that of the local Chamber of Commerce's—to restore Foucart's old buildings to their former glory. By 1977, when the news of McCurdy's discovery in Los Angeles reached the Saturday morning coffee klatch, work on the historic preservation of Guthrie had been under way for three years.

The thread that linked the men who met that Saturday morning in January 1977 was a passion for history. Bill Lehman, editor of the *Daily Leader* and an amateur historian, often hosted the gatherings. Fred Olds was the curator and chief administrator of the Oklahoma Territorial Museum. Glenn Shirley, who drove down from Stillwater, was, by some estimates, the most authoritative scholar then writing on western outlawry. Lastly, Ralph McCalmont, the banker. Each knew that if Guthrie were to survive, it would have to find a way to make people want to stop and visit. It would have to cash in on its history and pursue whatever might bolster or burnish that legacy. Guthrie would have to become an attraction of sufficient density to pull people off the interstate. It was in this way, in this setting, that Elmer McCurdy entered their lives, blown on a gust of nostalgia, with Bill Lehman holding up a copy of the *Daily Oklahoman* in which the wire-service story of the Long Beach fun-house mummy appeared.

"What do you think about this old dead fellow they found in Los Angeles?" Lehman said.

Glenn Shirley had seen the story, too, which had prompted him to dig into his cavernous system of files. He'd guessed, as had many newspapermen since the story broke, that the body belonged to Oklahoma outlaw Elmer McCurdy.

Fred Olds leaned forward. "What do you reckon they'll do with that body?"

"I'll tell you what they'll do," said Lehman, "they'll incinerate him and scatter him somewhere out in the Pacific."

Snow was falling lightly outside. The street below was quiet, but for the occasional purr of a passing car. The Pacific Ocean seemed about as far away from central Oklahoma right then as the moon, so that when Fred Olds began rummaging around the office for a telephone directory, which he found, and then picked up an office phone, then dialed up information and got himself connected to the Los Angeles County Coroner's Office, the men looked on—for half a moment—as if Fred were some marvelous creature that had magically appeared before them.

"That's just terrible." Fred Olds said, cradling the phone to his ear.

Suddenly, it seemed only right that they should try to retrieve this body, and even though it was Saturday, and nobody was at the Coroner's Executive Office, Fred left a message, to which the

Coroner's Office responded by letter. The following Saturday, the men reconvened at the newspaper offices, Olds waiving the letter in front of them, reading it aloud. Noguchi had struck a characteristically dour, skeptical, off-putting tone meant to deter the many dozens of oddballs and crazies. Anyone interested in the body, he wrote, had to satisfy three requirements.

The first was to assemble a team of forensic experts, who would join with Noguchi's team in Los Angeles in an attempt to positively identify the body. This was more than a little wrinkle in the plan, as few among the men present that Saturday morning had any working knowledge of what a forensic team might look like, "though most of us, if pressed, could have correctly spelled the term," McCalmont later recalled with a laugh. The other two stipulations set the bar even higher. The successful claimant would need to secure the approval of the state medical examiner, the only person to whom Noguchi would release the body. Finally, the city fathers of Guthrie would have to agree to and pay for a secure and dignified burial. About this latter point Noguchi was adamant. The days of mistreatment and abuse were over. No city or municipality was to benefit or profit or derive any boosterish attention on the national stage as a result of interring McCurdy. There would be no "Roman Holiday."

Noguchi's stipulations, daunting as they seemed, had a reverse effect on the men, made them lean forward into the problem, their eyes agleam. Each of the men had special skills that could be used to unlock the puzzle of bringing McCurdy back, which was, for starters, a forensic mystery. Fred Olds, who seemed to know everybody, called upon a paleontologist and forensic anthropologist named Clyde Snow, in Norman, Oklahoma, who agreed to help out in the matter if someone paid for his ticket to Los Angeles. No problem, said Ralph McCalmont, the banker, who agreed to underwrite all their expenses. Glenn Shirley, the outlaw historian, would help with archival research crucial to identifying the body. The task was also political because it involved maneuvering through state and local authorities, especially the Guthrie City Council, which oversaw the "boot hill" section of Summit View Cemetery. Here, Bill Lehman, with his newspaper connections, would help out considerably. He called upon the state medical examiner, A. Jay Chapman, who expressed interest. Lehman also began an editorial campaign in the *Daily Leader* to drum up local interest, casting McCurdy as a fellow Okie held captive in a bureaucratic no-man's-land. Each, in short, was expert in the ways of the world, in moving and shaking, as it were, in cutting through entanglements.

Returning McCurdy's body to Oklahoma would satisfy two primary motives: It would allow the men of the Saturday morning coffee klatch to dabble in the subject of western history, which was something they all loved and was perhaps the main reason the men gathered in the first place. But perhaps more pressingly, it would serve the cause of greater Guthrie. To sponsor their endeavor, they turned to a variety of historical societies, but none so happily mirrored their own views as a group called Westerners International.

In Westerners International, the spirit of historical inquiry met the spirit of glad-handing, chamber-of-commerce boosterism over plates of chicken à la king. The tone and tenor of Westerners International was set in 1944 by newsman Elmo Scott Watson and Leland D. Case, editor of *The Rotarian* magazine, who formed "corrals" and "posses" of western history enthusiasts in an organization that began meeting in Chicago. For a few hours each month, men could find a place where "western traditions prevailed." Their shrine and eventual mailing address—the Cowboy Hall of Fame in Oklahoma City—suggested the kind of traditions and the brand of west that did the prevailing. They elected officers: a "Sheriff" and his "Deputies"; an "Ink Slinger," or editor; a "Recorder of Marks & Brands," or secretary; a "Keeper of the Chips," or treasurer; and a "Trail Boss," or sergeant-at-arms. They ate and drank and listened to an invited guest speak on some topic of western lore, and they published a newsletter called the *Buckskin Bulletin*. The original meetings of the Chicago Corral, which bore a decidedly Rotarian stamp, were not officially open until two members uncovered "Old Joe," a drawing of a buffalo skull by Charles M. Russell, and everyone stood, "with right hand in Napoleonic posture," and said, "Hello Joe, you old buffalo!" At the end of the night, all would stand and say "Adios, Joe, you old buffalo!" In time, there were corrals in New York City, London, and Paris. Today, in Belgium, one can mosey into the Liege-Les Hommes de L'Ouest and talk turkey with "Sheriff" Cloude Boutigny. There are 120 members of the Mnisek pod Brdy Pony Express Corral and more than 400 members scattered elsewhere in the Czech Republic.

The Westerners' mission statement avows "a dislike for stuffshirtism, over-seriousness, and shiftless thinking." From the start, they displayed a general wariness of academe, long known to be a pocket of equivocation. Yet more or less by default, Westerners International found itself part of the emerging Western Studies scene in the 1970s, which, according to Larry McMurtry, was then made up of "country editors, prairie schoolmarms, county historians, retired lawyers, lone professors here and there, and not a few raving eccentrics." He might have been describing the Indian Territory Posse of Oklahoma Westerners, whose members gathered every month in a banquet room of Val Jean's Restaurant in Oklahoma City. Fred Olds was an elected member, as was Glenn Shirley. Also included among their ranks were professors from Oklahoma State University and the University of Oklahoma as well as members of the Oklahoma Heritage Association and the Oklahoma Historical Society. To shore up these weaknesses, the posse included a number of prominent Oklahoma businessmen, one of whom owned a world-class collection of antique firearms, another a substantial collection of Native American artifacts.

The story of Elmer McCurdy lent itself to the Westerners International sensibility in part because it was, at bottom, not a tragedy but a comedy, one ending with resolution, *after considerable delay*, a comedy of the high macabre. No matter how anyone tried to dress it up, it would remain a comedy, played out, perhaps, under Noguchi's strictures against misbehavior. That Guthrie might become part of that story by bringing it to its logical conclusion was at the front of the minds of the men who were elected to venture forth, like knights-errant of western nostalgia, to Los Angeles. They would bring back McCurdy, who would become an attraction, not exactly in the carnival sense, but not too far from it, either, a piece of history to help build up historic Guthrie. Noguchi, like a schoolmarm, had ordered them to be serious, and so they would wear their serious faces, like Will Rogers scratching his head in mock solemnity. They were connoisseurs of just this sort of posture. They would play down the joke and play up the earnestness. It was the perfect recipe, the clarion call itself, for the Okie put-on, and there could be no clearer sign of a put-on in progress, that a lark had gone a bit further than anyone could have guessed, than the two men walking together down the airport terminal in Los Angeles.

Ralph McCalmont was well suited for his role as "town father" of Guthrie, the sober banker, the civic leader, and in spite of Noguchi's injunction against malarkey, there was a shrewdness in Olds's canoodling cowboy getup, a visual intelligence at work that recognized the rhetorical value of a ceremonial, walkin', talkin', signifyin' cowboy manqué. If in real life Olds was a fund-raising, paper-pushing museum administrator, his hat and boots sought that extra bit of leverage by gesturing toward a past to which McCurdy had never belonged, but by whose symbolic authority Olds nevertheless sought to claim him for greater Guthrie. His was an awareness, finally, of how all of this would play—and look—in print and on television: It would be *cowboy rescues cowboy.*

A public-relations man for the Medical Examiner's Office met the two Oklahomans at the airport and took them to a nearby Holiday Inn. Tomorrow everything would be decided. Their adventure had spun out of itself and become something else, though it also retained, silently, among those who knew better, the germ of its original whimsy. It had gotten serious. And that, McCalmont guessed, was part of the meaning of the big grin on the face of Fred Olds.

Clyde Snow, the third member of the Oklahoma team descending upon Los Angeles that February, also had something to smile about, and in his profession a smile was a rare desert flower. He was a physical anthropologist, one of the few, it was

safe to say, presently working for the Federal Aviation Administration, an agency disinclined for obvious reasons to advertise
too loudly that it had a bone man under its employ. Yet the facts
were what they were. The unlikely, the unthinkable event—a
plane falling from the sky—happened frequently enough, and
when the FAA called his home in Norman, Oklahoma, the news
for Clyde was seldom good.

He was a chain-smoker and drank coffee all day, late into
the afternoon. When I visited him in Norman, Oklahoma, he lit
one cigarette after the other and spoke in a soft Texas drawl that
he wrapped around the terms of his trade. He quietly petted
three large-bodied dogs, a weimaraner and "two road dogs," as
he called them, each as big as a manatee. They breathed
steadily, sighing now and then, nuzzling his shin, as if to say
that, by way of recompense for a life spent climbing into and
out of the grave, one got to have dogs like these dozing and
dreaming at one's feet.

He handed me a coffee mug with a Mexican Day of the
Dead motif—skeletons dancing, singing, making merry—and
spoke about the mood of the investigation. "Well, in the first
place, it was turning into a fascinating case, and everybody was
having fun," he said, pausing for a puff. "I hate to put it that way,
at poor old Elmer's expense, I guess, but it was kind of light-
hearted."

As it happened, Snow had been attending a conference of
the American Association of Physical Anthropology in Seattle,
so it was nothing, really, to stop over in Los Angeles on his return trip to meet with Olds, McCalmont, and the forensic team
that Dr. Noguchi had assembled. Snow explained that he had
been experimenting with a technique called *medial superimposition,*

a useful but time-consuming process by which an unidentified skull, for instance, was superimposed on a photographic image of a missing person. To the trained eye, such a comparison made it clear whether the skull matched the person.

The technique arose, he said, from a lurid murder trial in 1935 in which a prominent English physician, Buck Ruxton, was convicted and hanged for the murder, dismemberment, and scattering of the remains of his wife and nanny all across the English midlands. In the Ruxton case, two pioneers of forensic medicine, John Glaister and J. C. Brash, successfully compared the skulls of the wife and nanny to family photographs.

Up until the 1970s, most superimposition was done using still photography, the skull mounted and arranged in the precise position of a sample photograph. It was painstaking work requiring three or four days to eliminate a single skull from contention, but Snow was often faced with dozens of bodies identifiable only by superimposition. To streamline the process forensics experts incorporated a video camera and a special-effects blender and were soon able to process a skull in fifteen minutes, within a margin of error of 5 percent. With a few phone calls, Noguchi was able to summon from Hollywood the proper equipment and technical support and have it all ready and waiting for Dr. Snow when he arrived.

Dr. Joseph Choi had previously determined the cause of death, a gunshot wound to the chest, and the ticket stubs found in McCurdy's mouth had led the investigation backward in time along a chain of custody to McCurdy's last moments as an active agent of his own will, the shoot-out on the Caney River in 1911. But this chain of custody was, at best, a paper trail

made up almost entirely of hearsay. For the doctors and witnesses standing in the examination room that morning in 1977,
the bottom line was that in 1911, someone who answered to
any number of different names, including Elmer McCurdy, had
been killed. That no death certificate was ever issued suggested
a degree of uncertainty, an unwillingness to commit pen to paper, to legally document, and hence fix, the identity of the bandit under Joseph Johnson's charge. And so, like an open parenthesis, the body had vanished for half a century into the hands
of a group rarely recognized for its allegiance to fact: the
sideshow operators, ballyhoo artists, and cinematic charlatans
of the world.

For Dr. Noguchi, the body's chief custodian in a long and
hapless chain of custodianship, the claim that the Long Beach
mummy was Elmer McCurdy satisfied no reliable, legal, actual,
positive proof of identity. The ticket stub—casually stuffed into
the mouth of the body so many years ago—had led investigators to the former custodian of a body—Dan Sonney—but
whose body was it? Sonney's claim did not constitute positive
proof. Rather, it underscored the degree to which such basic
questions are tethered to pieces of paper. We assume a natural
correspondence that does not exist in nature between the identity in question and the papers that "prove" it, forgetting that
identity is established by convention, is almost entirely based
on somebody's say-so, as Clyde Snow might put it, which can
be truthful or not. When we vanish, we vanish *without a trace*, for
it's the trace or traces that carry the force of identity for an
adopted child, for instance, or for someone in the Federal Witness Protection Program. Yet we know that no matter how we

shuffle the paper, the actual parent or the actual witness still exists—*out there, somewhere,* under a guise, a legal fiction.

As for the body that Clyde Snow was examining, the fact was that no positive proof could be made in 1977, as DNA analysis was still something in the future. What Snow was looking for was a cluster of correspondences between the body in question and certain more or less reliable pieces of paper—Bertillion records, for instance, the system pre-dating fingerprint analysis that required a catalog of physiognomy—height, weight, eye color, scars, tattoos, and any other distinguishing features. Fred Olds had photographs taken of McCurdy after he was killed as well as the photos and the Bertillion records that had been taken after Elmer McCurdy's arrest by the police in St. Joseph, Missouri. These records listed several distinct features, which were compared with the body in the examination room. The St. Joseph records mentioned a deep scar on McCurdy's right wrist, the scar he'd received in the drunken knife fight in Coffeyville after the Iron Mountain train robbery, and also several significant foot bunions.

"There were two things that we knew about Elmer," said Snow. "First, we had his photograph. Secondly, we knew that he had a scar on the right wrist. We knew something about his stature, his age, and sex and race. And the only physical description was a scar either on the right or left wrist, a deep wound.

"So when I got to Noguchi's lab, there he was, his face shrunken some in pretty good shape. We had a photograph of him laid out in profile." This would have been the "casket shot," in which McCurdy had been formally dressed and laid out as if for a funeral. "We also used the image taken of McCurdy when he was standing in the corner of the Johnson Funeral Home," he added. This would have been the photograph taken much later, in which Johnson changed McCurdy back into his old clothes and propped him next to a storage shelf containing embalming supplies. Sometime back in the 1930s, someone had turned this image into a postcard, perhaps in the spirit of the jesting sub-genre whose focus is on some regional point of pride—an Idaho potato, loaded onto a Mac Truck, a Maine lobster as big as a house—or like the old postcards that sideshow freaks sold of themselves for a little extra money—McCurdy transformed into a mummified joke, circulating throughout the U.S. Postal Service system.

"In that photograph," Snow continued, "McCurdy's hands are closed together, in a mummified position. Since there are an infinite number of ways in which the hands of a dead person might be placed, the position of McCurdy's hands would be pretty unique. That was helpful. We were able to get a good match with the cadaveric images of the hands."

Snow and Noguchi worked quickly through the morning, taking photographs, making measurements, using the video equipment, bent to the task at hand, oblivious to everyone else in the room. They were serious, disciplined. McCalmont the banker watched the men work, still a bit woozy from his tour of the security floor below.

After a break for lunch, everyone reconvened to discuss their findings and the evidence before them: his age, determined by sections of the hip bone called the *pubic symphysis*; his general physical description, including scars, bunions, and other tell-tale signs; the images from the superimposition of his skull and hands. All of the evidence coming directly from the body itself was utterly consistent with the Oklahoma team's paper trail of evidence. Snow and Noguchi were convinced, beyond a reasonable doubt, that this was the body of Elmer McCurdy.

Three long-outstanding issues remained in the McCurdy case, two of which were to be completed in an adjacent room, where a lawyer had drafted the necessary documents to return Elmer McCurdy back into the human community. McCurdy had never officially been declared dead, for instance, so Noguchi had the novel experience of filling out a death certificate sixty-six years after the fact. It was a form important for the standard sameness of its questions—date of birth, date of death, cause of death—questions that in the fullness of time will be asked about us all. One of the questions gave Noguchi pause, before he filled it out, gave the document his signature, and passed the form around the room for all to see. The troublesome question had been: Last Known Occupation. The correct response—"train robber"—would have seemed glib. Instead, he wrote "unknown."

The second issue involved the various claimants to the body. Apart from all the crank calls and assorted oddballs inquiring about the Oklahoma mummy, a western history museum in Missouri had made a serious offer to install McCurdy as a permanent exhibit; a number of mortuaries in the Los Angeles area had offered free burial services; and the Long Beach Amusement Company, whose the Laff-in-the-Dark fun-house ride had tripled its business, had placed a discreet request for the return of its mummy. But Noguchi's lawyer, invoking legal precedent going back hundreds of years to Blackstone's formulation, that a cadaver was no one's property, rendered these claims moot. Neither could the Oklahomans present in the room possess or claim McCurdy. Rather, the body would be officially placed under the protective custody of the Los Angeles Coroner's Office to be released only to Oklahoma's state medical examiner, Jay Chapman, or his designated agents—in this case, to Olds, Snow, and McCalmont. But Noguchi required official clearance from Chapman himself. To do this, Fred Olds had to call Bill Lehman in Oklahoma, who then called Oklahoma Senator John Dahl, who in turn placed a call to Chapman. As a final security precaution, to insure that it was, in fact, Chapman and nobody else giving the okay, Chapman then sent a coded message via telegram from his office in Oklahoma City to Noguchi in Los Angeles. Only after decoding the message did Noguchi formally release the body of Elmer McCurdy.

With all the legal paperwork completed, including a freight bill of $127 to ship the body to Guthrie, which Fred Olds paid out of his own pocket, it was time to consider other questions that the examination had raised about McCurdy's death. An earlier histological report prepared by a paleopathologist, Dr. Theodore A. Reyman, in Michigan, analyzed tissue taken from McCurdy's lungs, among other organs, and shed some remarkable light on McCurdy's physical condition in the final hours of his life.

"There was a lot of polymorphic nutrifilic infiltration in the tissue of the lungs," Snow told me. "White blood cells that mobilize during infection. The slides are fantastic. Basically, Elmer was pretty sick when he showed up at the Revard ranch. I guess he'd been going cross-country for a few days, living on whiskey. He may have gotten a little pneumonia."

Along with evidence of incipient pneumonia, Reyman's report indicated that McCurdy was suffering from trichinosis, the result of consuming partially cooked meat such as pork—McCurdy was said to have been living on whiskey and smoked pork while laying idle at the Revard ranch prior to the M, K, & T robbery. Lastly, the slides of his lung tissue suggested a legacy from his days shoveling ore in tri-state zinc mines, the tell-tale calcification of the lungs that signals tuberculosis, the pain of which, like so many before him, he'd tried to ease with a steady flow of alcohol.

Taken together, Reyman's report suggested that McCurdy was in very poor health at the time he was killed, too sick, perhaps, to even mount a horse, let alone make the forty-mile round trip from Revard's ranch to the robbery site near Okesa and back. Reyman's report flew in the face of the mythopoetic juggernaut of McCurdyana—the dozens of newspaper reports at the time of the M, K, & T robbery that identified McCurdy as a participant, perhaps the ringleader; his afterlife career, which had thrust him into the company of mythic western outlawry; and the recent story of his discovery in the Long Beach fun house, which seemed to require, if not demand, a Hollywood scenario—comically inept holdup man flees from the posse, gets killed in final shoot-out—a scenario that made the slow negation of his identity in afterlife all the more poignant. But the physical evidence before the men at the Coroner's Office seemed to flatten out the story considerably, demoting McCurdy from the swashbuckling bandit underdog that we wanted him to be to the sick and defeated alcoholic—the helpless and convenient scapegoat—that he probably was.

For Noguchi, the McCurdy case seemed to excite a number of neural pathways, as it were, which an autocratic, stentorian manner only half obscured. For no matter how much Noguchi might stress the unprecedented opportunities McCurdy's body offered to practice the latest techniques of forensic science, and no matter how much one might argue that Noguchi's penchant for media coverage increased public awareness of the role the Medical Examiner's Office played in public affairs, it was still Noguchi's handsome, telegenic image that was never far from the center of the frame. The televised press conference, for good or ill, had become his pattern, his *metier*, and it was, of course, not a spokesperson, not some subaltern stand-in, but Noguchi himself who chose to reveal the shocking disclosures therein, to shatter expectations, to lower the boom on the American iconography, from Kennedy to Belushi. And when it came to McCurdy, the western outlaw, Noguchi would feel compelled to put his stamp on the moment.

The four of them—Olds in his cowboy garb, Snow, McCalmont, and Noguchi—filed into a large multitiered room and sat down at a table on a small stage to face the glare of the Los Angeles media vortex. There were about 150 press reporters, wire-service writers, and broadcast beauties with their notebooks and microphones and hair spray, along with photographers and cameramen standing elbow to f-stop, all of them radiating a beastly combination of body heat, cologne, and cigarette odor that was nearly tactile. The major network affiliates were there. Lesley Stahl was reporting for the CBS Evening News.

With the press cameras rolling, Noguchi announced that the Coroner's Office had positively identified the body of the fun-house mummy as belonging to Elmer McCurdy, the outlaw from Oklahoma. In his hat and boots, Fred Olds presented a summary of McCurdy's life and afterlife, and he assured the press that the intentions of the Oklahoma delegation were honorable. "Preservation of our history is a big thing with us," Fred Olds said. Clyde Snow addressed the finer points of positive identification. Then Noguchi launched a new theory about McCurdy's death that would trump his own announcement and upstage the rest of the panel. McCurdy, he argued, had been set upon or "bushwhacked" by someone—perhaps the sheriff's posse, perhaps one of McCurdy's associates—while he had lain asleep in a drunken stupor. According to Noguchi, there had been no dramatic shoot-out between an outlaw and the men who put themselves in harm's way to see that justice was done. Rather, this was a simple case of murder.

Ralph McCalmont remembered the moment. "Earlier, before the news conference, Noguchi had broached his theory, to see how we would react." "I don't know if you Guthrie people— you Oklahomans—are going to like this," McCalmont remembered Noguchi saying of the shootout at the Revard ranch, "but I don't think the story is true."

Now, in front of all those cameras and reporters, "you could see the *Quincy* consultant coming out in him," McCalmont recalled. Noguchi waited for Olds to finish recounting the shoot-out at the Revard ranch, then he turned to his colleagues and, in measured tones, brought the hammer down upon a piece of western mythography.

Noguchi's debunking theory gave credence only to the evidence revealed by the autopsy—the track of the bullet downward from the upper right of the chest through the torso and into the hip bone, which Noguchi read as a bullet track made by someone firing a gun while standing over McCurdy, shooting the man while he was down. There was another explanation for the track of the bullet, one that was far more likely, but it required that Noguchi consider the eyewitness statements of people who weren't scientists, of neighboring farmers who were drawn to the Revard ranch by the sound of gunfire and who personally witnessed a shoot-out. Noguchi's experience had long since taught him to discount eyewitness reports, although in this case, statements of the posse members themselves that McCurdy had opened fire *from a position above them* in the Revard hayshed might have urged Noguchi toward a different response.

Of the dozens of witnesses, only one, Frank Revard, Charles Revard's brother, claims that McCurdy was ambushed without so much as a knife to protect himself. It was a strange, incongruous utterance, however, that no other witness corroborated and that no other newspaper in the region repeated. Frank Revard, a mixed-blood Osage, was married to the sister of Lige Higgins, who, for a time, was considered a coconspirator in the robbery. Clearly it was in the family interest to cast aspersions on the methods of Sheriff Freas and his men, to make McCurdy, and by extension, Higgins and his compatriots, appear to be victims of reckless vigilantism.

Another sticking point to Noguchi's murder theory was that it could not explain why the posse would willingly forfeit its reward money, which could only be claimed by the capture of McCurdy, alive. A final scenario—that Amos Hays, or Dave Sears, or perhaps someone else shot McCurdy to keep his mouth shut—suffers for the many complications it introduces into the ordinary run of things while failing to explain something as basic as why a bullet from Stringer Fenton's pistol was taken from McCurdy's body. The fact was that Noguchi's hypothesis required an abundantly complicated and unlikely conspiracy among law-enforcement officials, farmers, ranchers, and other eyewitnesses, none of whom had any interest or incentive to fabricate a shoot-out, in order to cover up a murder. But lights, and cameras, and microphones will do funny things to facts—and, anyway, it was just an educated guess Noguchi was advancing in front of all those people, couched in carefully qualified terms, with many a "maybe" thrown in.

Somewhere that afternoon, in another room, Joseph Choi, the man who had performed the autopsy, who had determined the cause of McCurdy's death, and had tracked the trajectory of the bullet through McCurdy's body, kept his thoughts to himself. He would remain circumspect about many things throughout his career under Noguchi, even after Noguchi underwent a protracted but failed legal battle to retain his post. Even years later in retirement, in a little oasis of avocados and eucalyptus trees in Fallbrook, California, after an afternoon of golf, Choi would not contradict his old boss. Yet, to demonstrate the probable trajectory of the bullet that killed McCurdy in a way that I could understand, Choi would lie prone on the floor of his own dining room, pretending to fire a rifle, as McCurdy had done from the top of the Revard hayshed. When I asked Choi about Noguchi's "bushwhack" theory, Choi paused for a moment. "It is possible," he said, in the way a career scientist might allow that other, similarly extraordinary things might also be possible in this world—angels, for instance, or flying saucers—"it's possible," he said, "but not likely."

## ❧ 11 ❧

# A Dignified,
# If Not Entirely
# Complete, Burial

The mist and rain falling over Guthrie the day of the funeral, clouds backed by more clouds, offered not so much a dawn, per se, as a slow and steady apportioning of light—as if there were an accountant involved in the matter. Nothing jubilant, just a kind of dull, weaselly, parsimonious light, which, in the era of the Kodak Instamatic, had its very own shutter setting: *Cloudy Bright*. It was enough, at any rate, to wake all the cowboys of Guthrie—which included, that day, a cowboy banker, a cowboy museum director, a cowboy newspaper editor, and a cowboy high-school history teacher, among others—and to set them to their cowboy business. Some of them, donning hat and boots and heading out the door, grabbed their Instamatics, and some brought Polaroids. For this would be a big day in Guthrie.

There were other, noncowboy types who brought fancy, expensive-looking gear that went *click-click-click*. These were strangers, journalists mostly and professional cameramen, some

of whom had come, as the locals said, *from as far away as Germany.*
They peeked through the curtains of their motel rooms,
stubbed their toes, and rummaged through their camera bags
making last-minute adjustments of lens and film speed. Others
from local television stations converged from Oklahoma City in
vans and cars, among them a crew from the local CBS affiliate,
presently unaware, as they drank coffee, smoked cigarettes, and
looked out over the bleary, dreary, godforsaken flats of central
Oklahoma, that the story they were about to shoot this morning would, by dinnertime, go national.

Meanwhile, at the Territorial Museum, a cluster of the Indian Territory Posse of Oklahoma Westerners had gathered
around a percolating coffee pot. With slight flourishes and a
varying commitment to "period" garb, everyone wore the standard, hat-and-boots cowboy getup. Bill Lehman added a
sidearm and a fancy black tie and vest; Ralph McCalmont made
up for his businessman's loafers by strapping on a holster and
six-gun; Glenn Shirley's rifle, marshal's star, and a fancy bolo tie
seemed at odds with the professorial effect created by his pipe,
corduroy jacket, and narrow-brimmed hat; John Dahl, U.S.
Senator for the State of Oklahoma, wore a dark business suit,
white shirt, a dark tie, and, for this occasion, the white Stetson,
which picked up his silver sideburns nicely.

By late morning, when it got to be picture-taking time
graveside, and all the photojournalists would swarm upon the
assembled buckaroos, Senator Dahl, with his handsome, chis-
eled features, would look fabulous and comfortable in the saddle, like something out of a Marlboro Man Senior Tour. For
now, though, Senator Dahl readied himself to ride with a cup of

funeral-parlor coffee. His companions in the saddle—George Wayman, the beaked-faced, tobacco-chewing sheriff of Osage County; Jim Cummings, the bespectacled state representative; and Robert Ringrose, Guthrie's mayor—had also spent part of that morning readying themselves for their roles as mounted escorts, or "outriders," who would form the advance guard for the funeral procession of Elmer McCurdy.

At the Summit View Cemetery, a cement truck stood off to the side of a gathering crowd, its great disc turning slowly. Having a cement truck standing by was just one item on a long list of arrangements that the Oklahoma Westerners had been working on at fever pitch for the past few weeks, few more busily than Fred Olds. Indeed, there had been no busier cowboy than he, who had contacted all the dignitaries, written press releases, received the blessing from all the many historical societies. He'd looked far and wide for someone to perform the burial service—all of the local clergy had refused after a *Guthrie Daily Leader* headline editor had innocently substituted the phrase "Christian Burial" for "Decent Burial," in a story Bill Lehman had written about the funeral preparations. The mistake caused such a contretemps, such a rolling, withering blast of high Christian editorial scribbling, that Olds spent weeks smoothing the ruffled feathers of the faithful.

Eventually, he prevailed upon Glenn Jordan, the executive director of the Oklahoma Historical Society and a lay preacher, who agreed to do the graveside honors. With Bill Lehman's help, Olds, among other tasks, had found a horse-drawn, glass-sided hearse that had been sitting in a barn in Stillwater—last used in 1918—and arranged for Truman Moody, who supplied rolling stock for parades around the state, to deliver and drive the hearse. He had found a beautiful coffin, handmade from white pine. He had arranged for the donation of a large tombstone of local pink granite. He had supervised the digging of McCurdy's grave, and he had made arrangements for the cement truck to be at the cemetery on the day of the funeral. He had hung oil portraits of western outlaws on the walls of the Territorial Museum so that when the VIPs arrived that morning the event took on the flavor of an art opening. He'd even thrown in a portrait he'd painted of McCurdy—a stylized, romanticized version of a cowboy who looked very much indeed like Fred Olds himself.

His was an attention to detail fueled by genuine affection. And this, of course, was in part the source of the smile among the men who remembered that first phone call Olds had made to the Coroner's Office on that snowy day back in January. Olds had been kept busy ever since, had managed to rouse an entire region from its sleep, and its representatives from far and wide were arriving that morning looking for coffee to drink and having a good-natured laugh at Olds's expense. After months of work, after all the coordinating and planning, after sitting in on tedious City Council meetings, after cajoling state senators and representatives, after all the paperwork and politicking, Guthrie would enjoy a few minutes of publicity far greater than anything it deserved, whereupon the cement mixer would pour enough concrete into McCurdy's grave to entomb him forever beneath the sod.

More than any of this, however, McCurdy had spent so much time among the living that he'd become a talisman of sorts, his body a visible, oblivion-thwarting artifact, a familiar with peculiar powers, something that stood up fairly well against time, a partial triumph over death. For this alone, one could come to love a mummy. To return him to the earth must have seemed, then, almost like a violation. It had even prompted a poem, set to the tune of "The Streets of Laredo," entitled "Bill Lehman's Lament," a ditty written in jest, but the joke, like the laughter of the men at the museum that morning, admitted the strangeness of the story that was now coming to a close. The song reflected, albeit obliquely, a sadness about McCurdy's imminent departure from the realm of the living, the attachment people felt toward him. It was a rueful separation—and it was as absolute and final as anything could be.

Thus, a little voice of temptation began to work at a few who had gathered there. The thought may have drifted among them listening to the rain in the lull of conversation that a last look at the corpse they'd come to call "Ole Elmer" might be a good idea. One last look, it seemed, for the handful of insiders, the Oklahoma Westerners, the Saturday-morning coffee club that had started all of this mess in the first place. Nobody would ever know the difference, anyhow, and so the motion for a brief, impromptu open-casket viewing was broached, in a joking sort of way. This was quickly shot down by Olds and Jay Chapman, the Medical Examiner for the State of Oklahoma, without so much as a word of explanation. Anyway, it was almost nine o'clock—time for the press conference.

There were reasons for keeping McCurdy's coffin sealed, reasons that transcended propriety. For Chapman and Olds had taken custody of the body the night before on the tarmac of

Will Rogers Airport, and when they'd opened the shipping container, they noticed something was awry. The entire dentition, as pathologists call it, was gone. Someone had forgotten to replace—or had filched—Elmer McCurdy's mouth. The men blinked in disbelief—but there was no mistaking it. His chin was gone. It looked like his neck went straight into his upper lip. With his mouth removed, McCurdy looked like the old cartoon character Andy Gump.

Olds walked to the front of the Oklahoma Territorial Museum to address the press. He wore a dark, broad-brimmed hat, a vest, from which dangled a watch fob, and cowboy boots, into which he'd stuffed his pants. He kept his pipe lit. He was as nervous as a hen worrying over its brood, trying to hold everything together, and perhaps because of this neither he nor Lehman wore a coat that morning. There was just too much to do. Theirs was an attempt to frame the event in terms that would satisfy Noguchi's third mandate, the injunction against a Roman Holiday. What Olds did not say to the assembled press corps, what he could not address without pointing to his own disingenuousness, was what made it a story of its time: its absolute and complete contrivance, shaped and molded for the media, to be covered by the media, which Fred Olds had courted for weeks.

Yet if there was any reason for a news conference—if ever there was something new and newsworthy about this story—surely it would have been the announcement of McCurdy's missing mouth. But this of course would have completely derailed the occasion and distracted everyone from the ceremony, the purpose of which was to do a very simple thing, after all: to bury a body.

There may have been a simple explanation for the missing mouth. According to Jim Njavro, the Los Angeles County Medical Examiner's chief of forensic support, who personally photographed McCurdy's body from head to toe, the jaws of unidentified bodies were routinely held indefinitely by the Los Angeles Coroner's Office, whereas the bodies themselves were sent to the crematorium. Such would have been the fate of Elmer McCurdy had Fred Olds and company not intervened. McCurdy's body had been positively identified, and so the jaw should have been returned. But procedural snafus had occurred before—the body of a John or Jane Doe identified, claimed, and sent back to the family, the jaws inadvertently left behind. In such cases the Coroner's Office would send the jaws by post, where they'd be reunited in a funeral home, wherever the body happened to await interment. If this had happened with McCurdy, then the Coroner's Office would have a record of such a shipment. But no such record exists. McCurdy's jaw may have been left behind by accident and then cremated, or placed in storage, shelved in an archival crypt somewhere—or it may have found its way to someone's home or office, a McCurdy memento mori.

In any case, the missing mouth, so symbolically loaded, would have disrupted the western mythopoetic pageant-in-progress that Fred Olds was so carefully orchestrating that April morning of 1977. Such a disclosure would have amounted to a final indignity visited upon the past by the present. It would have eclipsed the town of Guthrie itself and cast the entire state of Oklahoma in a laughable light. The funeral was just beginning, just developing its own momentum in the clop of hooves and the roll of buggy wheels and the scuffle-shuffle of cameramen trying to keep apace. Now it was too late. The great event was at hand. Now the rhetorical force of ritual, the public spectacle of it all, would become too powerful a disincentive for anyone to speak further of the missing mouth.

Senator Dahl and Sheriff Wayman rode side by side at the head of the procession, followed by several other horsemen, then the glass hearse in which McCurdy rode in his pine coffin, followed by a cortege of buggies carrying McCalmont, Snow, and other dignitaries, then more horsemen, then people walking on foot and cameramen chasing them all, taking aim. Slowly, the procession made its way to the cemetery, where hundreds of people were waiting, and came to a stop near a freshly dug grave, the imprint of the backhoe visible in the reddish Oklahoma clay. The grave was soon encircled. George Wayman, the sheriff of Osage County, had stuffed his cheeks with chewing tobacco, and high upon his horse he was discreetly ruminating from both barrels. Earlier, a photographer had captured Don Odom, a local high-school teacher and history buff, conducting an experiment with his tongue, which he'd torqued hard against the inside of his right cheek to create a passable "tobacco plug" effect. Odom was no tobacco chewer, but he was a stickler for verisimilitude, it seemed—and as the photographers worked the assemblage and pressed lenses into their faces, and the television crews lowered their boom mikes just out of frame and above their heads, Odom worked his tongue to the left, then to the right, with an uncommon assiduousness bordering on valor. And there on the cold, rainy morning, with the wire-service reporters and the local affiliates of all the major networks, and all those cameras and microphones pointed at them, it may have been difficult not to feel a bit ridiculous.

Indeed, the photographs from the funeral capture how often we mean so much more than we intend. One in particular—a group shot with the men lined up like statues. It's almost certain that Odom at the time was simply interested in maintaining his mask of faux chaw—but looking at the photograph, years later, Odom's expression is one of those small details that, once noticed, washes over everything in the frame, undermines the solemnity of the moment to betray the Okie put-on. In this case, it's a visual pun. You can see it in his face, which bears—and delivers—an old expression: *his tongue is firmly planted in his cheek.*

Eighty-one years earlier, a few feet from this very spot, on a late August evening, under stars and the cover of darkness, the time which custom reserved for the internment of paupers, indigents, wards of the community, and other abominations, a widow had held her toddler son and watched as a pine coffin containing her husband was lowered into the ground. Although the widow was the daughter of a local minister from nearby Lawson, no minister of any sort stood by her, and no congregation gathered to comfort her. Just a couple of deputy marshals and a handful of curiosity seekers, who looked on as the sexton filled the grave, one shovelful at a time, the earth drumming off the top of the coffin lid as the widow said, to no one in particular, "Poor Bill. Why did they kill him?"

Her name was Edith Doolin, wife of the late Bill Doolin. Her graveside question was, of course, rhetorical, but other, less sympathetically disposed observers could have provided ample motivation for the death of the most notorious outlaw of the 1890s. There was the matter of the $5,000 reward money for Doolin's capture, dead or alive, which had the effect of turning everyone around him into a potential assassin. Indeed, his own neighbors, Charley and Tom Noble, spied upon Doolin as he made preparations with his family to start a new life in New Mexico, but so formidable was Doolin's reputation as a marksman, the brothers did not dare to make a move against him on their own but instead quietly set up their neighbor and joined in with the ambushing posse led by U.S. Deputy Marshal Heck Thomas. During the gun battle, Tom Noble was so frightened he pumped his unfired cartridges onto the ground. For this, the Nobles received $36.00 apiece.

Bill Doolin had intercepted express trains, had robbed banks, and had outrun, out-shot, and outsmarted the local authorities for four solid years. It was, by comparison to the paths taken by other, better-known outlaws, a career of considerable longevity. Indeed, Doolin's greatest outrage, it seemed, was his efficiency, his ability to regularly interrupt the transfer of wealth from west to east. He was bad for business. Thus, more than any other outlaw of his time, he became the target and primary obsession of a manhunt, the greatest one in the history of the Indian Territories. The search, involving thirty-two deputy marshals and three of the best lawmen in history—Chris Madsen, Heck Thomas, and Bill Tilghman, ended in his capture, by Tilghman, at a health resort in Arkansas Springs. Doolin was brought back alive to Guthrie and paraded around the town for all to see, after which, as if in a sideshow exhibit, thousands of curious citizens passed through Marshal Evett Dumas Nix's office, ogling and shaking the hand of the great outlaw. It was on this occasion that a young woman is said to have remarked aloud, upon meeting Doolin, "That's not him. I just know it isn't. He doesn't even look bad. I could capture him myself," whereupon Doolin supposedly replied, "Yes, ma'am, I believe you could!"

Like so many of his kind, he had been a cowboy for a number of years, a trusted ranch hand, a reliable foreman who had seen to the construction of the 10,000-acre Bar X Bar ranch just north of present-day Guthrie. Then he had run afoul of the law and for a time participated in the depredations of the Dalton gang, until it was wiped out in the ill-conceived double bank robbery in Coffeyville, a raid that he avoided out of orneriness or a twist of fate—nobody knows for sure. He survived at least five gun battles, but they'd left him with a shattered right heel and a bullet that had struck his temple and lodged over his eye.

After Tilghman captured him, Doolin escaped from the Guthrie jail and fled to his wife and child. In August 1896, having loaded his family onto a wagon, he got on his horse and rode just 500 yards into his new life before being ambushed. A blast from an 8-gauge shotgun knocked him off his horse, killing him. Tom Noble took Doolin's body to the Rhodes furniture store in Guthrie, where an undertaker put the body on public exhibition before thousands of people, and a photographer named Bruce Daugherty took the famous picture of the bearded, bedraggled Bill Doolin, naked to the waist, eyes open, buckshot the size of twenty-five-cent pieces riddling his chest, in what has become a standard image of the end of the western outlaw.

As with other endings—the end of the buffalo, the end of the frontier, the paddlewheel steamer, the railroad—when the public sensed that something had been lost, it triggered a nostalgic wind swirl, which in this case lofted Doolin upward into American iconography. In nearly every popular anecdotal instance, Doolin is remembered betraying a dignity and honor beneath a tough veneer. He was courteous, apologizing to the farmer whose wagon he and Dynamite Dick stole during the Guthrie jailbreak. He was magnanimous in the old Robin Hood trope. At an isolated water stop near present-day Perry, Oklahoma, Doolin reimbursed E. Bee Guthrey, a Stillwater newspaperman, for what amounted to taxi fare for the last leg of his trip home, rather than leave the man stranded in the middle of nowhere. In a second run-in, Doolin asked the price of subscribing to Mr. Guthrey's newspaper. Guthrey told him it was a dollar a year, whereupon Doolin lobbed a handful of coins from a bulging sack. Eleven silver dollars fell to the ground. When Guthrey asked where he should send the newspapers, Doolin is said to have answered, "Send it to Ingalls until you hear that I'm dead, then send it to hell." George W. Stiles recalled a boyhood encounter with the Doolin gang that would, by today's standards, amount to kidnapping, but back then it seemed, to the young Stiles at least, like an evening's grand diversion. Fleeing from a recent crime, the outlaws scooped up the boy by the roadside and told him that the gunfire he'd heard was just them "shooting to hear the old dog bark." They offered the boy a drink of whiskey, which he declined, and then, after considerable debate about what to do next, let the boy go, commending him for his bravery. Whether or not the stories are true seems beside the point, which was, after all, about the creation of a myth—about people investing the better part of themselves into the life that Doolin led.

Bill Tilghman, in his 1915 movie, *The Passing of the Oklahoma Outlaws,* contributed to Doolin's continued notoriety, although local sentiment remained guarded. For six decades after his death, the Guthrie community deemed it fit to mark Doolin's grave with nothing more than a buggy axle. Then a longtime admirer and biographer bought a handsome tombstone of pink granite. Of course, Doolin had done much to earn his place in the roster of famous outlaws. But now, directly beside Doolin, a second, identical tombstone of pink granite had been erected, a crowd having closed in around the pine casket resting on two-by-fours over the grave, lowering ropes at the ready, cameras clicking away.

"Such a moment as this," Glenn Jordan said, his voice muffled by the surrounding hundreds of onlookers, "causes us to remember the past which spawned such a man and our ancestors, many of whom were his contemporaries."

Jordan reiterated a past that was familiar to everyone standing there—the Indian who "struggled in vain to maintain his land, . . . the soldier who came to pacify, control, and faithfully serve, . . . the cattleman who laid the foundation of the great Oklahoma cattle industry." It was the high-school textbook litany, the historical pageant of homesteaders, ministers, miners, lawmen, and outlaws, all receiving silent approval from the bowed and hatless heads standing around McCurdy's grave. All was quiet but for Jordan's voice and the whir and click of film rushing to record the moment under the darkening Oklahoma skies.

Then Jordan turned the formulaic historical palliative upon itself. He leveled his gaze upon the selfsame cattlemen, farmers, miners, and roughnecks and reminded everyone present of the shame and folly of much of Oklahoma history. The town of Guthrie separated the unwanted dead from the respectable dead, and Boot Hill was the last place of rest for the miscreants of the past, of which McCurdy had to be counted, but Jordan's eulogy also reminded everyone present that that distinction was a social nicety that wouldn't bear up today under much scrutiny. This was the Sooner State, after all, a term designating those who, to attain a share of the franchise, lied, cheated, or stole their way in advance of honest folk. "Do not judge others, and God will not judge you," Jordan had said at the beginning of his eulogy, quoting from Luke. Then he said Amen, and everyone put their hats on, and they lowered McCurdy into the ground. A young girl dropped a single rose onto the coffin. And when everyone had more or less dispersed, the cement mixer backed up and dumped two yards of concrete into the grave.

It was April 22, 1977. The funeral coincided with the annual 89ers Day parade in celebration of the famed Oklahoma land run. In a matter of hours, Guthrie, Oklahoma, would be writ large across the region and would make *The Evening News with Walter Cronkite*, even as McCurdy's name flashed over the wires. But not everyone was pleased with what they saw that day. On April 26 the Guthrie Chamber of Commerce received a letter from B. J. Thatcher, of Lawton, Oklahoma.

"Sirs," Thatcher began. "I viewed the burial of the Outlaw McCurdy on television last evening and I have never seen a more blatant display of commercialism and vulgarity in my long life. I am reminded of a former Comanche, Oklahoma, funeral director, who displayed the body of mass murderer Billy Cook in his funeral home. Placed at the foot of the casket was an offering plate in which viewers could place a 'contribution' to help 'defray expenses.' One cannot help but wonder if this same funeral director has moved to Guthrie."

It was a minority opinion that went unrecorded and unheard, despite Jordan's own thoughtful remonstration, which soon enough gave way to the 89er Day festivities—as the drums and the marching bands from across the state and the food stalls and the mock shoot-out held every hour, on the hour, helped to complete McCurdy's long-awaited election, just this side of apotheosis, into the bandit hall of fame.

## ✎ 12 ✎

# McCurdyana:
# Swirl and Vortex

In years to come, when the subject came up, people spoke with greater candor about the return of McCurdy's body to Guthrie, in the way that one might confess to one's parents, long after the fact, some youthful indiscretion. With McCurdy safely buried in perpetuity, some Guthrie residents would recall, with a smile, the delegation that was sent to Los Angeles, the high-minded speeches thereafter, the antiquarian burial procession, the whole Okie put-on that Fred Olds had orchestrated so many years ago. "We thought it would bring interest to our community," Olds told a reporter in 1991. To see McCurdy's grave, Olds said, "people came from all over the world." One couple got married in front of McCurdy's tombstone. Noguchi himself had inspected the site on a later visit to Guthrie that coincided with the annual 89er Day Festival, in which he'd served as a parade marshal, waving to the crowd in his cowboy hat and boots. Notwithstanding McCurdy's missing mouth, a fact long forgotten these many years, the grave had become a cool, weird, and free tourist attraction that benefited Guthrie indirectly. According to the economic mantra of heritage tourism, each tourist dollar Guthrie captured circulated up to seven times within the greater Guthrie community. But it took an aggressive player like Becky Luker, an outsider from Santa Fe, New Mexico, to discover how to connect the dots, as it were, to profit directly from McCurdy's enduring, residual fame, and in the process to stir up a controversy that launched McCurdy again onto the national stage.

Luker was a take-charge kind of woman in a take-charge kind of time—during Guthrie's renaissance as a tourist town. The aluminum siding was coming down, the beautiful red brick buildings of Foucart were emerging, and the era that would make Guthrie the official bed-and-breakfast capital of Oklahoma was just about under way. The only problem was that few Guthrians cared much about tourism, or understood the dynamics of the tourism game, and by the time they did care they were obliged to do so on terms that Luker, the outsider, the arriviste, had set for them.

Luker arrived in 1986, purchasing, restoring, and opening the Stone Lion Inn just months before a group of local investors could open an establishment called the Harrison House. Luker thus beat out the hometown crowd for the distinction of being Guthrie's first bed-and-breakfast establishment, and in the process she made for herself some instant and powerful enemies.

She was the kind of person who tended to raise eyebrows, a slender, self-possessed woman with a degree in philosophy and theology who was also completely at ease working with a construction crew. She could curse like a sailor, discuss St Augustine, hang Sheetrock, and harangue a subcontractor, often simultaneously. She had money and ambition, and she was, for some, that most worrisome sort of stranger, *a divorcee*. Worse still, she was an innovator, and she was anything but low key about her innovations.

Her idea for a Murder Mystery Weekend, for instance, was unique to the entire region, let alone to the people of Guthrie. To those still bound by the constraining codes of small-town life, Luker's brand of advertising may have seemed a little slick, perhaps even a little indecorous. She was media savvy. She understood the bally. She cultivated spook-house rumors about the Stone Lion Inn—stories that appeared in the *Daily Oklahoman* one Halloween in 1989, the year she began writing her murder mysteries—about the ghosts of dead children walking the floors at night. It was all meant, of course, to appeal to the wide world beyond Guthrie itself, to dentists and bank managers in Oklahoma City and the enlightened, college-town folk of Stillwater and Edmond, but her ghost stories cut the wrong way at home. Not only was she unsubtle, her style challenging the modest way one was supposed to go about one's business in a small town, she also seemed tone deaf to the fact that Guthrie had long since become a stronghold of hard-shell Christian fundamentalism of the sort that could be deeply troubled by cavalier talk about ghosts and devils.

Hoping to attract weekend business, the former English teacher wrote a script for the first Murder Mystery Weekend that revolved around Elmer McCurdy and included a funeral-like motorcade procession to the graveyard, the guests' car headlights turned on as they drove through Guthrie. At the Summit View Cemetery, Luker would sketch the outlines of

McCurdy's outlaw life and afterlife and sometimes conduct seances or ask guests to pray over McCurdy's grave. Next, someone would find a dead body (a life-sized, rag-stuffed doll) in the trunk of a car. Back at the Stone Lion Inn, Ouija boards and skulls and other ghoulish paraphernalia would be employed as the guests solved the murder mystery that Luker directed and choreographed. Having studied their roles in advance, the guests would be handed an index card on which Luker had typed scripted lines, to be read and "acted out" in the library, with Luker as "Kate Curare"—as in, the blackish tropical resin used for poisoning arrows—poking and prodding the program along. It was a new kind of chemistry. She pushed the forced intimacy of the whole bed-and-breakfast experience to its absurd extreme and lobbed enough bawdy suggestions and double entendres into the evening to make grandmothers and even churchgoing middle managers shriek with delight.

Luker's brochure trumpeted "bathrooms with clawfooted tubs," a library with "leaded glass bookshelves," and grounds in which one was invited to "sit in the gazebo and enjoy watching the squirrels." Her success was based in part on her shrewd targeting of a generation for whom "squirrel watching" might be an actual item on a day's agenda of things to do, and upon the insight that people generally enjoyed being bossed around, being scolded and ridiculed and mocked in front of others. When her guests stood up and botched their lines or proved that their eyesight was failing them, when they over-performed and Kate Curare sent the bad actors packing, the peals of laughter that followed them for having run the evening's gauntlet of humiliation was the product that Luker delivered each weekend along with after-dinner dessert and breakfast in the morning.

The Stone Lion Inn became a tremendous success, which many Guthrians noticed with varying degrees of irritation. Guests at the Harrison House would see the motorcades going out to the cemetery and ask about the murder mysteries and may have wondered why they weren't being offered something similar. Even if they wanted to, which they did not (such behavior was deemed unprofessional), the Harrison House proprietors could not respond in kind, of course, without seeming to copy Luker. To make matters worse, Luker had more business than she could handle. She sent business to the Harrison House in the form of spillover guests, whom the Harrison House put up—or put up with. It was just plain irksome. Others in town were alarmed by the ritualistic goings-on at the cemetery. Rumors began to fly, even as the regional press celebrated Luker's innovative business style. Luker also began moving upward among Guthrie's social and political power base, eventually getting herself elected to the Guthrie City Council. With the help of like-minded progressive council members, she pushed forward a tourism-friendly agenda that by October 1990 began to backfire. Old-time Guthrie residents began calling for her ouster. Suits were filed, a recall campaign was mounted, and then, in late January 1991, the first shot in the Bed-and-Breakfast War was fired.

One of Luker's guests was so traumatized by the bawdiness of a murder mystery script that he wrote a letter of complaint to the Guthrie Chamber of Commerce about "the adult nature of Luker's murder mystery." The man, who happened to be staying as an overflow guest at the Harrison House, complained to Phyllis Murray, the Harrison House's manager. Luker, it seemed, had finally stepped far enough over the line of bed-and-breakfast professionalism to warrant action. And so, according to the *Daily Oklahoman*, which covered the story, Murray wrote her own letter complaining of Luker's unprofessionalism and sent it to the City Council, to local banks, to the Chamber of Commerce, to the board of the Harrison House, and many other places. The return volley from Luker was swift. She promptly filed a $200,000 suit against Murray and the Harrison House for defamation of character. Then, in March 1991, someone—it is not clear who—unleashed a devastating salvo, revealing to the City Council that Luker was a convicted felon who could not legally hold public office as a City Council member.

It was all true. In 1981, while in New Mexico, Luker had apparently falsified collateral for a $10,000 loan from a New Mexico savings and loan. The case had dragged on until 1989, three years after Luker had moved to Guthrie, when she pled guilty and was sentenced to four years' probation. Strangely enough, in that same year, Jane Thomas had written a letter on Luker's behalf recommending leniency—that is, probation—for her. Since then, however, things had obviously soured between the two women, and now Thomas watched as her business rival was forced to resign from her City Council seat in disgrace.

Her enemies smelled blood. Luker and her guests were soon heckled at the Summit View Cemetery during performances of Elmer McCurdy murder mysteries. A group of protesters had formed, some with Bibles in their hands "This is nothing but devil worship," one protester shouted. "This is a cemetery, not a public place." Others sat in their cars and scowled. Luker's guests apparently thought it was all part of the show. "Where did you get those actors?" one of them asked. "They're fabulous!"

Then, at a special session of the City Parks and Cemetery Committee, Luker and her attorney, Richard O. Burst, faced her accusers. The latter were upset that Luker's guests wore black into the cemetery. They were upset that, as part of the Murder Mystery Weekend script, a body was discovered in the trunk of a car—never mind that it was a dummy stuffed with rags. They were upset that the script called for mock prayers at the graveside, conducted by mock priests—one of which was supposed to be an American Indian. It was disrespectful and blasphemous and enough was enough. The churchgoers seemed to have the sympathy of the Parks Committee chairman, Bill Reed.

"Nothing would burn me more than to pull over for a funeral procession and find it wasn't," Reed said.

Luker explained that the car lights helped prevent her guests from getting separated on the drive across town. She had stipulated a black dress code, she added, so that her guests would not show up at the graveyard wearing cocktail dresses, for instance, which, she said, would be disrespectful.

"You find cocktail dresses offensive but not mock prayers?" Bill Reed asked.

Someone suggested that Luker take her guests somewhere other than the cemetery, but Luker responded that Elmer McCurdy and his grave were central to the script she had written. He and the grave were the very reason her guests had traveled to Guthrie in the first place. "McCurdy's grave," she said, was "real, it was located at the cemetery, and was meant to be there as a tourist attraction."

The problem facing her detractors, it seemed, was how to write public policy narrow enough to target Luker specifically while honoring the language and the spirit of the Bill of Rights. The sticky issues of equal protection under the law, freedom of speech, and due process had all become, in the heat of the moment, fanciful and meddlesome ideas, imposed by outsiders having nothing to do with goings-on in Guthrie. City Attorney Ron Hudson tried to mollify the crowd. The Parks Committee chairman turned in his seat.

"The whole thing is pretty narrow," Reed said. "I'm about to change the hours at the cemetery and put a stop to the whole thing."

"You just killed the Edmond Girl Scouts' retreat out there every year."

"You can't take away someone's rights. If you get too strict it will keep the American Legion and VFW out."

"Does this mean that passion plays no longer will be allowed in the cemetery?"

The silence that followed seemed to rise up in Becky Luker's defense. Could the people of Guthrie prevent her from visiting Elmer McCurdy's grave yet allow Girl Scouts to frolic among the tombstones? Luker and Burst were facing a group of neighbors rallying each other like a herd of cornered musk oxen, each making a fearful little charge against the two strangers with their dangerous, disrespectful voodoo Bill-of-Rights high jinks. It was two against twenty-five, including one of Luker's most vocal critics, Jim Rosencutter, whom the *Daily Oklahoman* seemed to capture just as the Holy Ghost took possession of his mind. "What the Bible says could happen to her if she practices witchcraft," Jim Rosencutter thundered, ominously.

The brimstone and thunder would carry over into the City Council meeting the next week, where hundreds of spectators packed City Hall chambers to hear the debate over the proposed changes in the cemetery ordinance. CNN was covering the story by now, and all the local affiliates to the networks were there. Jim Rosencutter was there. He singled out Richard Burst and wondered aloud if Burst's own father were not now ashamed of him. Burst and his father were anything but ashamed. Nor was Burst intimidated by the crowd spilling out into the halls. He had, after all, recently and successfully argued a First Amendment case in the U.S. Supreme Court. What he saw here in the City Council chambers was nothing more than a spectacle, a prairie fire. The challenge, for him, would be to hold his tongue. He looked around the room. Fred Olds was trying his best to smooth everything out, but the situation had gotten beyond Olds's considerable diplomatic scope. Olds stood up to speak.

"We want Guthrie to be a great little city. Let's not spoil it with something stupid. People all over the country will sit back and laugh at us."

The boosterish gospel that had brought McCurdy to Guthrie in the first place, so many years ago, was now laced, as anyone could tell by looking at Olds, with a mixture of fear and exasperation. A week before, CNN had descended upon Guthrie for its first installment of the Bed-and-Breakfast War, a story that threatened to paint the town as a kooky hotbed of witch burners and religious nuts. Olds needn't have worried, for the dimensions of this particular story would be foreshortened, its absurdity flattened into mere quirkiness by the narrowing prerogatives of the television sound bite. CNN would flash but a few seconds of Luker's detractors, each of whom drawled their Okie drawls behind oversized sunglasses that seemed designed to dim the Second Coming. The last shot of the broadcast showed Luker standing at McCurdy's grave giving her spiel to her weekend guests, all dressed in black, who in turn were surrounded by a watchful, hovering group of people holding Bibles and listening intently lest any blasphemous line squeak past and disturb the dead. But the broadcast riled up Luker's antagonists, who arrived in force at City Hall. Fred Olds finished speaking, and Jane Thomas took the floor.

"There is no history in the cemetery," she said, adding that the headstones of McCurdy's and Doolin's graves were new and of "no visual historical significance." Thomas may have been a bit flustered. She had refused comment to the press, which had, in turn, focused itself on the media-friendly Luker. In point of fact, McCurdy had had nothing to do with Guthrie. Moreover, McCurdy's tombstone, identical to that of Bill Doolin's, had a visual effect that, indeed, to a historian like Thomas, so overstated McCurdy's place in history as be a gross misrepresentation; that is to say, a lie. But the point that Thomas was trying to make about historical authenticity was lost, it seems, in the heat of the religious squabble that was about to boil over.

When Luker spoke up to defend herself, she was roundly jeered by the crowd, who called her "a spawn of the devil" and "the devil's concubine."

It was a strange thing to have to say, here, in the last decade of the twentieth century, but Richard Burst rose up as well and addressed the Guthrie City Council. "My client is not involved in witchcraft," he said. Burst explained that the cemetery was public property, like City Hall, like the Public Library.

"Now, can you keep a Catholic from entering the public library?" he asked the crowd. A balloon of silence drifted by.

"Can you keep a Jew from entering city hall?" The answer, of course, was no. The town could not prevent anyone from entering these places—including the cemetery—based on who they were or what they believed in. "She can worship a box of Tide detergent," Burst concluded with a flourish, "and there isn't a damn thing you can do about it."

The squabble continued for weeks. Thomas, appearing before the Chamber of Commerce, bragged that she could get Luker's federal case in New Mexico reopened. But the Chamber demurred, and, after all the fuss, it turned out Luker had never, in fact, violated the terms of her probation. A milder city ordinance was passed that did not forbid Luker from taking tours into the cemetery, but charged her a usage fee, which Luker thwarted by purchasing the lots next to McCurdy's grave. Now that she owned a grave site, she could come whenever she wanted, it seemed, and nobody could do a thing about it. Her enemies within the community continued to pester her with citations for building-code violations and other thorns designed to make her life miserable, but Luker held her ground and walked through Guthrie's cleansing fire of opprobrium.

I pulled up in front of the Stone Lion Inn, a large, two-story, white Victorian house just west of Cottonwood Creek, a deep gully dividing the more fashionable Red Brick Historic Guthrie from a residential neighborhood that had seen better days. Indeed, the house seemed like a historic island that had been surrounded by houses of an almost ahistorical blandness. A series of steps led from the curb past a large, overhanging pecan tree, then up to a wraparound porch where a dozen or so people stood in awkward groups of two or three.

It was a warm, balmy evening in June, the sound of cicadas rising and falling in dozing, hypnotic waves. It was seersucker and sarsaparilla weather, yet everyone on the porch looked ready for a ball in October of some previous century, which is to say, they were wildly overdressed in dark formal frills, in Gibson Girl gowns, and coats too heavy for the season. The house had a widow's walk with a view across the street of yards strewn with plastic kiddie toys and children staring at the odd people dressed up on the porch. All was hushed, and my arrival seemed to present something of a distraction from the general funereal awkwardness. I sat in my car. I was not quite ready for this, not quite able to unbuckle my seatbelt, put on my sunglasses, and assume the role I had been assigned to play for the entire evening. I wasn't ready, though a few months before I had asked for this to happen, had practically begged Becky Luker to arrange for my benefit an Elmer McCurdy Murder Mystery Weekend.

The name itself had been too much to resist. I knew that if I went to Oklahoma and failed to participate in the Elmer McCurdy Murder Mystery Weekend, it would hound me the rest of my days. So I booked a room but was told by Becky Luker's secretary that the staff rotated through different murder mystery scripts, depending upon the number of guests, and so she couldn't promise me anything, McCurdywise, which caused me no small amount of worry. Then, just a week before my departure, Becky's secretary left me a message: "Okay," she said, in triumph, "I have you down for the 23rd, *and we will do Elmer on that night.*"

*Doing Elmer*—the phrase stayed with me for the two weeks I spent car camping in the Osage, a trip that was funded, after all, *because of* Elmer McCurdy. Because he had once existed, because he had then stopped existing. Because he had, moreover, stopped existing and had continued for such a long time to stop existing and in such a miraculous and spectacular way that do-ing Elmer had become over the years a cottage industry for so many. From Joseph Johnson, the funeral director of Pawhuska, displaying McCurdy for a nickel a throw, to the smooth-talking, body-snatching Mr. Avers of the Great Patterson Shows, to the many nameless, mid-century sideshow operators and exploita-tion filmmakers, to a dozen other latter-day artists and -interested parties—playwrights, balladeers, documentary film-makers, poets and writers—Becky Luker and myself included—the doing of Elmer continued into the third millennium, holding out the promise of profit, of windfall, of career opportunity at McCurdy's expense. In the constellation of meaning around the phrase, there was a gangland, murder-for-hire sense at work, and there was also, inescapably, the odd, pornographer's boilerplate for raw, gratuitous sex, such that *doing Elmer* attained an ex-tremely awkward conflation of senses that somehow, at least metaphorically, described the biographer's business of appropri-ation. It was not beyond the scope of most biography, it seemed, to kill and screw the subject. All of this meant, for the corpse in question, getting *screwed over, exploited unfairly, messed with,* and there I was, his most recent beneficiary, glancing over my shoulder along the great daisy chain of Elmer's doing, feeling both ashamed of myself and enthralled by what would happen next.

I had received a fax from the Stone Lion Inn that gave me my first taste of the weekend ahead. "Upon your arrival," it said, "you will assume the role of VITO MATUCCI. When you arrive, assume your character and do not leave that role for the entire evening. A short biography of your role and the other guests is attached." There were dozens of additional characters on nine pages of single-spaced paper. They had names like Bobby Burnes, Gloria Goodbody, and Thornton Pennypincher. There was a Paula Pureheart and a Doris Dimwitty and a Barbie Dohl, and in keeping with the Agatha Christie–like *whodunnit* scenario, each had something to hide, not the least of which was the desire to chisel each other out of a share of the inheritance of Elmer McCurdy.

"It is imperative," the fax continued, "that you study your role and the other bios thoroughly. Do not discuss your role with anyone prior to the event. You must reveal to no one your true identity or that of your spouse or mate. (Do not discuss your real-life job, children, pets, nothing!) STAY IN CHARACTER!" Included with the fax was an "Elmer McCurdy Genealogy," which was to McCurdy's actual life what the Easter Bunny is to the crucifixion of Christ. In a day or two, it seemed, I would engage in a bit of dress up and weekend role playing with some couples from Oklahoma City, and I had nobody but myself to blame.

The light of an early summer evening vanished quickly into shadows, and I could tell that the people on the porch were watching to see who I would be. The trouble was, I wasn't sure myself. On the fourth page of the information packet, I saw the name Vito Matucci—"Rather shady background. Vito is in Guthrie visiting his sister and looking into some business opportunities. Rumor has it he has Mafia connections." The dress code for men was black—dark suit and bow ties preferred. All I had was a pair of dark sunglasses and a cigar I'd bought to smoke under the stars. I had sandals and a pair of dark socks. I had a rumpled gray sport coat that I'd worn on the flight from Newark. Everything else was camping gear. From this I constructed the best Vito Matucci I could. Distilled to its essence, it was a sort of casual Sammy "The Bull" Gravanno look, had Sammy pursued the great outdoors in the witness-protection program.

I walked up the steps—in character—and cut through the crowd without saying hello. It was rude of me, but I didn't think Vito Matucci would bother to say hello to a bunch of Okies. I thought it best to say as little as possible, but I could not avoid the young woman who approached me where I sat alone in the library.

"Vito?" she said. "Vito Matucci?"

"Who wants to know?" I said.

"It's me, Victoria," she said.

I looked at her blankly. I had not studied my role and the other bios thoroughly. This was all starting to feel like a bad dream.

"Victoria, your sister, who lives in Chicago?" she said, helpfully.

"Oh, yes," I said. "Of course. Sweetheart! How are ya?"

What can one say about a weekend dress-up party with strangers other than that it was no less strange, I imagined, than a spouse-swapping session, say, no less odd than if a woman dressed as a nun had buttonholed me—as she did, later, at McCurdy's graveside, when she placed her foot on the bumper of my rental car and suggestively showed me some leg. It was all in good fun, of course. The woman was playacting. It was her way of conveying her part in a story line that included me. According to Luker's script, she was Sister Anna Tornick, who years ago had been Vito Matucci's lover. She'd been hit by a car, however, and remembered nothing of the affair or the child she'd had by me. She was also a drunk, and the woman playing Sister Anna expressed this by listing slightly over my car as she winked lasciviously and pulled her dress above her knee with all the subtlety of a whorehouse come-on, exposing a pale ham hock of thigh, by which gesture I was meant to understand, it seemed, that "Sister Amnesia," as she was also called, was getting her memory back.

It was just one of many moments that night in which I was jolted back into my Vito character, as if I were attached by a length of chain to the bumper of the farce that Luker had written for us. I straggled along behind, trying to keep apace, but every now and again received a sharp yank as the chain grew taut. By the time we'd solved the murder mystery, we'd shucked off our characters and were chatting amiably about life in Oklahoma City, which was where most of the guests were from. There was a banker and a bookseller, and an undertaker who had once been an investigator for the Los Angeles County Coroner's Office. The undertaker presented Luker with a plaque bearing the official shield of the Coroner's Office, which he'd purchased from its gift shop, "Skeletons in the Closet." I sat in the kitchen with Luker, who told me stories about growing up in the Southwest with a father who believed in The Bomb. He'd helped build it at Los Alamos and died at a young age of cancer. She'd grown up with a bomb shelter in the backyard. "You could buy them at the local state fair," she said. Soon it was late. The banker and the undertaker had gone to bed, and the rest of us went our separate ways for the night.

The next morning I felt *off task*, in the extreme. With the Murder Mystery Weekend, I had strayed about as far from my stated subject as one could, I had found myself floating at the apogee of a broad elliptical orbit of McCurdyana, as far from the real McCurdy, it seemed, as Pluto from the sun, and I was looking for some way back to the man.

I drove through Guthrie under the kind of sky that must have always seemed strange to him. There was just too much of it, and while it was sunny in town, a line of anvil-headed clouds to the north lofted themselves several miles straight up into the atmosphere and rolled across the plains, their colossal shadows gobbling up whole sections and townships, the wheat fields of the countryside throwing off light in battered waves of rust and coppery swirls and unripened, half-acre pockets of wind-clobbered, key lime green.

I'd learned that the resident prognosticators at the Center for the Analysis and Prediction of Storms in Norman, Oklahoma, use real data from whatever real storm they happen to be tracking to

construct the storm's double, which whirls around inside a computer and helps scientists guess where the storm will go and what
it will do next. But these same scientists couldn't tell you, of the
hundreds of big, angry storms blowing across the state each year,
which will blow over like an angry, chained-up dog, and which
will suddenly land on your head, dealing death and destruction
from the sky. Sometimes, a small event in the calculus blossoms
into a computer model that has nothing to do with the actual
winds knocking down farms and destroying trailer parks, a state
of affairs known as a "bifurcation."

I pulled into the Summit View Cemetery, looking at the
sky and thinking about my own peculiar wind swirl of fact and
fancy, my own congeries of error and degrees of bifurcation,
the shade of exploitation in my own project that suddenly
seemed not as far removed from the McCurdy Murder Mystery Weekend as I would have liked it to be. I thought of the
tug of myth that had kept a body on the sideshow circuit for
so long, that had brought it back to Guthrie under the guise of
"historical interest," and that was simply—and mostly—
another version of the bally, the one gravitational constant
you can count on in this world, that made McCurdy's story a
fable for our time. The wind swirl of McCurdyana seemed
clear to me that morning. What did not seem clear at all was
the man I'd been tracking for so long.

His mug shot had been on the wall near my desk back home
for two years and I hadn't bothered to really look at it for a long
time. It was taken, of course, by a policeman in the Buchanan
County Jail in St. Joseph, Missouri, 1910. McCurdy appears
slightly disheveled but handsome, and there's still something of

a spark in his face. The police photographer probably ordered McCurdy to look straight ahead into the camera, and it says something that his eyes, instead, dart downward slightly and to the right. He may have felt, being just out of the Army, that he didn't have to take orders from anyone anymore, his incarceration notwithstanding. He does not stare, as other outlaws did, in outward contempt. And in truth, he was not yet an outlaw. He still wore his army uniform. He was in between careers, on the cusp, the pointed end of something nobody could have invented, and he'd temporarily hit a rough patch, it seemed. But this instant had him cornered, captured, caught undeniably on the wrong side of things, and there was no remedy for it but to look away, his gaze a form of flight from the click of the shutter and the lock and the key of the slammer. And there for anyone with eyes to see is how he felt about himself. He was ashamed. He would hide from it in other ways, mostly in drink, stumbling along for the next few months, until he was literally cornered and could run no more. His lips make a thin line, turned down at the ends—not a frown exactly, and not exactly a sneer. It's not resignation, nor bemusement, but an option on an emotion to be named later, say, when hell froze over.

His body, for those trained to read the signs, spoke oceans about the man. As a matter of course, he seems to have put up with an amount of daily physical discomfort that few of us today would tolerate for any length of time. And he found his remedy in alcohol, which addressed several ailments at once— the painful bunions on his feet, the trichinosis in his stomach, the pneumonia and tuberculosis in his chest. But alcohol preceded all of that; alcohol, the one constant theme running through his short life. That he liked to drink, that he drank to excess, is the one, slender piece of information about him that his contemporaries noticed and remarked upon. And it doesn't seem accidental that his penchant for drink asserted itself at age fifteen, with the revelation about his questionable parentage. Charles Davis, Sadie McCurdy's cousin, was rumored to have been Elmer's natural father, a claim that one might discount, rumors being what they are. By the time Elmer learned the truth about his mother—that Sadie, not Elizabeth McCurdy, was his actual mother—Charles Davis was long gone.

It seems more than coincidence that Elmer's drinking career began shortly after this, and hardly surprising that his first scrape with the law shortly thereafter—the barroom brawl in Belfast, Maine—was fueled by alcohol. It claimed him, in its ineluctable way, and changed him, and by the time he was twenty he began using "Charles Davis" and various anagrammatic permutations as aliases. In name, at least, he sought the protective cloak of the vanished man who might have been his father, and he moved west, like so many others, to escape that part of his past. But his emptiness moved with him, and try as he did, no amount of alcohol would fill it. The west and its frontier that helped shape the American character destroyed McCurdy and spat him out.

What McCurdy would have said—had he a mouth to say it with—was anybody's guess. The missing mouth was indeed another puzzlement, among so many, complete closure forever beyond him. Indeed, larger forces than anyone knew seemed to be pushing McCurdy into the realm of the emblematic, perhaps even into a kind of mythically comic incompleteness, an updating of Zeno's Paradox. I foresaw a time when McCurdy's name would be used for a variety of phenomena that as yet did not have a name, a "McCurdy" or perhaps an "Elmer" as that last bit of a sandwich, for example, left on the plate, that last half swallow of milk lingering in the carton, that stub of a pencil abiding forever in a desk. Was it possible that now, in circulation somewhere, a mouth was being quietly held and hoarded by some keeper of last-but-not-least fragments? Perhaps I would never know.

I got out of my car, took the pillow I'd brought with me from New York, and walked over to the twin tombstones of McCurdy and Doolin, which stood out among the low-lying plaques of Boot Hill, where I found Doolin's other gang members, Little Dick West, "Killed April 13, 1898," and Charlie Pierce, "Killed by Officers, May 5, 1895," along with Tom Capers, "Shot by Ben Howard Nov 6, 1897," and Bert Casey, "Killed Nov 8, 1902." And somewhere nearby lay a man named Ned Shaw, and somewhere a man identified in cemetery records only as "Jennings," and somewhere else a man named Van Arsdale, gunned down while trying to escape the territorial prison. A swath of grass separated the paupers' section from the rest of the cemetery, where Guthrie's notable citizens lay, the Schwakes and the Frisbes and the Griffins and the Blands. It was late afternoon on a weekday of the early twenty-first century, and a soft breeze was blowing across eternity. I walked my way to the shade of a large poplar tree, listened to the wind sift through its canopy, cows lowing in a pasture nearby, and though there may have been an ordinance on the Guthrie books against what I was about to do, I aligned myself with my neighbors, put my head upon the pillow, and gazed for a while through the branches at the Oklahoma sky.

# Notes

## CHAPTER ONE

(page)

7    The article in which Chris Haynes gives his version of the prank pulled on Long Beach Fire Department paramedics appears in "Mummy Brings Out Dry Sense of Humor," by Steve Harvey, *Los Angeles Times*, Dec. 17, 1997.

21    References to the story of Elmer McCurdy in the culture at large are as follows: "The Oklahoma Outlaw," written and produced by Jonathan Gili, was broadcast on BBC 2, April 21, 1998. The Kansas professor was Richard Basgall; his book is *The Career of Elmer McCurdy, Deceased* (Lawrence, Kans.: Trail's End Publishing, 1989). "The Ballad of Elmer McCurdy" appears on *5 Miles or 50,000 Years*, by Mustard's Retreat, Mustard's Retreat Palmetto Records, 1993. "The Cowboy Outlaw" appears on *Brian Dewan Tells the Story*, by Brian Dewan, Bar-None Records, 1993. Glenda George's chapbook *The Corpse of Elmer McCurdy* was privately published in 1977.

## CHAPTER TWO

23–24    The westward migration of culture—and the particular details used in this chapter—are part of the central theme addressed in illuminating detail by Jan Willem Schulte Nordholt in *The Myth of the*

*West: America as the Last Empire* (Grand Rapids, Mich.: William B. Eerdmans Publishing Company, 1995).

24    For a complete account of British travel narratives, see Robert G. Athearn, *Westward the Briton* (New York: Charles Scribner's Sons, 1953).

25    The skirmish at Cozad comes from David Haward Bain's *Empire Express: Building the First Transcontinental Railroad* (New York: Viking, 1999), pp. 292–293.

25    For other essential items to bring on your trip west, consider Emily Post, *By Motor Car to the Golden Gate* (New York: D. Appleton and Company, 1917), pp. 253–254.

26    *Chicago Tribune*, April 27, 1893, found in Richard White, "Frederick Jackson Turner and Buffalo Bill," in James R. Grossman, ed., *The Frontier in American Culture* (Berkeley: University of California Press, 1995), p. 7.

26    The anecdote about Will Rogers and Vicente Oropeza comes from Larry McMurtry, "Inventing the West," in his book *Sacagawea's Nickname: Essays on the American West* (New York: New York Review of Books, 2001), p. 31.

26    Twain's quote about the booming nineteenth century is found in Justin Kaplan, *Mr. Clemens and Mark Twain: A Biography* (New York: Touchstone, 1966), p. 255.

27    I take the phrase "ephemeral west" and the vagaries of its location from Robert G. Athearn, *The Mythic West in Twentieth-Century America* (Lawrence, Kans.: University Press of Kansas, 1986), p. 10. The plurality of "wests" is a guiding theme of his book.

27–28    Richard Basgall traced McCurdy back to Maine and uncovered the story of his parentage and the sad drama that led to McCurdy's eventual departure from Maine at the turn of the century. Found in Basgall, *The Career of Elmer McCurdy, Deceased* (Lawrence, Kans.: Trail's End Publishing, 1989), p. 43.

28    Horace Greeley's imagined itinerary (from *Essays on Political Economy*, 1874, p. 286) for the westering young man of the mid-nineteenth century mentions Montana. McCurdy, too, is said to have ventured as far west as Colorado, where several sources say he killed a

man. But since no one has ever been able to place McCurdy west of Oklahoma, I take his "appearance" in Colorado as an instance of westward mythography.

28–29   The migration statistics are taken from Table C 25-73, "Estimated Net Intercensal Migration of Total, Native White, Foreign-Born White, and Negro Population Surviving from the Preceding Census Date, by States: 1870 to 1950," in *Historical Statistics of the United States, Colonial Times to 1957* (Washington, D.C.: U.S. Department of Commerce, Bureau of the Census, 1975), p. 44.

29   Gilbert C. Fite, *The Farmers' Frontier, 1865–1900* (New York: Holt, Rinehart and Winston, 1966), p. vi.

29   The comments by an observer on industrial capitalists were made by Brooks Adams. These, and other statistics on wealth in 1900, are from Page Smith, *America Enters the World: A People's History of the Progressive Era and World War I,* Vol. 7 (New York: Viking Penguin, 1985), pp. 9–10.

30   Stanley Lebergott suggests that the ups and downs of unemployment in the nineteenth century have been largely, perhaps even melodramatically, overstated. From *The Americans: An Economic Record* (New York: W. W. Norton, 1984), pp. 396–397.

30   Sadie McCurdy's brief career as a door-to-door seamstress comes from Basgall, *The Career of Elmer McCurdy, Deceased,* p. 45.

31   The views of the land openings in Oklahoma come from Evett Dumas Nix, *Oklahombres, Particularly the Wilder Ones* (Lincoln: University of Nebraska Press/Bison Books, 1993), pp. 88, 91–92, and A. M. Thomas, "The Story of the Strip Opening," from the Tonkawa Public Library Collection, Box T-3, Folder 620, Western History Collection, University of Oklahoma, Norman, Oklahoma.

32   Charles Moreau Harger, "To-Day's Chance for the Western Settler," *Outlook Magazine,* Dec. 17, 1904, p. 981.

33   The estimate is of Josiah Flynt, who spent a carefree eight-month vacation as a recreational hobo, during which time he was aided, assisted, and mentored by hoboes into the hobo lifestyle. He returned the favor by working for the railroad companies, posing as a hobo, in order to help drive hoboes from the rails. From the published

account, "The Tramp and the Railroads," *The Century Illustrated Monthly Magazine,* June 1899, p. 263.

33–34   The statistics and insights that counter the stereotypical view of the homeless in the nineteenth and twentieth centuries come from Kenneth L. Kusmer's fabulous book, *Down and Out, on the Road: The Homeless in American History* (Oxford: Oxford University Press, 2002).

35   Most of the information about Iola and the gas boom can be found in "The Boom Years of Iola, Kansas: 1896–1907," a master's thesis by Michael Edward Haen, 1968. I found this in the Kansas State Historical Society archives, Topeka, Kansas.

37   Basgall places McCurdy at the Eagle Cornice Works and Plumbing Shop in *The Career of Elmer McCurdy, Deceased,* p. 49.

38   The details about Elmer's life in Iola come from an article published after his death in the *Iola Daily Register,* Oct. 10, 1911.

38   The quote about Elmer being "addicted to drink" is by William Root, as quoted in the *Iola (Kans.) Daily Register,* Oct. 13, 1911, p. 5. The note about Elmer gaining access to the better circles of Iola society is from the *Fort Scott (Kans.) Tribune,* Oct. 9, 1911. Thanks to the Kansas State Historical Society, Topeka, Kansas.

41   Basgall places McCurdy in the Davey Mine #1 in Carterville, in *The Career of Elmer McCurdy, Deceased,* p. 53.

44   W. T. Sherman's report on the opening of the west to immigration is from Report of the Secretary of War, 1883, House Executive Document No. 1, pt. 2, 48 Cong., 1 sess., pp. 44–46 (Serial 2182), found in Athearn, *Westward the Briton,* p. 11.

44–46   The sketch of MacArthur's early career comes from my reading of William Manchester, *American Caesar: Douglas MacArthur, 1880–1964* (Boston: Little, Brown, 1978), pp. 69–71; Carol Morris Petillo, *Douglas MacArthur: The Philippine Years* (Bloomington: Indiana University Press, 1981), pp. 101, 106–107; and D. Clayton James, *The Years of MacArthur* (Boston: Houghton Mifflin, 1970), pp. 98–105.

46   Robert L. Eichelberger's vivid description of MacArthur comes from Manchester, *American Caesar,* p. 71.

46   The jaunty description of MacArthur's annual two-week demonstration in military demolitions is from the *Fort Leavenworth News,* Sept. 30, 1910.

## CHAPTER THREE

51    The help wanted ads are quoted from the *St. Joseph News Press*, Nov. 23, 1910.

52    The facts of McCurdy's service in a machine-gun detachment are from the *Leavenworth Times*, Nov. 30, 1910.

52    The unemployment figures are from an investigation by the board of the Bowery Mission in New York City, as reported by the *St. Joseph News Press*, Nov. 21, 1910.

54    The "Yeggs" quote is from the *St. Joseph Gazette*, Nov. 21, 1910.

56    The court records for the hearing and subsequent trial of McCurdy and Schoppelrie, and police records related to the arrest, booking, and photographic and Bertillion identification of the men, were destroyed, along with thousands of other records of the St. Joseph Police Department, in a flood during the mid-1980s. In *The Career of Elmer McCurdy, Deceased* (Lawrence, Kans.: Trail's End Publishing, 1989), Richard Basgall seems to have used these records before they were destroyed. He also cites the account of Captain Murphy's testimony (p. 69), though I found no mention in the *St. Joseph Gazette* or the *News Press* of Captain Murphy's statement, Elmer's violent "lunge," nor any mention of his having been restrained by court officers.

58    I take the term "social bandit" and much of the information about this subject from Richard White's essay "Outlaw Gangs of the Middle Border: American Social Bandits," *Western Historical Quarterly*, October 1981. For Bill Dalton's Chicago Saloon gambit, White quotes the *Oklahoma State Capital*, April 29, June 10, 1893.

59–60    *Ardmore (Okla.) State Herald*, March 14, 1895, quoted in Glenn Shirley, *West of Hell's Fringe* (Norman, Okla.: University of Oklahoma Press, 1978), p. 265. The James brothers' note is from Richard Patterson, *Train Robbery: The Birth, Flowering, and Decline of a Notorious Western Enterprise* (Boulder: Johnson Books, 1981), pp. 29–30.

62    The insight into the sibling dynamics of the Jarrett brothers comes from Richard Basgall, interview with Wayne Jarrett, the nephew of Walter Jarrett, Papers of Richard Basgall.

62    The particulars of the St. Joseph trial of McCurdy and Schoppelrie cannot be accurately confirmed as most of the trial documents

were destroyed by the mid-1980s flood. I have relied on Basgall's citation of a Buchannan County Record Book, in particular, for McCurdy's own testimony, the only known occurrence of McCurdy speaking on his own behalf.

62–63   The details about the Jarrett brothers selecting their own grave plots is from an interview with J. T. Ball and others conducted by Alfred F. Hicks, The Ball Cemetery, #6408, Indian Pioneer Papers, Western History Collection, Norman, Oklahoma. J. T. Ball's account of the Jarrett brothers' pact is probably apocryphal, perhaps the product of romantic whimsy on Ball's part. It suggests that the brothers made the pact prior to joining the Al Spencer gang. Most sources agree that the Spencer gang began in 1916. Walter Jarrett was killed in 1912, however, four years prior to the formation of the Spencer gang.

66   The description of the Iron Mountain train robbery comes from the eyewitness account of A. G. Green, mayor of Sioux City, Iowa, and published in the *Muskogee (Okla.) Times-Democrat* and the *Vinita (Okla.) Daily Chieftain*, March 24, 1911.

66   Statistics for total mail delivered are from James E. White, *A Life Span and Reminiscences of Railway Mail Service* (Philadelphia: Deemer & Jaisohn, 1910), pp. 263–264. Total track mileage is taken from "Bulletin No. 31 of the Bureau of Railway Economics," as found in *Sayings and Writings About the Railways by Those Who Have Managed Them and Those Who Have Studied Their Problems* (New York: The Railway Age Gazette, 1913), p. 203.

66   Net return figures for railways ($824,241,301, divided by 365, then adjusted for inflation) is from "Bulletin No. 39 of the Bureau of Railway Economics," found in *Sayings and Writings*, p. 236. Other information about the Iron Mountain train robbery is taken from H. B. Pinkney's testimony in the trial of the three surviving defendants, Walter and Lee Jarrett and Albert Connor, as reported in the *Muskogee (Okla.) Times-Democrat*, Jan. 18, 1912.

69   Information on safe-blowing techniques can be found in Patterson, *Train Robbery*, p. 66. *The Express Gazette*, a railroad trade publication, reported only six train robberies in 1910.

74–75   Walter Jarrett's death was reported in the *Lenapah (Okla.) Post*, Oct. 17, 1912. A story about Frank Curtis appears in the *Fort Leavenworth News*, July 1, 1910.

## CHAPTER FOUR

78    Information about the trial of David Sears and Amos Hays comes from *United States v. David Sears*, Case #723, April 22, 1912, U.S. District Court for the Western District of Oklahoma, National Archives and Records Administration, Southwest Region.

78    Amos Hays's name has been misspelled—as "Hayes"—in almost every account of the McCurdy story, although census records list Amos Hays as a dependent of Adam Orr Hays. Amos is also listed as a dependent in a petition for pension of Adam Orr Hays's widow and second wife, Melinda Higgins Hays.

Eugene Hayes was the name of the man Amos killed in Kansas City in 1905, probably in retribution for the murder of Amos's brother, Edward. Amos Hays was a cousin, by marriage, to Elijah ("Lige") Higgins. From a letter to Richard Basgall from Sandra H. Hays, July 13, 1989, Papers of Richard Basgall.

78    The "family story" of Dave Sears's entanglement in the M, K, & T robbery is from an interview with Mary Ellen Parker, granddaughter of George David Sears, Jr., June 27, 2001; and from Richard Basgall's interview with Phyllis McKay, granddaughter of Dave Sears' son, Charles Preston Sears, November 21, 1989, The Papers of Richard Basgall.

81    The phrase "legacy of conquest" comes from Patricia Nelson Limerick's eponymously titled book *The Legacy of Conquest: The Unbroken Past of the American West* (New York: W. W. Norton, 1988).

83    Statistics about the Klondike gold rush are from Jack London, "The Economics of the Klondike," *The American Monthly Review of Reviews*, January 1900, pp. 70–72.

83    Jefferson's comment about the Osage is from a letter from Jefferson to Secretary of War Dearborn, in *Letters of the Lewis and Clark Expedition, with Related Documents: 1783–1854*, 2nd ed. (Urbana: University of Illinois Press, 1978), p. 200.

83    According to Louis F. Burns, author of *A History of the Osage People*, most histories of the Osage greatly overstate the amount of influence that the Chouteaus and others had upon the Osage tribal politics.

84–85    Figures on the Treaty of 1808 are from Charles J. Kappler, comp. and ed., *Indian Affairs: Laws and Treaties* (Washington, D.C.:

Government Printing Office, 1904), 2:95–99, found in Terry P. Wilson, *The Underground Reservation* (Lincoln: University of Nebraska Press, 1985), p. 7. Another source, Louis F. Burns, *A History of the Osage People*, suggests that it is difficult to know which Osage chiefs were present at the treaty signing, and that because of either intentional or inept interpreting on the part of Pierre Chouteau, the Osages may have had little understanding of what it was they were signing away. Burns, *History of Osage People*, pp. 226–228.

86    The quote about the Osage being "the richest people on earth" is from William J. Pollock, Commissioner's Report, 1898, p. 241, found in Louis F. Burns, *A History of the Osage People* (Fallbrook, Calif.: Ciga Press, 1989), p. 465.

86    The quote from the *Hominy News-Republican*, Aug. 25, 1909, is found in Wilson, *The Underground Reservation*, p. 135. Quote about the depredations of the Osage is from Laban J. Miles, uncle of Herbert Hoover, in the Commissioner's Report, 1889, Vol. 2, p. 193. For more accounts of the institutionalized fraud visited upon the Osage, see Burns, *History of the Osage People*, p. 561.

87    Osage tribal population figures from Terry P. Wilson, *The Osage* (New York: Chelsea House Publishers, 1988), p. 56.

87–88    Osage oil production statistics are from David T. Day, "The Production of Petroleum in 1911," from *Mineral Resources of the United States, Calendar Year 1911*, Department of the Interior—U.S. Geological Survey (Washington, D.C.: Government Printing Office, 1912), pp. 73, 75, 76. Osage royalty payment figures from Wilson, *The Osage*, p. 74.

94    An account of the Chautauqua Bank robbery was reported in the *Sedan (Kans.) Times-Star*, Sept. 28, 1911.

94    Facts about the hazards of nitroglycerin in the Oklahoma oil fields are from Paul Lambert and Kenny A. Franks, *Voices from the Oilfields* (Norman: University of Oklahoma Press, 1984). The chapter from which the information was taken, "Shooters Don't Make But One Mistake," is taken almost verbatim from the WPA Project files in the Western History Collection. It is the record of an interview with "Shorty" Moses, a shooter for the Acme Torpedo Company, conducted by Ned DeWitt in the late 1930s.

95    The account of McCurdy's arrival at the Revard ranch is from Richard Basgall, *The Career of Elmer McCurdy, Deceased* (Lawrence, Kans.: Trail's End Publishing, 1989), pp. 110–111.

101    Information about George David Sears, Jr., is from *The History of Chautauqua County*, Chautauqua County Heritage Association, Curtis Media Corporation, 1987, pp. 657–58; from an interview with Mary Ellen Parker, granddaughter of George David Sears, Jr., June 27, 2001; and from Richard Basgall's interview with Phyllis McKay, granddaughter of Dave Sears' son, Charles Preston Sears, November 21, 1989, The Papers of Richard Basgall.

103    Elijah "Lige" Higgins's name appears on court documents as a witness for the prosecution, which suggests that Higgins may have received clemency in exchange for testimony against his cousin. Higgins was never indicted for trial. Sightings of McCurdy, Higgins, Hays, and Sears together prior to the robbery of the M, K, & T train are from the *Sedan Times-Star*, Nov. 2, 1911. According to the *Oklahoma City Times*, Oct. 4, 1911: "The tracks [of the robber's horses] were to be seen plainly as rain had fallen recently and the trail led in a southeasterly direction. It is only about a mile in the direction of travel to the prairies."

107    The M, K, & T robbery beer-fest was reported in the *Bartlesville Morning Examiner*, Oct. 5, 1911. The séance conducted to apprehend McCurdy was reported in the *Iola Daily Register*, Oct. 11, 1911. The opium den and other related discoveries after the M, K, & T robbery were reported in the *Pawhuska Capital*, Oct. 12, 1911.

108–9    The *Daily Oklahoman*, Oct. 8, 1911, and the *Fort Scott (Kans.) Tribune*, Oct. 9, 1911, suggest that Sears was followed back to his farm by the Fenton brothers and Dick Wallace. The *Pawhuska Capital*, Oct. 12, 1911, suggests that a neighbor had spotted a "suspicious looking stranger," probably Elmer McCurdy, lurking about the Dave Sears place just after the robbery. McCurdy's drunken bragging about the M, K, & T robbery appears in the *Bartlesville Evening Enterprise*, Oct. 7, 1911.

110    Details about the movements of David Sears the night prior to McCurdy's death come from the "Application for Witnesses, Sears-Hays Trial," April 22, 1912. "The defendant, Dave Sears, believes the

witness, J. Waters, will testify that he knows that one McCurdy . . . was taken by defendant to the home of one Revard at night instead of in the day time because Waters had asked him to do so in order that Sears could help Waters the following morning on an oil well." Case #723, The *United States v. David Sears*, U.S. District Court for the Western District of Oklahoma, National Archives and Records Administration, Southwest Region.

110    Charles Preston Sears' involvement on the eve of McCurdy's death is from Richard Basgall's interview with Phyllis McKay, granddaughter of Dave Sears's son, Charles Preston Sears, November 21, 1989, The Papers of Richard Basgall.

112    Richard Basgall, in particular, subscribes to the theory that Elmer McCurdy was murdered, perhaps by Amos Hays, in *The Career of Elmer McCurdy, Deceased*, pp. 130–131.

115    Stringer Fenton dictated his firsthand account of the Revard shoot-out to a reporter by telephone from Pawhuska on the afternoon of the shooting. The *Daily Oklahoman*, Oct. 8, 1911.

115    William Floyd Davis's account is from an interview with Davis archived in the Indian Pioneer Papers, Western History Collection, Norman, Oklahoma. Davis gets some of the details wrong in his account, given when he was fifty-eight years old, twenty years after the shooting, but unless he was embellishing to impress his WPA interviewer—not beyond the realm of possibility—the level of specificity here seems credible.

## CHAPTER FIVE

118    Ancient burial rights were described by John Weever, "Ancient Funeral Monuments," in Percival E. Jackson, *The Law of Cadavers and of Burial and Burial Places* (New York: Prentice-Hall, 1936), p. 7.

122    The congressional bill to recover the reward for the capture of Elmer McCurdy comes from the Papers of Thomas O. Berry, grandson of Stringer Fenton, Oklahoma Territorial Museum, Guthrie, Oklahoma.

123    Justice Joseph Henry Lumpkin's puzzlement over the legal status of a corpse found in *Louisville & N.R. Co. v. Wison*, 123 Ga. 62, 51

S.E. 24, 25 (1905), is found in Kenneth V. Iserson, *Death to Dust: What Happens to Dead Bodies* (Tucson, Ariz.: Galen Press, 1994), p. 556. The legal obligation of a community to bury unknown or unclaimed dead is also explored in Iserson's book, p. 558.

123–24    Jackson, in *Law of Cadavers*, p. 35, states, "So there is a duty on strangers to bury a man killed by accident far from home, with consequent reimbursement from his estate." Johnson cites *Rogers v. Price*, 3 Y. & J. 28, 148 Eng. Rep. 1080.

124    There were any number of legal precedents forbidding the arrest of a dead body for debt. Jackson, *Law of Cadavers*, p. 130, cites *Jefferson County Burial Soc. v. Scott*, 218 Ala. 354, 118 So. 644; *American Express Co. v. Eppley*, 5 Ohio Dec. (Rep.) 337; see also *Jones v. Ashburnham*, 4 East 455, 102 Engl. Rep. 905; *Reg. v. Fox*, 2 Ad. & El. (N.S.) 246, 114 Eng. Rep. 95; *Reg. v. Scott*, 2 Q. B. 248, note b, 114 Eng. Rep. 97. In recent years there has been a notable exception to this general rule. J. Merril Spencer, owner of the House of Spencer Mortuary, held—and may still be holding—the body of James McDill, who died on February 26, 1989. The McDill family owes Spencer $3,605.29 in unpaid funeral expenses. There are no Michigan state laws requiring burial if there has been no payment. "Held for Ransom," *Mortuary Management*, February 1992, p. 20. For Oklahoma case law prohibiting the practice of arresting or detaining a dead body upon a debt, see Jackson, *Law of Cadavers*, p. 183.

127    The phrase "spectacle of the real" belongs to Vanessa R. Schwartz, from her fascinating look at the culture of the Paris Morgue in *Spectacular Realities: Early Mass Culture in Fin de Siècle Paris* (Berkeley: University of California Press, 1998). The works cited below are found in Schwartz, pp. 60–61: The comparison of the morgue to a serial novel, George Montorgueil, in "La morgue fermée," *L'Eclair*, Sept. 7, 1892; the quote about the "retina," from the poem "La Vitrine," by Clovis Pierre, the morgue registrar from 1878–1892, in *Gaietes de la morgue* (Paris: Gallimard, 1895); the English visitor was E. V. Lucas, *A Wanderer in Paris* (London: Methuen, 1909), pp. 54–55.

127    Joseph Johnson's comments were published in the *Pawhuska Journal-Capital*, Sept. 30, 1928.

129    The quote from Luke Johnson comes from Richard Basgall, *The Career of Elmer McCurdy, Deceased* (Lawrence, Kans.: Trail's End Publishing, 1989), pp. 156–157.

130    The description of McCurdy as "a desperado who refused to surrender" appeared in the *Daily Oklahoman* on Oct. 8, 1911. He was called "a notable criminal" and "a leader of a gang of outlaws" in the *Fort Scott (Kans.) Tribune*, Oct. 9, 1911.

## CHAPTER SIX

131    The Burne-Jones anecdote comes from Georgiana Burne-Jones, *Memorials of Edward Burne-Jones*, Vol. 2, 1868–1898 (New York: Macmillan, 1904), pp. 114, 175. The name of Burne-Jones's estate was "Westward Ho!"

132    The rhapsodic qualities of "Egyptian Brown" are found in Heather Pringle, *The Mummy Congress: Science, Obsession, and the Everlasting Dead* (New York: Theia/Hyperion, 2001), p. 174.

132    The quote from Henry Fielding is found in Frederick Drimmer, *The Body Snatchers: Mummies, Mysteries, and Mayhem* (New York: Citadel Press, 1992), pp. 27–28. The information about body snatching as a crime and about the Ben Crouch gang is found in Martin Fido, *Body Snatchers: A History of the Resurrectionists, 1742–1832* (London: Weidenfield and Nicolson, 1988), pp. 10, 37.

133    New York City grave-robbing statistics are found in Christine Quigley, *The Corpse: A History* (Jefferson, N.C.: McFarland & Company, 1996), p. 296.

134    Hemingway's disdain for biographers and biography is discussed in Robert Hendrickson, *American Literary Anecdotes* (New York: Penguin, 1990), p. 107.

## CHAPTER SEVEN

141    Braithwaite, *English Fairgrounds*, pp. 16–17, quoted in "The County Fair Carnival: History and Self-Definition," by Leslie Prosterman, in Lee O. Bush, ed., *The County Fair Carnival: Where the Midway Meets the Grange* (Elmira, N.Y.: The Chemung County Historical Society, 1992), p. 22.

141   The Lincoln, Nebraska, editorial use of *ballyhoo* is found in *Random House Historical Dictionary of American Slang* (New York: Random House, 1994), vol. 1, p. 81.

145   H. L. Mencken's etymological attempt with *ballyhoo* is found in *American Language* (New York: Alfred A Knopf, 1936), p. 188. The source for the use of the nautical term in Melville's *Omoo* is found in Atcheson L. Hench, "Possible Clue to the Source of *Ballyhoo* and some Queries," *American Speech* 20 (1945), pp. 184–186. Author Charles Wolverton, however, seems quite convinced that *ballyhoo* originated at the Columbian Exposition. Although he acknowledges the bewildering difficulties of his theory, he declares, "There is gratification, then, in being able for once to trace one of the most characteristic words of our language to its source and to bring clearly into the light the manner in which a new word comes into being. There is even more gratification in being able to find the actual American who, forty-two years ago, brought that rich and gorgeous word, *ballyhoo*, into the speech of our people." In "Ballyhoo," *American Speech* 10 (1935), pp. 289–291.

143   Information on paradoxography and wonder is from the immensely readable book by Katharine Park and Lorraine Daston, entitled *Wonders and the Order of Nature, 1150–1750*, New York: Zone Books; Cambridge, Mass.: Distributed by the MIT Press, 1998.

148   This actual bally from the James E. Straits shows was recorded by Charles Harrell for the Radio Research Project, Washington, D.C., 1941. It is in the Archive of Folk Culture Recordings, AFS 4701, and quoted in an essay by Amanda Dargan and Steven Zeitlin entitled "Turning the Tip: The Art of the Sideshow Carnival Talker," in Bush, ed., *The County Fair Carnival*, p. 38.

148–49   The anecdote about the "girl show" carnival talker comes from a conversation with sideshow scholar Warren Raymond, June 13, 2002.

150   The quotation from Dan Sonney about his father's way of setting up the wax figures is from Richard Basgall, interview with Dan Sonney, 1979, Papers of Richard Basgall.

152   Emmett Dalton's career in film is traced in Kevin Brownlow, *The War, the West, and the Wilderness* (New York: Alfred A. Knopf, 1978), pp. 288–289.

156    In the 1920s, the preserved corpse alleged to be that of John Wilkes Booth was on display at the Minnesota State Fair midway.

160    A first instance of *ballyhoo* being used in print was supplied by Stuart Berg Flexner, *I Hear America Talking: An Illustrated Treasury of American Words and Phrases* (New York: Van Nostrand Reinhold, 1976), p. 16.

160    Stories and articles on the Transcontinental Footrace appeared on a nearly day-to-day basis in the *New York Times* from April 1 to June 19, 1928. For a good overview of the race, published just after its completion, see "The 'Bunion Derby' Glorifies the American Hoof," *Literary Digest*, June 16, 1928, vol. 97, pp. 52–56. For biographies of the racers themselves and an extensive history of distance running of the period, see Harry Berry, *from l.a. to new york, from new york to l.a.* (England: 1990).

161    C. C. Pyle's endorsement campaign on behalf of his client, Red Grange, is from James H. Thomas, *The Bunion Derby: Andy Payne and the Transcontinental Footrace* (Oklahoma City: Southwestern Heritage Books, 1980), p. 10. "Running and Walking Records," *International Transcontinental Footrace Official Program*, 1929, pp. 4, 17–19.

169    The description of Bunion Derby racers entering a small town is from *The Literary Digest*, vol. 97, June 16, 1928, pp. 56 and 86. The harsh conditions that Bunion Derby racers faced is described in Thomas, *The Bunion Derby*, pp. 55, 86, and in passim.

182    Luke Johnson's encounter with the Ocean Park carnival talker is found in Richard Basgall, *The Career of Elmer McCurdy, Deceased* (Lawrence, Kans.: Trail's End Publishing, 1989), pp. 190–191.

## CHAPTER EIGHT

188    All uncited quotes from Friedman are from my interview with him at the Chiller Theater Convention in October 1999 and 2001. I have also relied on David Chute's two-part interview, "Wages of Sin," *Film Comment* 22, no. 4 (July–August 1986), and have used other sources, as noted, for all other quotes.

189    Friedman's quote of H. L. Mencken is from the *Atlanta Journal-Constitution*, Jan. 27, 1991, Section M, p. 1.

190    Statistics on wage increases, etc., are from Judith A. Adams, *The American Amusement Park Industry: A History of Technology and Thrills* (Boston: Twayne Publishers, 1991), pp. 60–64. For most of these figures, Adams cites Julius Weinberger, "Economic Aspects of Recreation," *Harvard Business Review* 15 (Summer 1937), pp. 452, 454, 456.

191    Friedman's early life in Anniston from Chute, "Wages of Sin," p. 44. Information about traveling wax museums in France in the 1850s from Vanessa R. Schwartz, *Spectacular Realities: Early Mass Culture in Fin de Siècle Paris* (Berkeley: University of California Press, 1998), p. 97.

191    Eric Schaefer's thesis is that these World War I hygiene films were the precursors to later exploitation films. Schaefer notes, among other things, the wide popularity of such films, despite the much-publicized "outrage." See Schaefer, *Bold, Daring, Shocking, True: The History of Exploitation Films, 1919–1959* (Durham, N.C.: Duke University Press, 1999), pp. 17–28. The ersatz, official-sounding organization—The John D. Rockefeller Foundation of the National Public Health Association—is also mentioned in Schaefer, p. 170.

191    The Madame Tussaud connection comes from Schwartz, *Spectacular Realities,* pp. 93, 95.

193    Dan Sonney refers to Esper as a "fifth-of-scotch-a day" drinker in Richard Basgall, interview with Dan Sonney, August 1979, Papers of Richard Basgall. Esper's drinking is also described in Millicent Wratten to Bret Wood, in the Introduction to Bret Wood, *Marihuana, Motherhood & Madness: Three Screenplays from the Exploitation Cinema of Dwain Esper* (Lanham, Md.: Scarecrow Press, 1998), p. xv.

193    David Friedman's joking anecdote about the way Dwain Esper was said to answer the phone ("I'll sue!") appeared in the introduction to Wood, *Marihuana, Motherhood & Madness,* p. xiv.

194    Joseph I. Breen's outrage is described in Wood, *Marihuana, Motherhood & Madness,* p. xvi.

194    Joseph Breen, file memo, April 9, 1935, *The Seventh Commandment,* PCA files, found in Schaefer's *Bold, Daring, Shocking, True,* p. 136, and in the Introduction to Wood, *Marihuana, Motherhood & Madness,* p. xvii.

194    The Louis Sonney/Dwain Esper business connection is told in many places, but perhaps no better than in an interview with Dan Sonney, August 1979, recorded in Papers of Richard Basgall, p. 4.

195   This latter-day sighting of Elmer McCurdy on film occurred in the early 1940s in Pawhuska and was recounted in an interview with Johnny Johnson, December 3, 1979, recorded in Papers of Richard Basgall, p. 11.

196   Friedman's intimate knowledge of the American film-distribution network is recounted in the Chute interview, "Wages of Sin," p. 44.

197   Friedman's experiment in 1956 with the film *The Story of Bob and Sally* comes from my interview with him on Oct. 23, 2001.

198–99   His contraception spiel, from the same interview, was delivered in his hotel room, more than forty years after the fact, which I found impressive. It is almost identical to the spiel that appears in Chute, "Wages of Sin," p. 42. The "simpatico" quote is from Chute, p. 46.

201   Friedman's use of "planted" stories comes from "David Friedman," an interview with Jim Morton, from *Re/Search #10: Incredibly Strange Films*, 1986, p. 104.

201   The facts of *Blood Feast* are from Eddie Muller and Daniel Faris, *Grindhouse: The Forbidden World of Adults Only Cinema* (New York: St. Martin's Press, 1996), p. 94; and Chute, "Wages of Sin," pp. 47–48.

201   Lewis's apparent indifference to film and contempt for his audience comes from "Herschell Gordon Lewis," by Andrea June, Mark Pauline, and Boyd Rice, *Re/Search #10: Incredibly Strange Films*, 1986, pp. 23, 31: "I was, and am, and probably always will be interested in what I call *force communication* . . . which is causing the rats to go through the maze the way you want them to. . . . Of course, I don't mean rats as rats; I mean rats as people."

## CHAPTER NINE

208   The quotations from Dan Sonney are from Richard Basgall's interview with Dan Sonney, August 1979, Papers of Richard Basgall, p. 6.

213   Basgall incorrectly places McCurdy in the Black Hills. Richard Basgall, *The Career of Elmer McCurdy, Deceased*, (Lawrence, Kans.: Trail's End Publishing, 1989), p. 196.

215    The quotation from John Purvis is from Basgall, interview with John Purvis, Aug. 28, 1979, Papers of Richard Basgall.

## CHAPTER TEN

218    This early puzzlement regarding the Okie put-on is recorded in Ben Yagoda, *Will Rogers: A Biography* (Norman: University of Oklahoma Press, 1993), p. 127.

221    The facts surrounding these first fraudulent citizens of Guthrie come from the *Kansas City Daily Journal*, April 24, 1889, found in B. B. Chapman, "Guthrie: From Public Land to Private Property," *The Chronicles of Oklahoma* 33 (1955), p. 63.

222    The description of the first day of Guthrie, Oklahoma, is quoted in Anne H. Morgan and Rennard Strickland, *Oklahoma Memories* (Norman, Okla.: University of Oklahoma Press, 1981), pp. 86–90. The quotation from Evan G. Barnard, from 1936, can be found in Howard R. Lamar, "The Creation of Oklahoma: New Meanings for the Oklahoma Land Run," in Howard F. Stein and Robert F. Hill, eds., *The Culture of Oklahoma* (Norman: University of Oklahoma Press, 1993), p. 34.

228    The description of the Western Studies scene is from Larry McMurtry, "The West Without Chili," found in his book *Sacagawea's Nickname: Essays on the American West* (New York: New York Review of Books, 2001), p. 4.

236    The request for the return of McCurdy to the Long Beach Amusement Company and the *CBS Evening News* segment on McCurdy reported by Lesley Stahl is from Richard Basgall, *The Career of Elmer McCurdy, Deceased* (Lawrence, Kans.: Trail's End Publishing, 1989), pp. 216, 237.

240    Noguchi's murder theory was told to me in an interview with Ralph McCalmont, July 23, 2001.

241    Frank Revard's account of McCurdy being unarmed was reported in local papers at the time of the shooting, and Joseph Johnson recalled it in his reminiscence published in the *Pawhuska Journal-Capital*, Sept. 30, 1928.

## CHAPTER ELEVEN

244    Information about the funeral procession and burial was obtained through author interviews and correspondence with Fred A. Olds, Glenn Shirley, Ralph McCalmont, Glenn Jordan, A. Jay Chapman, and Bill Lehmann and was further assisted by an extensive series of photographs taken by Gene Lehmann.

248    The fact of McCurdy's missing mouth was first broached by Dr. Clyde Snow in an interview in Norman, Oklahoma, 5/17/00, and later confirmed by Dr. A. Jay Chapman.

251    The facts of Doolin's outlaw career, his death, and his burial come from Baily Hanes, *Bill Doolin: Outlaw, O.T.* (Norman: University of Oklahoma Press, 1968), pp. 170, 195.

254    Doolin's subscription to the paper edited by Guthrey was reported in E. Bee Guthrey, "Early Days in Payne County," *Chronicles of Oklahoma* 3, no. 1 (April 1925), p. 78.

254    The account of Doolin and the young boy is from George W. Stiles, "Early Days in the Sac and Fox Country," *Chronicles of Oklahoma* 33, no. 8 (1955), p. 331.

## CHAPTER TWELVE

259    The quotation from Fred Olds, "People came from all over the world," is from Todd Mason, "A Corpse Is a Corpse, of Course, Unless It's Elmer McCurdy," *Wall Street Journal*, June 11, 1991.

259    Thomas Noguchi himself wrote a letter to Ralph McCalmont a few days before McCurdy's burial that spoke to the heart of things. "There has been considerable interest shown by the public in the story of the late Mr. McCurdy," Noguchi wrote, "and the press coverage has been excellent." Letter from Thomas T. Noguchi, M.D., to Ralph McCalmont, April 18, 1977.

259    The accounts of the Bed-and-Breakfast War are from a series of stories filed by Ellie Sutter for the *Daily Oklahoman.*

264    Regarding the leak to the Guthrie City Council about Becky Luker's felony conviction: Jane Thomas was one of the few

people in town in a position to know of Luker's former troubles. Although, considering the acrimony between the two women, it would not be unreasonable to surmise that Thomas may have been directly or indirectly involved in the disclosure, Thomas says in a letter to the author that she did not "share the story of Luker's felonious background with Guthrie. . . . I don't know who opened the case with the City Council." Letter from Jane Thomas to the author, June 18, 2002.

264 The Summit View Cemetery protesters were covered in a story with an eye-catching headline: "Guthrie Cemetery Tours Stir Claims of Devil Worship," *The Daily Oklahoman*, June 17, 1991.

265 The emotionally charged meeting before the Guthrie City Parks and Cemetery Committee was covered in "Guthrie Council to Consider Cemetery Rules," *The Daily Oklahoman*, June 17, 1991.

266 Jim Rosencutter's statement—"What the Bible says could happen to her if she practices witchcraft"—appeared in "Cemetery Spat Aired in Guthrie," *The Daily Oklahoman*, June 14, 1991.

267 Jim Rosencutter's attempt to embarrass Richard Burst is recounted in an author interview with Richard O. Burst, March 19, 2002.

267 Fred Olds's warning to Guthrie residents—"People all over the country will sit back and laugh at us"—appeared in "Cemetery Spat Aired in Guthrie," *The Daily Oklahoman*. June 19, 1991.

268 Jane Thomas's statement, "There is no history in the [Summit View] cemetery," was reported in "Cemetery Spat Aired in Guthrie," *The Daily Oklahoman*, June 19, 1991. Thomas later said (in a letter from Jane Thomas from the author, June 18, 2002) that she was talking about "visual history." Even so, Becky Luker had dryly noted at the City Parks and Cemetery Committee meeting that Jane Thomas's argument about the historic inauthenticity of the McCurdy grave was undercut by the city's own historic trolley tours, which used the recorded voice of Jane Thomas to point out and invite people to visit, among other things, the grave of Elmer McCurdy. "Hotel Rivalry Escalating into City Furor," *The Daily Oklahoman*, June 6, 1991.

269 Richard Burst's argument is recounted in an author interview with Richard O. Burst, March 19, 2002 and was reported in "Hotel Rivalry Escalating into City Furor," *The Daily Oklahoman*, June 6, 1991.

# Acknowledgments

I first encountered Elmer McCurdy in a BBC documentary produced by Jonathan Gili and based on Richard Basgall's book *The Career of Elmer McCurdy, Deceased* (Lawrence, Kans.: Trail's End Publishing, 1989). Basgall's book was an inspiration. For eight years he explored the curious realms and odd pockets of the American landscape. During this time, the number of people who knew or cared about his subject wouldn't have filled an elevator. I inherited a story line whose scope and strange dimensions Basgall was the first to trace at length. Because of him, I worked daily in the confidence that there was, in fact, a path to follow, a luxury Basgall himself could not have often enjoyed. Basgall died in 1989, but his wife, Eleanor, generously opened his papers to me, and to her I owe a special note of thanks.

I would also like to thank Nicholas Pearson, Sarah Chalfant, John Donatich, Don Fehr, and Sarah McNally for believing in this project. Thanks as well to Bucknell University for the generous use of its library facilities, and to the Bertrand Library staff, especially to Candice Busch for her valuable help, good humor, and forbearance, and to Mary Jean Woland, Jennifer Perdue, Isabella O'Neill, and Kimberly Palm.

A note of thanks also to Cindy Smolovik of the National Archives and Records Administration, Southwest Region, Fort Worth, Texas; and to the Oklahoma Historical Society, Oklahoma City; the Kansas State Historical Society, Topeka; the University of Oklahoma Western History Collection; and to the Chautauqua County Kansas Historical and Genealogy Society.

I am indebted to Eric Schaefer and David F. Friedman for their assistance with exploitation-film history; to Lisa Petrucci and Mike Vraney of Something Weird Video for the use of photographs from the exploitation film era; and to Ward Hall, Jerry Pickard, and Warren Raymond for their help with sideshow and carnival history. For the forensic aspects of this project, a special thanks to Dr. Thomas T. Noguchi, Dr. Joseph Choi, C. Scott Carrier, Bob Dambacher, and the office of the Los Angeles County Medical Examiner-Coroner.

I am deeply grateful to a number of people from Oklahoma whose good humor, insight, and memories contributed to this project, among them Ralph McCalmont, Louis F. Burns and Ruth Burns, Harvey Payne, Fred A. Olds, and Bill Lehmann. Thanks go as well to Billie Ponca at the White Hair Memorial, Nathan Turner at the Oklahoma Territorial Museum, Jeannie Wickware, Joe Kirshner, Jr., Phyllis McKay, Mary Ellen Parker, Michael Vaught, Park Ranger, Osage Hills State Park, Glenn Jordan, Rebecca Luker, Dr. A. Jay Chapman, Dr. Clyde Snow, and the late Glenn Shirley, historian.

# Index

303